WHITE HATS OF THE NAVY

By

George R. Sharrow

HELP KEEP OUR NAVY TRADITIONS ALIVE!

George Sharrow

CONTENTS

iii

ILLUSTRATIONS

PREFACE

This book is intended as a tribute to the American Sailor. "WHITE HATS OF THE NAVY" is a collection of true stories, poems, cartoons , and photographs about the United States Navy written and submitted by former Navy enlisted personnel.

Humor, battle-action, liberty, love, wit, wisdom, and a little Navy tradition, are the subjects of these stories. Most of us entered the Navy as boys and came out as men. It was truly an educational experience. We enlisted as strangers and were discharged as ship mates forever. A great bonding took place between these men and their ships. Memories were formed that will last a lifetime. It is termed, "the brotherhood of the sea".

Now, as senior citizens, we look back and reflect upon our Navy careers and feel that we must pass on to our present day generation this part of history that we lived.

If, while reading this book, you recognize the name of a shipmate, or took part in one of the stories, and you would like to contact one of the contributors, write me a letter and I will endeavor to get you in touch with that individual. I know that I would welcome hearing from any of my old shipmates. If you are a former white hat and would like information on a ship reunion association, the Shellback Association, The PT Boat Association, the National LST Association, the National LSM/LSMR Association, write me a letter and I will send you information.

The UNITED STATES OF AMERICA is the greatest country in the world and the men and women of the UNITED STATES NAVY help keep it that way. In some small way, I hope this book will help to pass on to future generations some of the tradition, heritage, and honor that is THE UNITED STATES NAVY!

Every school, library, and home should have a copy of this great book!

THE AUTHOR

George Sharrow
1040 Stoney Creek Road
Dauphin, PA 17018

E-mail: whitehats @ juno . com

ACKNOWLEDGEMENTS

MY APPRECIATION AND SPECIAL THANKS GO OUT TO THE FOL-LOWING ORGANIZATIONS. WITHOUT THEIR HELP THIS BOOK WOULD NOT HAVE BEEN POSSIBLE.

Van Watts Studio
1832 W. Commonwealth Ave
Fullerton, CA 92833-3014

The Shellback Association
57 Parcot Ave.
New Rochelle, NY 10801

United States LST Association
P.O. Box 167438
Oregon, OH 43616-7438

Charles J. Adams, Jr.
100 West 46th Street
Reading, PA 19606

Tin Can Sailors
P.O. Box 100
Somerset, MA 02726

National LSM/LSMR Association
237 Duquesne Blvd.
New Kensington, PA 15068

American Legion Magazine
5561 West 74th Street
Indianapolis, IN 46268

Veteran Of Foreign Wars Magazine
406 West 34th Street
Kansas City, MO 64111

Navy League Of The U. S.
2300 Wilson Blvd.
Arlington, VA 22201-33081

PT Boats, Inc. Museum & Library
P.O. Box 38070
Germantown, TN 38183-0070

OUR NAVY MAGAZINE
Jack Banks, Miami, FL
John Allen, Everett, WA

CONTRIBUTING AUTHORS

Adams, Charles Jr., Reading, PA.
Allen, Jack, Everett, WA.
Anderson, John, Mechanicsburg, PA.
Baker, Floyd, Essex, NY.
Banks, A.R.Jack, Miami, FL.
Bartholomew, Willie, Severna Park, MD.
Baughman, Willis, Burlington, WA.
Bohne, Henry F., Parker, CO.
Brown, Terrance, Chandler, AZ.
Case, Bernard E., Midwest City, OK.
Crofton, William Sr., Saginaw, MI.
Crosswell, Jack, Cripple Creek, VA.
Dawson, George, Wantagh, NY.
Decker, Edward, Costa Mesa, CA.
Deyo, H.B., Flint, MI.
Doyon, Joseph P., Tigart, OR.
Edwards, Donald, Cincinnati, OH.
Elshoff, Richard, Springfield, IL.
Engler, Frederick, Saginaw, MI.
Evers, Robert O., Irvington, NJ.
Fisk, Kenneth, Liberty, NY.
Giandana, Victor, Coconut Creek, FL.
Grimm, Larry W. Sr., Northwood, OH.
Grupe, Thomas V., Brook Park, OH.
Hagen, Franklin, Longview, TX.
Herring, Kenneth, Murray, KY.
Hoffman, Walter E., Greenville, PA.
Homan, David R., Racine, WI.
Kappes, Irwin J., Middletown, NJ.
Madsen, Robert R. Sr., Lena, WI.
Marks, James A., Braderton, FL.
McGrogan, John J., Union Beach, NJ.
McGuinness, William J., Oradell, NJ.
McMullen, Frank H., Palestine, TX.
Metcalf, Edwin L., Edmonds, WA.
Misiewicz, Stanley, Shrewsbury, MA.
Parrow, Robert, Pipe Creek, TX.
Patfield, Carl R., Las Vegas, NV.
Reed, Robert, Commerce City, CO.
Regenos, Allen D., Claypool, IN.

Rinaldi, John, Lodo, NJ.
Schatz, Richard S., Greenfield, MA.
Schorer, Bruce E., Nicollet, MN.
Scott, Walter, Aurora, NY.
Scott, Wilbur, Sacranento, CA.
Sharrow, George R., Dauphin, PA.
Spencer, Jack, Connersville, IN.
Stafford, Roy A., Schoolcraft, MI.
Stanoski, John, Natrona Heights, PA.
Stein, Paul, Bayside, NY.
Stull, Raymond, Citrus Heights, CA.
Thessen, Donald C., Albion, NE.
Thompson, William, vail, AZ.
Tuckhorn, Thomas, Cherry Hill, NJ.
Watts, Van, Fullerton, CA.
Wessell, Jack, Nineveh, IN.

THE CAPTAIN'S PIES

GEORGE SHARROW, Dauphin, Pa.   **USS DEUEL APA 160**

After the decommissioning of LSMR 517 in Orange, Texas, I was assigned to the USS DEUEL APA 160 in Norfolk, Virginia. It was like moving from an efficiency apartment into a big mansion.

I was not use to such luxury and conveniences on a ship. It had everything from an ice cream store to a gym. It had a hospital, a post office, and even its own brig. Wow! It took me a month just to locate and find everything.

The quartermasters on the USS DEUEL even fought over me. They were amazed that I had both signaling and navigational skills. On the small LSMR, a quartermaster had to do everything from using the signal light to shooting the stars for a fix. On the APA, they had a signal gang who just did signaling on the signal bridge and a navigation gang who handled all the navigation chores in the pilot house and on the navigation bridge. When they gave me my choice, I chose the signal gang as it was more fun, easier, and had less responsibilities.

They had a Chief and a First Class Petty Officer in the navigation gang with just a First Class in charge of the signal gang and he was about to be discharged. As it ended up, I made second class. The first class retired, leaving me in charge of the signal bridge.

As I became an integral part of the DEUEL crew, I practically lived on the signal bridge. The signal bridge was huge. It ran the width of the ship and was at least twenty-five feet deep. We had a small office with our own coffee mess plus another small room, which we called our barbete, that had a chart size desk and enough deck that you could sleep on it. We even had a small room below decks where we had a desk and stored our extra flags.

Even after taps if you went into the galley or mess hall, you would find a pizza or a large flat cake waiting to be eaten along with your spam sandwiches. Coffee, hot chocolate, even a coke machine. Wow! These sailors could easily become spoiled.

George Sharrow, UDT-2

1

Since the signal bridge was the upper most deck on the ship, with my berthing compartment two decks below the main deck, and all the stores, shops, and offices in between, it meant that I would be climbing up and down ladders all day long. Just to go to the head from the signal bridge, I had to go down five decks to find one. In good weather I used the outside ladders that were fastened to the superstructure with a landing on each deck. During bad weather or high seas, I used an inside ladder that went from below the main deck to the pilothouse, passing through officers' country and the Captain's quarters.

One day as I was going up this inside ladder and reached the deck that housed the Captain's quarters and his private galley, right there on the landing by his cook's pantry there were three pies on a shelf!

Since I usually stood the mid-watch, I seldom met anyone while using this ladder. Actually, I think it was mainly for the use of officers and ships control personnel.

One night while at sea, using this ladder on my way to the bridge, in the Captains pantry, I spied my favorite kind of pie. It was french apple, made using raisins, coconut, and topped with a white icing.

This particular night we had mutton stew and rice pudding for evening chow, standard fare when we had Marines onboard. I was still hungry. Seeing and smelling my favorite pie was just too

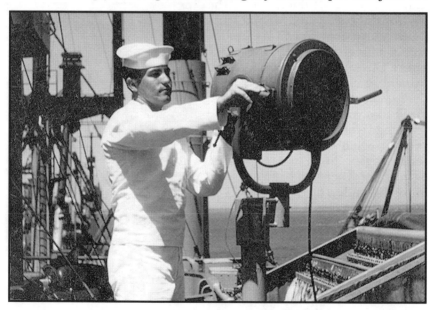

George Sharrow, USS DEUEL APA 160

much for me. The temptation was really great, so I lifted a pie from the shelf and with a growling in my stomach, I proceeded up the ladder to my coffee mess on the signal bridge.

I did not conceal the pie in any way. I openly carried it with one hand like a waiter would in a fancy restaurant. Anyone seeing me, and many did, no doubt thought I had picked it up at the crews mess hall.

The three men standing the signal watch refused to leave the bridge without a piece of my pie. I enjoyed a piece with them along with a cup of coffee. Then about midnight after we had enjoyed our traditional spam sandwiches, the O.O.D. who had noticed the pie as I passed through the pilot house, came up to my bridge and politely mentioned that a slice of that pie would sure taste good.

What could I do?

"Where's my Striker?"

About fifteen minutes later the Chief Quartermaster joined me on the bridge and helped himself to my pie. Next, our Communications Officer Lt. Baron showed up on the bridge. He never visited me on the mid-watch before he had some pie and coffee then disappeared. I am telling you that by 0100 the pie was all gone and I was lucky to have gotten my one piece.

The reason I keep referring to the signal bridge as my bridge is because I was in charge of that area of the ship, but mainly because all these officers and the Chief hardly ever came up to the signal bridge, especially after midnight when there is only one sig-nalman and a striker on duty. It is normally a quiet, peaceful place. Only word of my pie could have attracted them.

In four or five days I repeated my action and took another french apple pie from the pantry. The same thing happened as with the first pie. I was again joined by the same people and all enjoyed pie. The signal bridge was beginning to become a place to be during a mid-watch.

It was a long cruise and after we had been out to sea for three weeks strangely more french apple pies kept appearing in the Captain's pantry. So I started taking two, and at times three, pies to my bridge.

I had officers and chiefs visit with me that I did not even rec-ognize! One night the Chief Engineer even came up from the depths of the ship to visit and have pie. Another night the ship's executive officer, Commander Honeycutt, joined us. His parting remark to me was, "Sharrow, I compliment you. You serve the best damn pie in the Navy!"

I fast became a celebrity and no one ever questioned or asked where I was getting my pies!

Fortunately this was my last cruise in the Navy so the tradi-tion did not continue. Upon our return to Norfolk that Fall, I was honorably discharged from our great Navy and moved on to attend Millersville University in Central Pennsylvania.

ANGELS

GEORGE SHARROW, Dauphin, Pa.   **USS LSMR 517   UDT 2**

Have you ever seen an Angel? How do you know? If not in person, perhaps you saw one in your dreams? Many people say they have talked with God or an Angel in their dreams. Indeed, they may have done so! In the Bible it is stated that men have talked with the Lord and seen visions of Angels in their dreams. Have you ever called on an Angel to help you in times of sorrow or distress? I certainly have! Many a time when I was in a dangerous or life threatening situation, I have called on God to send an Angel to help me.... and He always did!

Have you ever felt that you had been protected by an Angel in any given situation? Have you ever felt that you have had your life saved by one? I sure have! Have you ever been in a situation where you felt that death was imminent and where you gave up all hope and accepted the fact that you were dead about to die? Then, in the twinkling of an eye, you are safe and out of danger. Your life has been saved and there is no explanation how it happened

This has happened to me, not once, but several times. My only answer is that Angels saved my life, for what purpose I do not know. However, I do feel that there is always a reason.

One such incident happened when I was a diver in the United States Navy serving with a UDT Team training off the coast of North Carolina.

We were standing in chest deep water about one hundred yards from shore when we received word that we were finished for the day and should return to the beach. We had been in the water about four hours and we were all very tired. The only equipment we had on were a face mask and swim fins on our sneakers.

Since the water was only chest deep and I was very tired, I decided to wade ashore rather then swim thinking that the depth of the water would get lower as I neared the beach. I was with a team of twelve men and some of them were already making their way towards the beach. Some swimming, some wading. We were all very good swimmers.

At this particular beach the tides and currents can get pretty rough. The strong currents sometimes washed deep gullies in the sand under the water. You could be standing in knee deep water one minute, take a step, and drop off into a ten or fifteen foot trench without warning. I knew all this, but was not thinking about it, as I started to wade ashore. This day the swells were about six feet high and starting to really pound the beach because a storm was fast approaching from seaward. The tide was coming in, so along with the high swells and the tide coming in, I figured all this would push me towards the beach.

It seems that I stepped off into one of these deep trenches in the sand just as one of these big swells hit me. Not expecting this, I did not have time to take a deep breath before I got hit. Down I went into a cloudy, murky, hole! At this distance from shore the swirling sand makes the water very cloudy and you can hardly see when underwater. The strong current had caused a whirlpool effect in the trench and I had a hard time reaching the surface again.

We had been taught that in a situation such as this we should dive for the bottom, when our feet hit sand, push off like a jet for the surface. It was either do this or let the current wash me out of the trench then swim away from the danger area under the water, surfacing when clear. I chose to bottom out and push off for the surface.

Almost exhausted, I reached the surface. Just as I opened my mouth to take in some air, it happened. Boom! I was hit with another tremendous swell. I swallowed a mouth full of salt water and down I went. When I broke the surface again, I got hit by another swell. This time it either knocked me to the bottom, or the current got ahold of me, I am not sure which. Down to the ocean floor I went again!

There I was, underwater, my lungs filled with salt water, and I could neither see the glow of the surface nor feel the bottom under me. I could hear the water gurgling all around me and I can not explain the horrible taste that filled my mouth and nose. It was a strange feeling and I knew that I was drowning. I no longer had control of my actions and was being thrown around underwater like a dead fish. I had no chance of ever reaching the surface. I gave it all up!

In an instant, the next thing I knew, I was lying on the beach in about a foot of water. I was coughing and sputtering water from my nose and mouth. It took a few minutes to regain my composure, but I was alive and well.

Some of my buddies came up to me as I was laying there and asked: "What happened to you Sharrow? One moment we saw you, then you were gone."

"I was gone alright!" I answered. "I thought I had bought it!"

Another buddy said: "That was sure some rough surf out there!" as he walked past me.

I know that an Angel saved me that day! There is no other explanation. At that time I was a young man of twenty, and young men of twenty do not reason things out. I guess I felt that it was just not my time to go. Now that I am older, and I hope, wiser. I can see that Gods Angels protect you when He has some future plan for your life. SO WHAT DO YOU THINK???

THE PENTECOSTAL RESERVISTS

GEORGE SHARROW, Dauphin, Pa.   **USS DEUEL APA 160**

I had just made signalman second class and was in charge of the signal gang aboard the USS DEUEL when my first crises arose.

About a week after taking charge of the signal gang, I was informed the DEUEL had been assigned the duty of taking twenty Navy Reservists on their annual two week cruise. My signal gang was to be assigned two of these reservists who were QMSN's.

My gang were all experienced signalmen, experts with signal light, flags, and semaphore. They considered themselves to be "old salts" and looked upon the reservists as "weekend sailors."

A small revolt ensued! My gang all refused to stand watch with the reservists. To appease them, I agreed to stand all the mid-watches and have both the reservists with me.

I figured it would be an easy cruise as we would be steaming up and down the coast independently, making regular liberty ports along the way. The other reservists were to be assigned to the gun-nery and deck divisions where they would be going through drills and training all day long. On the signal bridge, life was a little easier as we did much the same routine no matter what condition the ship was standing at.

At last the big day arrived and we watched as the twenty re-servists came marching down the pier looking more like a platoon of Marines than sailors except they were wearing dress blues and each was carrying a seabag on his shoulder.

They were brought onboard, quartered in one of the empty troop compartments, then each was taken to his assigned duty station to meet the crew of the DEUEL.

My two QMSN's were Ronald and Donald Walker, (I can re-member their names but not their home town). They were identical twin brothers. As we talked and became better acquainted, they soon let us know they were born-again Pentecostal Christians. They did not smoke, drink, swear, chew, nor mess with women. I really do not know how these guys ever ended up in the Navy as they were certainly not typical of any sailor I knew.

When I explained that we would be on the signal bridge from 0800 until 1800 each day that was alright with them. I told them they would both be standing the mid-watch with me every night, that was alright too. When I explained to them that the duty mes-senger of the watch would awaken them at 2345 so they could relieve the watch on time that was alright. EXCEPT! They wanted us all to know that if, when the messenger came to awaken them, they were not in their bunks, he should not be alarmed. It would mean that the end of the world, as we know it, was coming to its end, that Christ was returning and had called them up (meaning to Heaven) as that is what will happen to all born-again Christians those last days.

Looking back—they must have thought all the rest of us were sinners bound for hell and they were the only saints onboard. Any-how, that did it! Now my signal gang all proclaimed that these two reservists were absolutely crazy and wanted to have nothing to do with them.

We initiated the Walkers by giving them their "general quar-ters gear" which consisted of the steel pot of a helmet (no liner) and a big, bulky, kapok, life jacket like the Marines wore when we were disembarking them. They really did look like nerds.

For general quarters my regular signal gang wore just a hel-met liner painted light gray with their name and rank painted on it. We wore a neat belt like, tube type, life belt that was deflated, (you would not inflate it until after you were in the water). A lot of sail-ors had gotten their necks broken when jumping into the water wearing those big kapok jackets. This belt like life preserver also gave us more freedom to move our arms and body while carrying out our signaling duties.

So there I was stuck with these two fanatical Pentecostal Christians who were looking for Christ to return at any moment, and I would be with them night and day for the next two weeks. At that time I was twenty-one years old, a typical sailor. Although I had attended church and sunday school as a youth, I hardly attended church services since joining the Navy.

I must say that both Ron and Don Walker were good workers and anxious to become more proficient as signalmen and tried hard to carry out all assignments I gave them. They told me that when they attended reserve meetings they had no signal light nor flag bags to practice with. They did, however, make some semaphore flags and practiced that method of signaling. One thing is for certain, when they returned to their home base they would know a lot more about signaling than they knew before this cruise.

The days went smoothly. Since we were steaming indepently, there was no one to communicate with visibly so we kept the boys busy with flag hoist drills and by giving them practical, hands-on experience at chipping and painting, or how to maintain a signal bridge.

At night, on watch, they would be preaching and teaching the Bible to me. When I tired of this, I would hand one of them a flashlight and send him up to the guntub on the bow and have him send prepared messages back to his brother on the bridge. After two weeks of this, they both became proficient with the signal light and the morse code.

Now for the good part! We tied up at four liberty ports those two weeks. It was just a twelve hour liberty, noon until midnight (1200 to 2400 to you old salts) and Ron and Don went ashore at each port.

I still remember that first liberty port, it was Baltimore. The twins departed the ship just after lunch. I stayed onboard and stood the signal watch. Around 2200 I saw Ron and Don return onboard. They were carrying a large box. As they walked up the gangway, they spotted me on the bridge and waved to me.

When they came up on the bridge with their box, I found it to be loaded with fudge, cookies, an apple pie, and a large cake... I immediately made a large pot of coffee.

As each member of my signal gang returned to the ship, they came up to the bridge where they found Ron, Don, and I enjoying all those goodies. Of course we shared with everyone. We still had a good bit remaining after everyone ate their fill so we stowed it in a safe place so we could further enjoy it on our mid-watch along with our regular spam sandwiches.

The next liberty port was somewhere on Long Island so once more the twins went ashore and this time they returned with a basket full of goodies. By now the rest of my gang who had refused to stand watch with the twins and thought they were crazy were now envious and jealous of me and of our midnight snacks.

I asked the twins where they were getting all this food and they told me that each time they went ashore they went to a Pentecostal Church and the congregation gave them all these goodies to bring back with them. All in all, we made four liberty ports and each time they brought back food.

So on that two week cruise, I gained five pounds and learned a lot about God, the Bible, and the Pentecostal Church. Now at age sixty-five I look back at that episode and now I know that even then, some forty years ago, God was reaching out to me, and exposing me to Christians. No, I did not become a Pentecostal but twenty years and a few more such incidents later I saw the light, received the Holy Spirit into my life, and became a Christian.
THE LORD WORKS IN STRANGE WAYS!!!

THE TWENTY YEAR SEAMAN

GEORGE SHARROW, Dauphin, Pa.   *USS DEUEL APA 160*

Back in the old Navy of the forties and fifties there were men to be found on almost every ship in the fleet known as "twenty year seaman." This was a man who had been in the Navy twenty years or more and still held the rank of seaman. They were found mostly in the deck, gunnery, and commissary divisions. Occasionally one might be found in the ship's control division, but very seldom.

Most twenty year seaman were men who enjoyed being a sailor, loved the Navy, but did not want to assume the responsibilities of being a petty officer. Others were men who performed their duties well, became petty officers, but would lose their rank due to disciplinary action. Good men onboard ship and at sea but when they went ashore always got into trouble causing them to lose their rate, over and over again. These men found a home in the Navy, accepted their own actions as normal and were satisfied to remain as seaman forever. They truly enjoyed the Navy.

In todays modern, nuclear Navy, with all its modern technology, highly sophisticated equipment, plus down sizing; there is no place for a man with the attitude problems of a twenty year seaman. Today, if you do not continue to raise in grade, and keep your nose clean, they will discharge you.

Too bad, as these twenty year seaman were as much a tradition in the Navy, as the white hat and bell bottom trousers.

A darn good man and sailor, well on his way to becoming a twenty year seaman, was Joe Bealer. Joe was twenty-eight years old and had already been in the Navy ten years.

In 1943 right in the midst of World War II, Joe was a sophomore at a small college in Indiana. He was not doing real well in his studies, so with a fear of being drafted into the Army, he quit college and enlisted in the United States Navy.

With his college background and high grades he received in boot camp, Joe was sent to a class-A quartermaster school. In the Navy, quartermasters are responsible for signaling and navigational duties working hand in hand with the ship's officers on the bridge. It takes a certain amount of intelligence to perform these duties. So you can see that Joe was no dummy! In fact he was an intelligent, highly motivated, young man who did his job well and got along good with all his shipmates including the ships officers that he was in daily contact with.

By the end of World War II, he had attained the rank of quartermaster third class aboard the USS Randall APA 224.

Joe had one great fault common to many a sailor, he loved to go on liberty and get drunk. Booze was his downfall! When drunk, Joe was an entirely different person. His personality changed completely. He would become bold, mean, arrogant, and aggressive. He would then do things he would never think of doing when he was sober.

It was because of a riot he instigated at a bar in Shanghai, China in 1946 that caused Joe to lose his first crow. From that bar room brawl until I met Joe aboard the USS DEUEL in 1954 he had gained and lost his crow three more times. He was a QMSN on the signal bridge when we met. I was third class at that time.

In those days the running of a ship was far less sophisticated and more tolerance was granted to guys like Joe who truly loved the Navy and served it well but had the problem of

"As my assistants I will need two lieutenants, three jaygees, four ensigns and two chiefs—and oh yes, send along one seaman also, to do the work!"

getting into trouble now and then. Good seaman were needed in every division aboard ship. At that time it was understood that some men are not born leaders or willing to accept responsibility and are satisfied to do the menial tasks of swabbing the decks, chipping the paint, and do the other constant maintenance tasks that are required on a ship at sea. Joe was a very good signalman being expert on the signal light and with semaphore.

The signal bridge is the highest deck on most ships. In order to reach it, you have to climb up several ladders. These ladders were on the outside of the superstructure with a small landing at each deck with a door, or hatch, leading into the ship at that point. As I remember, there were about six decks above the main deck on the APA 160 with the third deck being where the Captain's apartment was located. The Captain's apartment had not only sleeping quarters, but a living room area, a bathroom with tub, and its own kitchen and eating area. This apartment had its own hatch leading out onto the landing on the ladder mainly for the Captain's cook and stewards mate to use.

On the USS DEUEL, the Captains cook had claimed this landing as his very own private spot where, when taking a break, he could smoke, relax, and enjoy the salt air. For his convenience, he had placed a three foot high metal stool on this landing on which he sat.

The problem was, whenever a sailor went up or down this ladder at any hour of the day or night, he had to go around this stool as it was always there. Many a shin had been knocked open, many a curse uttered, while hurrying along in the dark when men would bump into this stool. It was indeed a major nuisance and did not belong sitting on this landing.

This stool created a problem and a hazard to every sailor using this ladder and with Joe Bealer having to use it several times a day it became a thorn in his side and he had many bruises to prove it.

One hot Summer evening after having been conducting landing exercises on one of the Caribbean islands, the USS DEUEL steamed into the harbor

"What did you miss most during your two years on the island?"

at San Juan, Puerto Rico and dropped anchor. It was to be a week-end of rest, relaxation, and liberty for the crew.

As usual, Joe went ashore and started drinking. When he re-turned to the ship late that night he was as drunk as a skunk. After navigating up the gangway, saluting the O.O.D., and the flag, he headed straight for the ladder leading up to the signal bridge where he knew he would find some hot coffee plus a place to sleep off his hangover without being bothered with noise.

Getting up the almost vertical steel ladder in his condition was a chore in itself. Upon reaching the landing where the cooks stool sat in the darkness, Joe did not see it and bumped right into it as he had done many times before, even when sober. It caused him to fall forward and almost over the guard rail, not only scaring the hell out of him but also adding a few more bruises to his already scarred legs. He was immediately struck with a burst of anger.

"What the #@!!*!" He mumbled out loud. "Its that damn stool!"

Without any hesitation, Joe picked up the stool and tossed it into the dark, murky, water of the harbor.

Up on the signal bridge where I was standing the mid-watch I heard a thump, a scraping of metal against metal, some mumbling and swearing, followed by a big splash. As I walked toward the gunnel to see what had happened, Joes head appeared coming up the ladder.

"#%^!!*, #!!%&* stool" Joe was still muttering to himself. "I took care of that ^%##!@ stool this time!"

I was amused seeing Joe in this condition and at his mumbling. Not being a drinking man myself, I could never understand why a person would drink so much to get themselves in this condition.

"What the hell did you do?" I asked, quite anxious to hear his reply.

"I fixed that cook's ass this time," Joe said to me. "I threw his precious #!!*^% stool overboard."

"You did what?" I exclaimed, not expecting this answer. "Your ass is grass. "I told him, "and the Captain will be the lawn mower."

"!!&*^# him too!" Joe was very mad not just for banging into the stool and almost falling overboard but it opened up some old bruises on his leg and it was bleeding. "What the #@!*^ can he do? Bust me to a civilian?"

"Holy cow!" I said "You are in deep shit this time."

Ignoring me now and not wanting to discuss the matter any further Joe climbed up on a flagbag and was soon fast asleep.

The night was soon quiet again and when my watch was over, Tim Jones relieved me and I told him that Joe was sleeping on the flagbag. I did not tell Jones about the stool incident.

When I returned to the signal bridge the next morning after breakfast, Joe was no longer on the flagbag. He had apparently gone below to his rack. On my way up the ladder I had noticed that the cook's stool was indeed missing and was amused that Joe had gotten revenge on it as he had often promised he would do.

Later that day when the Captain's cook came out on the landing and saw that his stool was missing, all hell broke loose. Knowing that I had been on watch that night, he questioned me but I told him that I knew nothing about where it went.

When they questioned the O.O.D. and messenger who had been standing the Quarterdeck watch, I guess they figured pretty much what had happened and Joe was called on the carpet. He confessed and received a Captain's mast a few days later.

Joe was busted down to seaman recruit and given two months restriction to the ship.

When I left the ship some six months later, Joe was back up to seaman apprentice. He was still a hero to the entire crew for getting rid of the cook's stool and I heard he received a lot of free drinks when he went on liberty.

I will never forget Joe Bealer and the stool incident.

SEASICK

GEORGE SHARROW, Dauphin, Pa.   **USS LSMR 517**

No Navy book would be complete without mentioning "seasick." In his New World Dictionary, Webster defines seasick as: Nausea, dizziness, etc., caused by the rolling of a ship at sea.

This is a fair description but I would say not just, "by the rolling of a ship at sea," but more like, "by the rolling, pitching, tossing, slamming, yawing, and other violent actions taken by a ship when underweigh in the sea while plowing, surging, blundering, through, above, and under the surface of the sea.

It is quite obvious to me that the person who wrote the description of "seasick" in Webster's Dictionary had never been to sea in a flat bottomed ship, especially during a storm.

It is the nemesis of almost every sailor who goes to sea and is oft times described as a feeling you never felt before and pray that you will never feel again. I have never gotten seasick the same way twice. Each time seemed different than the previous time. There are some sailors who claim that they never have been seasick, particularly those serving on large ships like battleships and aircraft carriers, while I have seen others who were experienced, seasoned sailors who got sick the instant the last line was tossed aboard from the pier.

I am thankful that with me, I only got seasick one time each cruise. After recovering from that first bout, which could last up to three days, I never got seasick again for the rest of that cruise.

Everyone got seasick when going around Cape Hatteras. That was one of the roughest areas of the Atlantic Ocean. Even when passing that point from a hundred miles out to sea it was rough, and I usually got sick.

I still shudder and a chill rushes through me as I sit here on dry land and remember how it feels to be on a ship at sea during a storm or in very high seas. Yes, those were the good old days!

The USS LSMR 517 was a small ship having a low freeboard and a flat bottom. It was a real seasick machine!

As a quartermaster, I spent about eighteen hours a day in the open air on the open bridge or conning tower. This was our navigation bridge and was the highest deck on the ship. Many times when I felt nausea and like I was going to become sick, the fresh sea air would settle my stomach, however, a man has to sleep sometime, and the only way to reach my berthing compartment and the comfort of my bunk on a rough day was by taking the below decks route which meant passing through the engine room.

Our engines were twin diesel and if you have ever been behind a bus in city traffic and smelled the fumes of its diesel engine you can imagine what it felt like when you are half sick and must pass through a room laden with those fumes. I would go below and stand outside the hatch leading into the engine room, hyperventilate, then undog the hatch and charge through that horrible smelling area.. I had to run on a catwalk that was just above the engines, the distance was about forty feet and I could never reach the opposite end without being completely overcome with nausea. I swear to God I do not know how the men who worked in that engine room all day could stand it. They must have become immune to the smell.

Many times I would fain off seasickness by eating just saltine crackers and drinking just enough water to get them down, then I would see a shipmate heaving into his puke bucket and that is all it would take. I would then get sick too.

We had one Captain, an old Mustang who had come up through the ranks, who had a really strong stomach and never got seasick. I think he actually received pleasure from seeing others getting sick. It would never fail, when we were plowing along in a high sea or in rough weather and everyone on the bridge were fighting off getting sick. (generally the OOD, QM of the watch, a striker, a messenger, two lookouts, and perhaps a Bosn) the hatch would pop open and up would come this Captain juggling in his hand, like a waiter in a fancy restaurant, a plate of spaghetti. It would be greasy looking and steaming hot. He would go to his chair, sit down and commence eating this spaghetti usually remarking so that all could hear, "umm, this sure tastes good" followed by, "would anyone like a plate of this fine spaghetti?" With our stomachs already feeling queazy and our heads feeling dizzy, the thought and sight of this greasy spaghetti entering our bodies was enough to make us sick. Then when the aroma finally hit our nostrils that was the last straw, we would all aim for our puke buckets. The Captain would just sit there enjoying his spaghetti and laugh at us.

Do you remember the old Chief saying to you: "Boy, when you feel a tickling in the back of your throat... swallow hard! That's your asshole coming up!"

I remember one time we were heading out to sea, had just cleared the bay and entered the ocean, the sea was as calm and smooth as I had ever seen it and the day was warm and pleasant. The type of day when you just want to relax and enjoy the beautiful ocean and its fresh breezes, feel the salt spray on your face, and all that. We were steaming alone so since I was not standing duty on the navigation bridge I decided to sack out, take a nap on the port flagbag on the signalbridge. The signalbridge on an LSMR is located a deck below, and just aft of the lookout stations on the deck above.

We had recently taken aboard, as part of our crew, two brand new sailors fresh out of bootcamp. Not only had they never been to sea before, they had never even seen a ship before coming aboard! This was their first cruise. Would you believe that the Boatswains Mate of the watch decided that since it was such a nice day, he would teach these two kids how to be a lookout on the bridge. Well, once we hit the ocean and the ship started to roll ever so slightly, the kid standing lookout on the port side got sick. He never thought of using the puke bucket that was there for him, instead he heaved right over the side of the ship. There I was laying, relaxing, with my eyes closed, enjoying the ride, when WHAMMO! I got hit in the face, all over my dungarees, all over the flagbag, even the bridge superstructure, with this kid's heave! I mean he must have had one darn good lunch because I never saw so much heave from one person before.

Infuriated, I got up cursing, wondering what had happened. It was one horrible mess and boy did it stink. As soon as I realized what had happened, I rushed to the bridge and really chewed out the dumb kid for not using his puke bucket. I had to go below, shower, and change my clothes. Everyone on the bridge from the Captain on down, had a good laugh at my expense that day.

Needless to say, the next day with the sea still calm and the sun shinning brightly, the young sailor had recovered from his bout with the ocean and I had him on the signalbridge cleaning up the mess he had made on the flagbag and the superstructure.

After we mothballed the LSMR 517 and I was transferred to The USS DEUEL APA 160, I never got seasick again. I did however watch as young sailors, especially reservists coming aboard for their two week cruises, got seasick when the sea was so calm you could not even tell that the ship was moving. So you see seasickness can be a horrible or a humorous incident. It all depends on if it is you or another sailor who is doing the suffering.

THE LOOKOUT

GEORGE SHARROW, Dauphin, Pa.   *USS LSMR 517*

"Periscope one hundred yards off the port beam!" The port lookout yelled out.

I rushed to the port side of the bridge not believing what I had just heard, when the port lookout yelled even louder: "Submarine one hundred yards off the port beam!"

I could not believe what I was seeing. There it was, just off the port beam, steaming along right beside us. I had never seen a submarine this close before. Everyone on the bridge had rushed to the port gunwale with remarks like: "Holy Shit!" and "What the hell?" and "Where did it come from?"

Then, as quickly as it had appeared, it disappeared below the surface and out of sight. Amid all the confusion among us white hats, I looked over to see that both the Captain and the O.O.D. had remained calm as if nothing out of the norm had just happened. Why were they not as excited at having the submarine surfacing right alongside as the rest of us? Then I figured it all out, the Captain must have arranged this little rendezvous to alert us all to the possibility that, when at sea, anything could happen. His little ploy really worked as everyone from the ship's cook to the senior quartermaster were on their toes the rest of that cruise.

One of the most responsible jobs on a ship at sea is that of standing lookout duty. On a small ship like an LSMR almost every non-rated man in the deck and gunnery divisions is trained to stand lookout watches on the conn or open bridge. It can be a tedious and boring task standing in one position for two and four hours at a time scanning the sea and sky with a pair of binoculars.

The quartermasters should be the best lookouts on the bridge as they spend almost their entire day on the bridge area plus regular four hour night watches. Everything that you see; usual, unusual, strange, odd, different, anything worth commenting about goes into the log known as "the quartermasters' notebook which is the responsibility of the quartermaster of the watch. Here are some of the entries I can remember putting into that log.

One time we spotted what we thought to be a dead man floating in the water about a mile from our ship. Upon closer investigation we found it to be a dead sea turtle. Its shell was about five feet in diameter and yellowish, from a distance it looked just like a body. We gave a gunners mate some practice with his twenty millimeter gun, sinking the turtle providing food for the fishes below and eliminating a hazard to navigation on the surface.

On another occasion we were steaming along on a bright sunny day with the sea as smooth as glass, when everyone on the bridge began hearing a strange slapping sound. It was as though someone was clapping their hands together four or five times, only louder. We scanned the horizon and could see nothing. The sound continued for more than a half hour so we began timing the sequence of the sound and headed the ship in the general direction the sound seemed to be coming from. With nothing on the radar and no visual contact we were baffled. After an hour we were close enough to the sound to see something on the surface which seemed to appear then disappear in time with the slapping sound. Closer and closer we got, with all hands eyes glued to the sighting. We finally could make out what we thought were two enormous fish fighting, we thought they were whales. They would seem to pop up out of the sea, stand on their tails in mid-air, and slap their bodies together, creating this clapping sound. They would sink back down into the sea still slamming and clapping, only to emerge in a few seconds, perhaps a few minutes, and repeat this act. We watched this show for quite some time then the Captain decided they were no threat to man nor navigation so we turned away and headed back to our original course we had been following before this folly began. We thought they were some species of whale but the Captain said they were "black fish" we still never figured out if they were playing, fighting, mating, or what? Just another oddity of the sea.

Another incident took place one peaceful day when on the bridge we heard a loud yell coming from the fantail area. The O.O.D. sent the duty messenger of the watch to go find out what had happened. When the messenger returned, he reported that a mess cook had been dumping garbage overboard when he spotted a shark that was as long as our ship was wide. Now our LSMR was thirty-five feet wide so that was one heck of a big shark. The O.O.D. had the lookouts train their binoculars on the ship's wake and sure enough they spotted several large fish or sharks that seemed to be following our ship. Bad omen you say? I don't know but I do know that no one did any sea laundry that day.

One more incident that I thought was humorous. Our ship won the coveted "Navy E" several times. One reason we were so efficient was that our Captain drilled us over and over again. This one day we were standing at general quarters for about two hours and I must admit things were a little dull and boring. For some reason I had trained my binoculars aft and was looking skyward when I noticed something strange. A seagull was following our ship, just one lone seagull! It seemed to be holding a steady position, height, and distance. Trained to report all strange looking sights, I asked the O.O.D. to check out the seagull. Pretty soon everyone on the bridge was watching that seagull. Then one lookout reported that it seemed like the bird had a string in its beak running to our aft forty millimeter mount. The O.O.D ordered the gun captain to report to the bridge.

It seemed that a young seaman apprentice had noticed that when garbage was thrown overboard the seagulls would swoop down, gulp it up, and swallow it. So when this young sailor had become bored while standing at his gun mount as a loader, he came up with the idea of tieing a piece of string to a potato peel, tossing it overboard, and caught himself a seagull. The string was like a roll of kite twine some one hundred yards long. So it worked, a gull took the bait and there it was flying along like a kite on a string.

The Captain was not amused at this incident as he was trying to teach us the seriousness of a general quarters drill. He really chewed the young sailor out and restricted him to the ship for a month with extra duty. He was just a seaman apprentice fresh out of boot and serving as a mess cook. How much worse could it get?

A hundred years from now when some Navy historian takes a look at the quartermaster notebook from the USS LSMR 517 he, or she, will probably think we were the wackiest ship in the Navy.

YESTERDAY AND TODAY

GEORGE SHARROW, Dauphin, Pa.   USS LSMR 517 & UDT 2

It was back in the mid-fifties while serving with a UDT Team on a ComPhibLant exercise in the Caribbean Sea when this incident all started.

We were to be a support group for a mock invasion that was to take place on a beach of Viegas Island. Usually a mock invasion would go something like this: On a designated day the fleet would appear on the horizon about ten miles off the invasion site just long enough for the intended enemy to see it. Then the fleet would do a disappearing act by heading out to sea giving the enemy the thought that nothing was really going to take place. Then, two or three days later, as the sun came up, the fleet would reappear back off the targeted beach and the mock invasion would begin.

As we all know, such an invasion is a heck of a lot of work for all ships and personnel taking part in it. For our team of six divers it was to be fun time. On the day the fleet withdrew from the area, an APD dropped us off about five miles from the targeted beach. We were to recon the beach, set our charges, then hide out somewhere until the pre-dawn hours of the proposed D-Day. At that time we would set off our pre-positioned charges blowing up beach obstacles, later we would rendezvous with the APD and be picked up for evacuation.

Our mike-boat had a canvas tarp covering its open deck area to protect us from the sun and rain as we would be living in this boat for the time we spent in the area. We had cots, sleeping bags, and almost all the comforts one could expect. Lots of canned water and food, or so we thought. We looked forward to lots of swimming, sun bathing, and a little fishing.

Two hours after dropping our anchor in a sheltered cove about a mile from the targeted beach someone got hungry and decided to get into our food box. Much to our surprise and dismay some wise guy had replaced our cans of food with gallon size cans of figs. Yes, figs! After the initial shock, since we were all chow hounds, we decided that we had to do something fast to replace our lost food supply. As with most of our assignments we were not to be seen, nor heard, by anyone until after our assignment had been completed. This presented somewhat of a problem, but in the teams we had a saying: "The difficult we do immediately. The impossible takes a little longer." To us, this was but a minor difficulty.

We had a Chief Boatswains Mate on our team who knew this area of the Caribbean well having spent a lot of time here. He remembered that on a nearby island was a small Naval installation known as Roosevelt Rhodes where a small tent city had been set up by a Marine unit. As a part of this tent city, the Marine officers had set up their own, shall we say, mess tent. The Chief figured there was enough food and beer in this tent to sustain us during our stay in the area. It is suggested that we carry out a raid on this officers' tent to replenish our supplies. A plan was soon sketched out.

Without going into great detail, we raided that officers' tent and managed to acquire a canned ham, other good food stuffs, and a case of beer. We did such a good job that no one saw or heard us during this escapade even though the area was heavily guarded by United States Marines. Returning to our boat we put all this loot into a large cargo net and sunk it near our anchor in fifteen feet of water near our anchor.

The next day all hell broke loose at the Marine encampment. They missed the ham and beer we had taken and it did not take them long to learn of our presence in the area. Suspecting us right away they put a squad of Marines in a boat and came looking for us. When they approached us they seemed all pissed and bad acting asses. I did not say they were bad asses. That is a term given only to members of UDT Teams. Anyhow, after finding nothing in our boat they all got back into their little boat and returned to their base very unhappy for they thought they had finally caught us doing something wrong.

That little incident took place some forty-four years ago when I was a lad of twenty years.

**George Sharrow,
USS LSMR 517**

Just this past year while attending a United States Navy League meeting at the officers club at the Mechanicsburg Navy Supply Depot, here in Mechanicsburg, Pennsylvania I was sitting at a table with seven other members having our after dinner coffee and telling sea stories. When it came to my turn, I related this story and it was well received by all. All, that is, except by one retired Marine Colonel who seemed to be mumbling to himself saying: "You *%^#+#!" He was visibly upset upon hearing my story.

"What the hell is wrong with you Steve?" Another man sitting at our table asked the Colonel.

"You #%^*!#+!" the Colonel said again, only this time it was aloud and he was looking directly at me. "I was a Captain back then and I was in charge of that officers' mess tent and its security." He was really pissed! "We figured it was you UDT *^%##! that did it but we had no proof. YOU #@!!&*!" He said again.

I bought a round of drinks for everyone at our table. Things started chilling down so then I went into great detail about how we had carried out the raid and we all had a big laugh at the Colonels expense. Everyone seemed to enjoy the story even more after learning about the Colonels involvement in it

Ironic isn't it? How our past seems to catch up to us!

CAPTAIN'S MAST

GEORGE SHARROW, Dauphin, Pa.   *USS LSMR 517*

Julius (J.J.) Jackson was the best Stewards Mate I have ever had the pleasure to meet in the Navy. I served with him aboard the LSMR 517 in the early fifties. He was a third class petty officer.

The LSMR was a small ship with six officers and two stewards mates to serve them. They were the best kept officers in the Navy thanks to Julius and his seaman striker.

Jackson had been in the Navy eighteen years and was thirty-six years old, about ready to retire. He was one of the most efficient and proficient persons I have ever known. Always neat and polished looking, he looked better in his undress uniforms than I did in my dress blues. Even his dungarees were starched and pressed with creases in them. His shoes always had a spit-shine on them. Everyone aboard ship loved J.J., he was a friend to us all. His personality, charm, and wit were the greatest I have ever seen combined into one person.

J.J. had two faults; women and booze! Both got him into a lot of trouble. I finally got a good example of this when I shared a "Captains Mast" with him one bright Spring morning.

On these R-boats the officers did not have their own galley they ate the same food as the enlisted men and it was prepared by the ships cooks in the ships only galley.. The wardroom shared a common bulkhead with the galley, it had a window between them that the officers food was passed through to the stewards mate who served it to them. The seaman stewards mate striker worked in the galley helping the regular cooks. J.J. always did the serving. Jackson maintained that wardroom in such a magnificent condition, it was like a first class restaurant.

The Captain of LSMR-517 at that time was Lt. James Rothermel from the Dutch country of Central Pennsylvania. We nicknamed him, "gentlemen Jim" as he was always neat and prim looking thanks to J.J. For instance: Every morning, even when at sea and in the roughest weather, when the Captain got out of his bunk each morning his uniform for that day was laid out waiting for him all cleaned and pressed, even his shoes were spit-shined! Then, as if by magic, Jackson would appear at the Captain's cabin door, knock, then present him with a fresh cup of coffee and a smiling, "good morning Captain."

Is it any wonder then, that whenever J.J. got into trouble either on ship or ashore and appeared before a Captains Mast he seemed to get away with murder. But, wait, I am getting ahead of myself with this story.

Although the joy and anticipation of going ashore on liberty is one thing every sailor shares and looks forward to, it can also be a time of ruin and destruction for many a good sailor who becomes greedy with wine, women, and other vices that are strewn before them.

This is how I came to be sharing a "Captains Mast" with J.J.

The 517 was slated to leave the Little Creek, Virginia area and head for the Caribbean Sea to take part in amphibious operations with other member ships of the fleet, and would be gone for two months. With this in mind all the sailors onboard wanted to take advantage of the long seventy-two hour weekend that was being offered to two-thirds of the crew the weekend prior to our departure. The weekend liberty was to begin 0800 Friday and expire onboard 0800 the following Monday. The ship was scheduled to leave the Little Creek amphibious Base about 1100 Monday, just after quarters.

Since all the officers were also taking advantage of this liberty leaving only the most junior officer onboard, Stewards Mate J.J. Jackson was not really need onboard ship, his striker could take care of this one junior grade officer. So J.J. borrowed some money from his striker, as he always did, and from one of the cooks who was staying on duty and then he too, took off for parts unknown to enjoy the long weekend.

I took advantage of this opportunity myself to drive home to Harrisburg, Pennsylvania to visit my mother and grandmother, plus say a sailors farewell to a few girlfriends in that area.

The weekend went well, but as I started back to Little Creek on Sunday night it was raining quite hard. There were no four-lane interstate highways in those days and all the major roads took a driver right through all the major cities and towns along the way. My route took me through Gettysburg, Pennsylvania, then Frederick, Maryland, Washington, D.C., and Richmond, Virginia, plus a dozen or so small towns along the way. It was a good eight to ten hour trip. When I reached Frederick, I was traveling down a cobblestone street, not macadam, the rain had made the stones very slippery, my car hit a bump, I careened into the bumper of a parked car. The police came and took me to the city jail where they locked me up. I guess they just hated sailors in Frederick. Anyhow, I was detained in that jail for several hours and then released. Just long enough to screw up my schedule. Knowing that my liberty time was running out and I had just a few hours remaining to catch my ship before it was to depart, I broke all speed laws trying to get back to the base in Little Creek in time.

I arrived at the parking lot just outside the base gates about 1100 that Monday, passed through the gate and started walking back to the pier where the LSMR-517 was tied up.

All of a sudden I heard the long blast of a ship's horn coming from the dock area. This sound indicated that a ship was backing away from its pier getting underweigh.

"Oh, my God!" I said aloud. "The damn ship is leaving!"

To miss your ship is one of the greatest crimes in the Navy and I realized at that moment I was in big trouble.

Now running at full speed I could see the 517. It had thrown off all its lines and had started backing away from the pier.

"Holy shit" I was yelling while running as fast as I could, "wait for me!"

I could hear some heavy breathing near my side and just a step behind me but I paid no heed, just kept running at full speed not caring what was behind me.

As I ran onto the pier the ship was still about two hundred feet away, still backing. Sailors standing on the bow of the ship were waving and shouting: "Come on Sharrow!" and "Come on J.J.!" It was then I realized the man running behind me was J.J. Then they shouted; "JUMP!" and jump, we did!

The ship was actually five or six feet past the end of the pier when we jumped and were pulled aboard by our shipmates. A loud cheer broke out all over the ship. I guess the whole crew had been watching and voiced their approval that we had made it by cheering.

Jackson and I rushed to our "special sea detail" stations and assumed our duties. Even before the ship had cleared the jetty we were informed that we would be having a "Captains Mast" later in the day.

This was to show me how good a standing Jackson had with the Captain and how I would lose out on a good conduct medal.

Once out to sea, the special sea detail was secured and the regular underweigh watch set. Things were settling down to our regular ships routine except for Jackson and me. We were standing at attention just outside the wardroom door waiting our visit with the Captain.

Since my duties called for me being on the bridge of the ship about eighteen hours a day working with the officers, and J.J. worked with them night and day, the Captain knew us both on a personal basis. However, missing your ship when it is headed out to sea is a court martial event. I was shaking in my shoes while standing there waiting, but J.J. seemed to be calm and cool. He had been here before!

The door to the wardroom opened and a voice we both recognized as the Captain said: "Sharrow and Jackson, get your troublesome asses in here!"

"Yes Sir!" we both answered at the same time. Entering the wardroom Jackson pushed me in, ahead of himself. We found ourselves standing at attention before Captain Rothermel and by his side, our executive officer Lt.(jg) Blake.

"I can understand Jackson," the Captain started, "but you Sharrow, you never get into any trouble and have a perfect record. What happened to you?"

The Captain obviously wanted to hear my story first so I told him exactly what had happened leading to my being late getting back to the ship. I later learned that when we landed on the ships deck it was 1115, since we were both three hours AWOL we had both been put on report as missing.

The Captain listened attentively to my story then said: "Sharrow, I am a little disappointed that you did not allow yourself more time to get back to Little Creek."

"Yes Sir!" I replied, still at attention.

That was it as far as I was concerned. The Captain focused his attention to Jackson "All right J.J." the Captain said looking directly at Jackson with a frown on his face.

"What is your sad story?" Jackson now standing at double attention, if that were possible, began his story.

"Well Sir, Captain," he began. "You understands the trouble I have with women?"

"I sure do!" The Captain replied sternly. "As well as with drinking, gambling, and a few other things." then he said to J.J.: "lets hear all of it!"

I was about to be entertained!

"Well Sir," Jackson began, "I was at the Anchor bar in Norfolk when I met this woman. She was a real beauty. We both started drinking and became a little tipsy. After awhile she took me to her apartment. This was on Saturday night."

J.J. was really getting into telling his tale, using his hands to articulate certain messages and facial expressions, even body language, to try and get his message across. He was a great story teller and this was to be one of his best performances. To tell you the truth, I was glad I was present to hear him in action and I would repeat this scene over and over, again to many people in future years.

J.J.'s story continued: "Once we got in her apartment she stripped stark naked and things just started to happen. Then she got out a bottle of scotch whiskey!" J.J. was really jumping around at this point. "This ole girl just spread the goofa-dust all over me and into my eyes." He was really getting into it now. "I'm telling you Captain this woman was something else! She sang! She danced! We drank and drank then we had the best sex I have ever had in my life. I mean, we screwed, screwed, and screwed some more and all this was happening while the dancing and drinking was going on."

J.J. paused and wiped his brow with a handkerchief he had produced from inside his jumper. Obviously, he had come to this Captains Mast well prepared. He continued his story; "It was like I died and went to Heaven."

The Captain interrupted J.J.'s story. "My idea of Heaven is a little different than yours. Continue your story. It is just starting to get good."

Lt(jg). Blake, who did not seem to be more than a year older than me, was standing by the Captains side taking it all in, as was I. I guess regulations called for a junior officer to be present at a Captains mast and the Captain wanted Lt(jg). Blake to gain experience in all aspects of Navy life.

"Well Captain," J.J. continued. "With all this shaking going on, the booze and all. I just passed out." J.J. looked around at all of our faces trying to read our reactions to his tale thus far, then he finished his story. "When I woke up it was 0800 this morning. I was naked, cold, and shaking. Here that woman had gone and left me and she took all my money with her!"

I could see that the Captain was enjoying J.J.'s tale, Lt(jg) Blake was standing there looking dumbfounded, as was I. The two of us had never witnessed a performance like this before.

J.J. was not finished yet! "I knew I was in deep trouble," he went on. "Not being able to find my shorts or socks I just threw on my pants and jumper, slipped into my shoes and took off running."

"You ran all the way from Norfolk to Little Creek?" the Captain asked with a frown still on his face. Apparently he was not as amused at J.J.'s story as Lt(jg) Blake and I were.

"No Sir," Jackson continued again. "I ran to Military Highway and hitched a ride back to the base. I got back just as the ship was backing. Then when I heard that horn blowing I knew it was for all the marbles so I jumped for the ship just like Sharrow did."

I think J.J. was enjoying telling his story as much as we were enjoying listening to it. "I jumped clear out of my shoes!" He exclaimed. "They is still back on the pier at Little Creek. I sure did not want to miss this ship. I knew that was serious."

Jackson was finished and I felt like applauding. What a performance that was. I would not have missed it for the world. I know I must have been standing there in awe at what I had just witnessed. My eyes were big and my mouth agape.

"Well Jackson," the Captain said to J.J. "That's your best story yet. Just what the hell am I going to do with you?"

"I just don't know Sir. I just don't know." Jackson was now standing with his head looking down at the deck, his arms drooping at his side, looking like a sick puppy. I could tell by all his new expressions that he was appealing towards the Captain for sympathy.

The Captain was in a good mood that day and was very lenient to both Jackson and me. Jackson was restricted to the ship for one month and I just received a reprimand. Since the ship would be in the Caribbean for two months it did not matter much. What an experience in life I had just witnessed!

TOWNS THAT HATED SAILORS

GEORGE SHARROW, Dauphin, PA.   **USS LSMR 517**

A lot of sailors talk about how they hated Norfolk, Virginia but by the time I got there in 1951, I found the town to be quite hospitable. It had a very picturesque downtown area that I really enjoyed and I did not drink nor go chasing women. I spent many a good liberty in Norfolk with my buddy, Michael Raymond Kiseluski, Ski or Mickey to his friends. Our typical liberty in Norfolk usually started off with a nice swim at the YMCA pool, then dinner at some nice restaurant, and ended up going to a movie or taking in the burlesque show on Main Street.

My recollections of Main Street are filled with bars, where tattooed women who worked in the bars were tougher than the sailors who drank there. Uniform shops where you could pickup a tailormade set of blues or whites at a good price and in an hours time. A lot of greasy-spoon restaurants, pan-handlers by the score, and of course, the prostitutes. I forget the name of the burlesque theater on main Street but it was a very popular place. The shows were not vulgar like todays "adult worlds" they were good strip shows with comedy acts in between.

A recent visit to Norfolk for a ship reunion was a shocker. Gone were all the old buildings in the downtown area including Main Street. I guess the locals looked upon all that as a detriment to society. No more bars, greasy spoons, women or even sailors walking the streets. I did not see one sailor in uniform in the downtown area. The waterfront area is all cleaned up, with neat and proper tourist attractions abounding.

We visited Norfolk Navy Base and the Little Creek Amphib Base .... I didn't recognize either one. They are now like a city within a city. Anything you would find in a small town was now located on the base within the gates. No need for a sailor to go outside the base for anything. Theaters, furniture store, bowling alley, pizza parlor, beauty shop, just everything you could think of. Security on the bases was very tight.

It seems like a different Navy today! Would you believe you could count the number of sailors in uniform on your hands. I guess as soon as they get off duty these days the Navy personnel change into their civvies. Perhaps they are not as proud of their uniforms as we were?

So Norfolk is not listed among my "towns that hated sailors!

Now Virginia Beach, Virginia, was a different story. I remember how we all stayed away from that town. Back in the fifties sailors definitely were not welcome there. Shore patrols roamed the streets in jeeps and on foot. If your hat wasn't squared or your neckerchief knot at the right position they would write you up or send you back to your ship. I definitely saw signs that stated, "sailors and dogs keep off the grass!" Besides that the restaurants were too expensive and the women too snooty.

Another town that sailors stayed clear of was Colonial Heights, Virginia. As I remember it was a small one-horse, two red light town. The speed limit was twenty-five miles per hour and if you were caught going one mile over the limit you were arrested and paid a stiff fine. The rumor was that at one time the town had normal speed limits then one day the police chiefs young daughter was hit by a car driven by a sailor. I really don't remember if the daughter was killed or what.

Back in those days hitch hiking and travel by car was the main mode of transportation for sailors headed home on weekends. A great number of sailors headed North from Norfolk towards Richmond, Washington, and points further North and the main route North went right through Colonial Heights.

A popular practice was to catch you speeding, take you before a justice of the peace immediately, actually ask you how much money you had on you, then fine you that amount. Many a sailors holiday ended right there and had to turn around and head back to Norfolk broke. It didn't take long for the word to get around. No sailors drove above the speed limit in Colonial Heights, Virginia.

My vote for the town that hated sailors the most was Frederick, Maryland. My initiation to the towns justice system came one rainey night in June when I was returning to Norfolk from a long weekend with a car full of sailors.

It was around 2200 on a dark, rainey, night when we reached the streets of Frederick. The route through the city led us down a narrow, cobblestone street with cars parked on both sides. As I proceeded down the street my tires slipped on the wet stones and the car slid to the left. My front bumper slid gently into the rear bumper of a parked car. I was only going about twenty-five miles an hour because of the treacherous driving conditions. The sound of metal hitting metal brought an Airforce Sergeant out of one of the houses. I had stopped my car, got out and was looking to see if there was any damage when he approached me. He said "Hi" and identified the parked car I had hit, as belonging to him. With the aid of a flashlight he examined the bumper and declared that no damage had been done so he said to me: "Its OK sailor, no damage done, you can take off!" With these words I returned to my car and resumed winding my way through Frederick.

About five miles on the other side of Frederick I was startled by the flashing red light of a Maryland State Trooper who pulled us over.

After checking my credentials he told my passengers they were free to go but that I was to get back in my car and follow him back to the jail in Frederick. He told me that I was under arrest for hit-and run! Naturally I told him that he must have mistaken my car for someone else. He then asked, "Did you hit a parked car back in Frederick?" I replied, "Yes, but I stopped and talked with the owner of the car and he had told me it was OK to leave."

"Sorry sailor," the trooper said, "thats not the report I received. You will have to follow me back to the jail and get things straightened out there."

So I got back in my car and followed him back into Frederick while my three buddies got out and had to start hitch hiking, in the rain, back to Norfolk.

When we reached the Frederick jail they impounded my car and threw me into the drunk tank. They would not listen to my side of the story saying, "The judge will hear your case in the morning!" This was Friday night.

The drunk tank was filled with drunks, derelicts, thieves, and queers! I caused some trouble when a queer approached me so they removed me to a cell where I spent the night. My cell was about six by ten feet with two metal slabs hanging from the wall that they called bunks and a wash bowl- commode fixture in the rear. The bunk had no mattress and the commode stank of urine. Here I was in my dress-whites in this filthy hole.

Around five a.m. the next morning they roused us up and had us (me and about ten other prisoners) form a line facing each others back with our left hand on the left shoulder of the man in front of you, then they lock-stepped us to the dining hall.

Breakfast consisted of a tin-cup filled with black coffee and a metal bowl half filled with cornflakes that had some corn syrup poured over it. No sugar, no milk! naturally, I did not eat anything. Then it was back to my cell where I spent the morning talking with my fellow prisoners; two thieves and a man who had beat-up his mother.

At noon, they once more had us line up and march to the dining hall, lock-step as before. Lunch was a real treat! It consisted of the tin cup of black coffee and the tin bowl, only this time the bowl contained a colored water and one bean, They called it bean soup. Once more I did not eat. We were returned to our cells as before.

At five p.m. the dining room procedure was repeated only on the table this time something new had been added. There was now a dry piece of bread with a hotdog laying on it. This was in addition to the coffee and water soup. Again I ate nothing! My fellow prisoners, seeing that I was not eating, quickly grabbed up my food and ate it as though it were a steak dinner. Once more we were marched back to our cells.

By now I had been in their lousy jail about twenty hours. My white uniform was filthy from laying on the metal-slab bed, I had no razor, toothbrush, or comb, so I was looking like a bum. No officer or guard had said anything to me about anything and I had not even been allowed to make a telephone call. I was starting to get pissed off!

Around seven p.m. a guard came to my cell and said I was to receive my hearing. Thank God, I thought, now I will finally get some justice. I was lock-stepped to a court room where I was seated before a robed judge along with ten other prisoners.

I watched as one by one my fellow prisoners were led before the judge. He had a thick accordion-type file on each one. All of these prisoners had committed, what I considered to be, serious crimes. Would you believe that all but one of them received suspended sentences and were set free!!!!! Then it was my turn.

As I stood before the judge I noticed that all the evidence he had on me was a three by five inch file card. So when he said to me: "Son.... this is a very serious offence!" I about crapped in my pants. Finally he asked me to explain exactly what had happened the night before and when I had gone into great detail about the accident. When he had heard my story the judge turned to the bailiff and asked if the complainant was in the room. He was, so the Airforce Sergeant stood up and confirmed my story.

"Why then, did you file a hit-and-run charge against this man?" The judge asked.

"Because my wife told me to, your honor" the airman said. "This sailor never told me his name,"

The judge had no alternative but to dismiss the charges and release me. But, it did not end there!!!!!

The judge turned his attention to me and stated: "There are no charges against you, however, there will be a fine of thirty dollars imposed on you for costs."

By now I am really getting my dander up! Here I am falsely accused, imprisoned, and abused..this guy is making me pay costs. "What costs, your honor?" I spoke out.

"Young man you stayed overnight in our jail and consumed three of our meals. That is the costs!"

That was it! I exploded! I told the judge about his filthy cell, his lousy food not fit for pigs, and of the inhumane treatment I had received.

"I now find you in contempt of court! The fine is fifty dollars, plus the costs, or thirty days in jail!" Since I had no money they sent me back to my cell. This was Saturday.

On Sunday morning as they lock stepped us to lunch we passed by an open office door and I spotted a telephone on a desk. Breaking out of line and into that office I grabbed the telephone and made a call to my home in Harrisburg Penn. Luckily, the guard understood my plight and let me make the telephone call.

My Aunt Ruth answered the telephone and upon hearing my story immediately passed out cold and fell to the floor. My cousin Thelma picked up the telephone whereupon she said she would wire the money to Frederick so I could be released.

The telegraph office in Frederick was closed on Sunday so I had to wait until nine o'clock Monday morning when the court received their money and finally set me free. It was eleven o'clock before I got back into my car and headed back to Norfolk. I knew my ship, the USS LSMR 517, was to be leaving Norfolk and headed out to sea at five p.m. so I really had to break all speed limits getting back to my ship.

I reached the pier just as my ship was backing, but I made it aboard. However I had been listed as AWOL. Once out to sea I had a "Captains Mast" and was acquitted. The officers on my ship were so mad at the injustice I had received from the Frederick Police that they wanted to take up a collection and go back to Frederick and sue the court but since we were going to be out to sea for six months they discarded the idea. They proclaimed that I had received a "kangaroo court trail" which was illegal and was happening all over the South.

To this day.. I still feel the city of Frederick, Maryland owes me, at least, an apology for the injustice and inhumane treatment I received from them.

Sometime later, someone did blow up a part of that jail in anger. It was not me! However I do applaud the person who did it!

TOSSING THE PRESIDENTIAL FLAG

JOHN STANOSKI, Natrona Heights, Pa.   USS LSMR 515

Serving as a quartermaster aboard an LSMR meant you did dual jobs of signalman and navigation. The good part was that you gained a lot of valuable experience in your rating. The bad part was that you only had a limited amount of space and equipment to carry out the job, yet you were to function with the same ease as a much larger ship like a cruiser or aircraft carrier. At times a herculean task! This, at times, presented quite a problem.

While serving aboard the USS LSMR 515 in 1953, we were assigned to visit the United States Naval Academy at Annapolis, Maryland so the midshipmen might come aboard and familiarize themselves with our type of ship.

At the Academy we shared a pier with a guest destroyer of the Fletcher Class who was there for the same purpose we were.

I was a quartermaster second class at the time.

Without much advance notice we were told that the President Of The United States was playing golf nearby and that upon completion of his game, and before returning to the USS WILLIAMSBURG he would be coming to the Naval Academy and would be visiting aboard either the destroyer or our LSMR.

This presented somewhat of a problem for us.

When a dignitary of flag rank or above comes aboard your ship you must display, or fly, his personal flag from your yardarm. I would say that very few ships carry a Presidential flag in their inventory aboard ship. Aboard our LSMR our storage area for extra flags was a metal box about three feet square and a foot deep that was stored under the Loran set in the pilot house. In that box we stored a dozen or so extra flags that we normally have in our on-deck flagbags that have a tendency to wear out, also two extra ensigns and a spare unionjack. No special flags except for our church pennant.

Somehow the quartermasters on the destroyer had acquired a Presidential Flag and had it on hand.

We expected the President to visit the destroyer, not us, so we decided to leave his flag aboard the destroyer. The understanding was that if he, the President, suddenly changed his mind and veered towards the gangway of our ship, the quartermasters aboard the destroyer would "throw" the flag to us on the LSMR.

Procedure for presenting a special flag is that it is folded, rolled up, then tied with a very thin thread that will break easily. In advance of its use, the flag is attached to a halyard, then run all the way up to the yardarm where it will await the arrival of the dignitary, then it will be displayed, the instant he steps aboard your ship.

The flag was in place at the yardarm on the destroyer. Our greatest fear was then realized! At the last second, the President Of The United States, Dwight D. Eisenhower, decided to visit our ship, the USS LSMR 515.

The Presidential Party had started walking down the pier headed directly for the destroyer when, all of a sudden, it changed direction and veered towards our gangway some twenty feet away.

A miracle was called for!

There was a sudden burst of activity on the signal bridge aboard the destroyer as the quartermasters had to lower the flag, unhook it from the halyard, then accurately toss it across the pier, some thirty feet, to be caught by a quartermaster aboard our ship who would take it to our flagbag, attach it to a halyard, run it up to the yardarm, (two block it using old Navy lingo), to be broken and displayed the instant the President stepped aboard our ship.

Again, all this had to be accomplished as the Presidential Party walked a mere twenty feet or so to our gangway.

Luckily we did catch the flag thrown to us and managed to get it up to the yardarm and broke it to fly in the wind just as President Dwight D. Eisenhower stepped aboard our ship.

The staff officer accompanying the President immediately looked up as the flag was being hoisted. Can you imagine the trouble we would have been in if we had not hoisted that flag? Incidently, the flag was thrown directly over the President's head.

Sounds like a scene from "Mr. Roberts" movie or the "McHales Navy" television show doesn't it?

THE SANDWICH INCIDENT

HAROLD WELCH, Mecosta, Michigan   USS FLOYD B. PARKS

While serving as Commissary Chief aboard the destroyer, USS FLOYD B. Parks, Chief Welch relates this story to us.

Serving aboard this ship at the same time was a Lt(jg) Robert Barker who was the gunnery officer. Lt(jg) Barker was hated by every white hat on the ship as he always went out of his way to irritate, discredit, and otherwise make life miserable for every enlisted man aboard.

Lt(jg) Barker was fully qualified as an O.O.D. and would stand a bridge watch when the ship was underweigh. The bridge watch on this size ship usually consisted of the O.O.D., one quartermaster, two lookouts, a boatswains mate who doubled as the telephone talker, and a duty messenger (usually a seaman or apprentice seaman).

On this particular night the ship was underweigh by itself. It was the mid-watch, about 0200. Only the engine room had its full compliment standing watch. In the galley was seaman Tom Spots who came on duty at midnight to make sandwiches and coffee for all enlisted men standing the midwatch throughout the ship as was standard Navy procedure for ships underweigh. He was also kept busy making pies and bread for the coming days meals.

Two weeks prior to this day Tom Spots had been a Commissaryman Third Class until Lt(jg) Barker (now on duty on the bridge) had his rank taken from him reducing him back to Seaman because he had neglected to dump garbage overboard at the proper time. So to say that Lt(jg) Barker was now at the top of Seaman Spots hate-list would be putting it mildly.

To better understand and enjoy this story you must know that in the United States Navy an officer is given money known as "food rations" apart from his regular salary. Officers in the Navy are an elite group and are treated as such. Using these "food rations" they maintain their own galley and have Stewards Mates whose duty is to care for them, (cook, serve food, make their beds, clean their clothes, etc.). Using this money the officers buy their own food and do not eat food prepared in the enlisted mens mess except on certain occasions. If an officer wants something during the course of his duty watch like a cup of coffee or a snack, all he has to do is call for the duty Stewards Mate and he will bring it to him, that is their duty assignment.

It is the duty of the Stewards Mate to serve the officers. This is not the duty of any other enlisted man aboard ship. They could do it as a compliment but never as a duty.

On this particular Mid-watch the sandwiches and coffee prepared by Seaman Spots had been served about an hour ago, at 0100. All hands on the bridge had enjoyed two spam sandwiches and coffee including Mr. Barker to whom it was complimentary.

Time goes slow on a mid-watch so an hour later, around 0200, Mr. Barker was still hungry and asked if there were any sandwiches remaining on the tray.

"No Sir," replies QM3 Jones, who was quartermaster of the watch. "They were all eaten Sir."

"Well I am still hungry," Lt(jg). Barker said. "Where is the duty messenger?"

QM3 Jones looked over to a corner of the bridge where Seaman Bauim, messenger of the watch, was having a conversation with one of the lookouts.

Jones nodded to Bauim and gestured towards Lt(jg). Barker who was standing by the electric compass. Bauim stopped talking with the lookout and approached the Lieutenant.

"Yes Sir," Bauim saluted. "Did you want something Sir?"

"Yes I do," Lt(jg) Barker spoke in a command type voice. "Go down to the galley and bring me back another sandwich."

"Aye,Aye,Sir!" The young Seaman replied as he looked toward Quartermaster Jones with a puzzled look on his face knowing that Lt(jg) Barker should not be doing this. In fact, he should not have eaten any of the enlisted mens sandwiches in the first place.

Jones just shrugged his shoulders as if to say, "hey, who am I to question this officers actions?"

So Seaman Bauim, messenger of the watch, left the bridge and headed for the galley to carry out Mr. Barkers order.

Upon his arrival at the galley Bauim found Commissaryman Spots busy making pies with flour all over hands and apron.

Looking up from his work Spots asked, "what is your problem Bauim?" Spots snapped at Bauim hating to be interrupted while he was working.

"Mr. Barker wants a spam sandwich!" Bauim blurted out.

"Screw Mr. Barker! Who the hell does he think he is?" Spots was pissed off that Mr. Barker, the prick as Spots called him, would expect to get a sandwich from the enlisted mens galley. "Tell the #*%@! to call his Stewards Mate." Spots was still very angry that Lt(jg) Barker had taken his rate away from him over the garbage incident.

The entire crew had a large disrespect and a bad feeling towards Lt(jg) Barker for his misuse and poor treatment of the enlisted men aboard ship plus he had frequently abused his privileges as an officer by ordering messengers of his watch to get food for him from the crews galley which was a "no, no."

After thinking it over for a few minutes Commissaryman Spots reconsidered and told Seaman Bauim to have a seat in the messhall and enjoy a cup of coffee while he made the sandwich.

Bauim heaved a sigh of relief for he knew how upset Spots was and he was afraid he might take his anger out on him. Bauim drew a cup of coffee from the urn, picked up a magazine, and sat down at a mess table. He was in no hurry to return to the bridge.

A quick get even scheme had started to take shape in the mind of Commissaryman Jones. As he looked around in his galley for some ingredients that would make a good sandwich for Mr. Barker. He had thoughts of teaching this officer a lesson that he would not soon forget and to perhaps even the score for the garbage incident.

He had recently cleaned the grill after making the hot spam sandwiches for the mid-watch using a piece of terrycloth toweling to wipe off the grease and debris.

Finding this piece of terrycloth rag, using a pair of boning shears he cut out a piece the size and shape of a slice of bread. Smelling it he was not satisfied that it was right for the job just yet, so he dipped it into the dirty grease pot that was under the stove. This was a pot where all the grease and waste from the grill was deposited for later disposal. Now he squeezed some excess grease from the rag and laid it aside.

Spots then put two slices of bread into the toaster, this was going to be a sandwich extraodinaire. He then spread mayonnaise on the toast, added a slice of tomato, some lettuce, then on top this, he placed the dirty, greasy, dish rag. He topped it with the second piece of toast and the sandwich was complete. Placing the sandwich on a nice clean plate along with two slices of pickle he called for the messenger.

"Here Bauim, take this to Lt(jg) Barker with my compliments!"

Happy that he could now complete his mission Seaman Bauim took the sandwich and headed for the bridge thinking that perhaps now he would make a few good points with Mr. Barker.

Up on the bridge Mr. Barker was getting very hungry and wondered why it was taking the messenger so long to get his sandwich.

When he finally saw Bauim approaching with his sandwich which looked and smelled so delicious he could hardly contain himself. Picking up the sandwich he charges at it with his mouth.

Biting into it he enjoyed the initial taste of the bread, lettuce, tomato, and mayonnaise. He bit into it again, and again. He seemed to be snarling at it as he twisted the bread from side to side.

All these actions by Lt(jg) Barker towards the sandwich seemed to delight the lookouts and Quartermaster Jones who had all watched with envy as Bauim had handed the sandwich to the officer.

Mr. Barker was really becoming frustrated as he kept biting into the dirty, greasy, dish rag that Commissaryman Spots had placed in the sandwich instead of spam.

Harold Welch,
USNTC GREAT LAKES

Finally, with one big lunge in his part, the bread pulled away in his hands, the tomato and lettuce fell to the deck, and the dirty dish rag, gripped tightly in his teeth, plopped sloppily onto his chin spewing grease onto Mr. Barkers hands, face, his uniform, and the deck.

"What the hell!" Mr. Barker exclaimed as he pulled the dirty rag from his teeth. "What is this #%^*@ thing?"

In the darkness of the bridge the dull glow of the electric compass and the tiny red light on the chart desk were the only light source. He could not immediately discern just what it was he had been biting on.

Taking a flashlight from the chart desk he shined its beam of light towards this thing he had now tossed onto the deck.

"Jesus, its a filthy rag!" He swore in rage and disgust.

As soon as he realized what it was, that someone had sabotaged his sandwich, he jumped up and swearing profusely, ordered that the duty cook and Chief Welch be brought to the bridge immediately.

Shaking in his boots but swelled with laughter Seaman bauim, the duty messenger, took off down the ladder to the Chiefs quarters, then to the messhall where he knew Seaman Spots would be waiting, expecting him.

Soon the messenger returned to the bridge with a sleepy eyed, bath robe bedecked, Chief Welch not far behind him.

"Chief Welch," Mr. Barker screamed, "just what the hell is going on here?"

"Gee, I don't know Sir," the beguiled Chief replied. "I don't even know what the problem is." Not one to get upset by an excited officer Chief Welch remained calm and cool, but he was anxious to find out what had happened.

Looking around, the Chief noticed that all the men on the bridge were either giggling like school girls or holding their hand over their mouth to keep from laughing. He figured it must be something funny.

"The messenger only told me that you wanted me on the bridge immediately," the befuddled Chief replied. "I don't know what is going on here Mr. Barker."

Mr. Barker then picked up the dirty, greasy rag from the deck and showing it to the Chief said: "This piece of crap was in my sandwich!"

Still calm and trying to figure out what had happened he turned and saw that Commissaryman Spots was standing on the bridge behind him. The Chief guessed in his mind what had happened. No matter what, he knew that he would be on Spots side.

"What is my baker doing here on the bridge?" Chief Welch asked the officer. "He is supposed to be down in the galley making bread and pies."

"He is the #@%^**+ who made my sandwich!" Lt(jg) Barker was still angry and seeking revenge.

Chief Welch had sized up the situation right away and looking Lt(jg) Barker square in the eye asked: "How come my baker made your sandwich? Why wasn't your sandwich ordered from the officers mess?"

"It is none of your #@^^* business what I do, or where I get my sandwich!" A now much angered Mr. Barker yelled at the Chief (which as an officer and a gentlemen, he should never do) "You are responsible for this man and his actions!"

"What do you intend to do about this Sir?" Chief Welch knew that this officer was out of line and he had him by the balls. He would now take charge of this situation.

"I am putting you both on report," Mr. Barker exclaimed. "You will answer to the Captain for this."

Upon hearing this the tired, and now bored, Chief Welch said to Lt(jg) Barker; "Will that be all Sir?"

Mr Barker still in shock over the entire incident plus the Chiefs calm attitude said with authority: "I will tell you when it is all!"

Ignoring Mr. Barker for a moment Chief Welch turned to his commissaryman Spots and told him to go below and get back to his baking duties.

This action by the Chief really infuriated Lt(jg) Barker who told Chief Welch "that smartness just added insubordination to your charges. You just stand-by here until you are dismissed."

By this time Chief Welch decided that Mr. Barker was acting out of anger and under duress with conduct unbecoming an officer of the United States Navy so he politely saluted, and turning, exited himself from the bridge.

"Good night Sir." He ended the charade.

The officer dumbfounded by this action by the Chief, walked to the center of the bridge, put his binoculars to his eyes and stared out at the empty ocean.

Quartermaster Jones picked up the components of the ill fated sandwich and cleaned up the grease using a paper towel. Seaman Bauim took a damp mop from its rack and mopped the surrounding deck, then returned to his perch near the compass.

Commissaryman Spots returned to his galley and resumed his baking of pies and bread.

Chief Welch returned to his bunk... and the mid-watch resumed on the bridge.

Two days passed without a word said about the incident.

Three days later both Chief Welch and Lt(jg) Barker decided to discuss their little altercation with the ships executive officer Lt. Sam Osborne to let him decide what punishment, if any, should result from the sandwich incident.

The discussion was held over cups of coffee in the officers wardroom with just the three of them present.

It took just three cups of coffee for Lt. Osborne to reach the conclusion that Lt(jg) Barker and Seaman Spots were both at fault. He further decided that the incident was brought about by the tension and stress put on both men from being at sea for such a prolonged period and that no serious action, or punishment, was necessary.

Mr. Barker was reprimanded for ordering sandwiches from the crews galley and he was ordered not to ever do this again. He was also told that he should be more respectful of the enlisted men and of his position as an officer in the United States Navy.

It was decided that Commissary Seaman Spots was to be restricted to the ship the next two liberty ports the ship entered. This in itself was no big deal as they would be returning to Norfolk, their home port, in three weeks.

Chief Welch was complimented by Lt. Osborne for keeping a cool head during this tense situation and for calming things down.

At the conclusion of the meeting Lt(jg) Barker was the first to leave the wardroom. Lt. Osborne motioned to Chief Welch to hang back for a moment.

"Chief," LT. Osborne said, "I want to thank you for handling this situation the way you did. It could have gotten nasty."

"Thank you Sir," Chief Welch replied. "Someone has got to watch out for the shit-heads in this mans Navy."

"True Chief," LT. Osborne agreed, "but this has got to be one of the funniest stories I have ever heard." He started laughing as he poured himself another cup of coffee.

"Aye, Aye, Sir," Chief Welch saluted. "Thank you very much Sir, "and he too departed from the wardroom, happy that the situation ended the way it did.

DEMPSEY DUMPSTER INCIDENT

HAROLD WELCH,   *Great Lakes Naval Training Center*
Mecosta, MI

Harry Albrecht enlisted in the United States Navy in September 1964 and reported to boot camp at Great Lakes Naval Training Center.

After one week of training and all the articles of the Navy had been read, and taught him, he was placed on barracks watch serving the mid-watch from midnight until 0400. Upon being relieved he was found to be sound asleep. The relief awoke the master-at-arms and brought him to Harry's post, who at this time awakened Harry and informed him that he was being placed on report for sleeping on watch.

The following morning when Chief Welch the commanding officer of Company 263 reported onboard he was informed of the incident. Chief told the master-at-arms to inform Harry that he would be appearing at Captains Mast at 0730. At Captains Mast Chief Welch found Harry guilty according to articles found in the UCMJ.

As punishment for sleeping on watch Chief Welch informed Harry that he could be shot, or confined to the brig for as long as five years. Instead Chief Welch told Harry that he was going to assign him to the "dempsey dumpster" watch. whereupon he would take a stool and his rifle and be placed inside a dumpster dumpster with its lid down, and when any one lifted the cover to deposit trash into the dumpster Harry was to come to attention, present arms, and sound off with, "Harry Ablbrecht, 515937421, Recruit Training Command, dempsey dumpster watch, Sir!" and then sit down.

Once the recruits in Company 263 were ready for drill practice Chief Welch took them to the parade field for drill. He was teaching the fundamentals of the nine-count manual and the sixteen-count manual. The recruits had been on the parade ground about two hours when first class quartermaster Hurd, who was also a Company Commander, asked Chief Welch if he had someone on dempsey dumpster watch. He was informed by Chief Welch that he did. Where upon quartermaster Hurd informed Chief Welch that the dumpster had been picked up and was being taken to the dump.

Chief Welch immediately asked quartermaster Hurd to take over his company as he ran for the parking lot along with his recruit master-at-arms to take his car and drive to the dump to try and stop Harry from becoming a pile of garbage.

Upon arriving at the dump the driver was ready to push the button which would tip the dumpster and empty it. When Chief Welch yelled to the driver. "DON'T DUMP THAT DUMPSTER! THERE IS A BODY INSIDE IT!" The driver immediately said, "What are you talking about man?" Chief Welch told him; "Look inside the dumpster!"

He lowered the dumpster to the ground, raised up the lid, right away Harry jumped up and gave his name, rate, service number, and that he was the dempsey dumpster watch. Whereupon the driver said; "Hey man! What the hell is going on here?"

When Chief Welch ordered Harry to get out of the dumpster and into his car, then the Chief walked over put his hand out to shake hands with the driver, but the driver wanted nothing to do with this Navy man. The driver told the Chief that he was going to take the truck back to the base and quit his job. That, he wanted no more to do with these crazy-assed Navy recruit trainers.

At the inquiry of a rumor that this incident had taken place they found no proof that it had ever occurred.

MY TEETH! MY TEETH

RICHARD ELSHOFF, Springfield, Illinois   USS VULCAN AR5

It was just after World War II when in 1946 we returned to New York City. Even now, some fifty years later, I can recall the scene most vividly. On the water tug boats, fire boats with streams of water shooting from their water guns, and fireworks seeming to erupt from everywhere. Ashore there was much celebrating and hoop-a-la going on. In the finest restaurants to street vendors selling hot dogs, you paid for nothing, it was all free! No matter what bar or club you went to, all drinks were free! It was a long, hard fought war, we won a victory, now we were home and it was all over now. Fathers, sons, sweethearts, they were all home now and it was time to celebrate.

A week later it was Armed Forces Day and big parade marched down Fifth Avenue. Sailors from every ship in the harbor and, I believe, all servicemen in the area marched in that parade! After the parade, it was one big, city wide, party. Everywhere you went food and booze was free, all you cared to eat or drink. I think we all over indulged. I know I did!

**Richard Elshoff,
USS DEUEL APA 160**

One of my fellow crewmen on the USS VULCAN gave up drinking that night. He always drank a lot but could not hold his liquor, so the first place he went to when back on board ship was the head. On these older ships you did not have commodes such as you have in your home. Instead, it was like along horse watering trough with slats across it for you to sit on. The sea water came in one end of the trough and right out the other end, carrying with it any body waste, or anything else, laying in the trough. It was quite a fast, steady current, of water passing through that trough.

Anyhow, after that big night on the town drinking everywhere in the city, we made it back to the ship in pretty good shape. All, that is, except for our buddy who could not hold his liquor. He went straight for the head, ran to this trough, and commenced heaving his guts out.

Then came a gargled scream and a long stream of curse words. We looked! It seemed like our buddy was trying to either swim in that trough, or he was panning for imaginary gold!

While heaving, his false teeth had fallen out of his mouth, into the fast moving water in the trough, and were being carried by the current, right out the scupper. Never to be seen again!

Somewhere on the bottom of New York Harbor in all that mud and God know what muck, lies a pair of false teeth stamped United States Navy.

IRISH COFFEE

RICHARD ELSHOFF, Springfield, Illinois   USS LIBRA AKA 12

We were working out of St. Thomas in the Virgin Islands when one of my duties was to go ashore daily, with a large pouch, and pick up the mail. On one trip my first class supervisor talked me into picking up a fifth of Jack Daniels Whiskey.

I was sweating all the way back to the ship and when going up the gangway kept wondering about the big bulge in my pouch which was very noticeable. I made a snappy salute to the flag and then the O.O.D. and when it looked like he was going for my pouch I said, "I'm sorry sir, this is classified mail." He just muttered something to himself, then said: "Carry on sailor!"

I gave a big "whew" and double timed it to the radio shack where my first class and chief relieved me of my extra carryon. We had a friend in the medical department who added some color to the brew and poured it into three bottles labeled "cough medicine."

Imagine, all this for some Irish Coffee!

When we pulled out for our regular cruise around the island we had on board a red headed Lt. (jg) from Alabama who had been a pilot on an aircraft carrier who was constantly trying to figure out how he ended up on board the Libra with nothing to fly. He was a typical "fly boy" with personality plus. I never saw him without a smile on his face or a joke to tell.

He always stopped by the radio shack for a cup of what he called the best coffee on the ship. This time he walked in while the three of us were having our Irish Coffee. He never said a word, just kept sniffing the air, then in his best southern draw he said: "Ah smell whisky!"

From that moment on we had to split our cough medicine four ways.

We all had special hiding places for our medicine, mine was way back in the pigeonhole housing our telegraph key. The first class kept his inside our large transmitter just behind the DANGER HIGH VOLTAGE sign. I have no idea where the chief and the Lt. (jg) hid their medicine but we all brought it out when it was time for some Irish Coffee in the radio shack.

RED OIL FOR THE RED RUNNING LIGHT

HENRY F. BOHNE, Parker, Colorado

We had just finished the sea trials after recommissioning the ship when we received a new draft of hands. One of these was Lenny, seaman apprentice and activated reservist.

Today in our political correct language we would have a different description for Lenny, but back in those days he was—well—dumb! I never knew what his IQ was, but it was rumored that it was in the low sixties.

Lenny was assigned to the deck gang and worked for one of the boatswains mates. He quickly became the butt of many jokes and pranks. Most everyone knew about Lenny, he tried hard, and worked hard, if the task was simple. We made allowances for him, but the jokes and pranks continued.

Once he was sent to get some red oil for the red running light. The engine stores sent him to the office to fill out a requisition. They sent him on a wild goose chase to find whoever had to sign the requistion, and so on and so on.

On another occasion he was sent to the fireroom to get a bucket of steam. Also, he went to the boatswains locker to get two fathoms of waterline.

Get the picture? Well, so did Lenny—finally!

Then came the day when the boatswain sent him to get half a bucket of diesel oil so some paint brushes could be cleaned.

You guessed it. Lenny thought this was another of the pranks. He ditched the bucket, went to the living quarters, crawed into his bunk and went to sleep.

When Lenny didn't return with the diesel oil the boatswains mate sent someone to look for him. Nobody thought to look in his bunk. Finally the boatswain became concerned and went on a search himself.

He found Lenny asleep. After getting dumped from his bunk and an immediate "chewing out" the boatswain put Lenny on report. On report for a whole host of things; violating or ignoring an order, sleeping when he was supposed to be on duty, and anything else the boatswain could think of.

I was on the Quarter Deck as Petty Officer Of The Watch when Lenny appeared at Captains Mast. First the boatswains mate was asked to tell what happened. He did, but it seemed that he now felt that the discipline report was a bit much.

After he finished, the Captain asked Lenny for his version of the story. Lenny recited the litany of the jokes and pranks, many more than I mentioned earlier. Occasionally during this recitation the Captains mouth would twitch, but he managed to keep a straight face. The Division Officer didn't succeed as well. At one point he had a coughing fit and had to smother his face in his hands and handherchief.

After hearing the evidence the Captain had a long pause as he thought about what he heard. Finally he handed down his decision. He asked the boatswains mate if he thought that restriction to the ship would be sufficient, without extra duty. The boatswain agreed and two days restriction was imposed.

Not too long after that we left the West Coast to join Destroyers Atlantic. Just before leaving Lenny was transferred to the Receiving Station for further assignment I never heard what

OH THOSE "SPAM" SANDWICHES

FREDERICK "FRITZ" ENGLER, Saginaw, MI   *USS STANLEY*

When our ship was tied up in San Diego four of us would always go on liberty together; Dodge, Gus, Red, and myself. We would always stop at a different restaurant for dinner.

One day as we approached a nice looking restaurant contemplating whether or not to go inside a tall, well dressed, elderly man approached us and asked if we would like to have dinner on him. We were all puzzled but did not hesitate to say yes. So he led us into the restaurant.

Once inside and seated at a choice table he asked if we would all like a drink before dinner? We refused as none of us were drinkers. He then told us to order anything we liked on the menu, which we proceeded to do.

As we all enjoyed a full eight course dinner, our newly found friend and benefactor carried on a pleasant conversation with us and was very congenial. After we finished dessert he asked if we would like a cigar? None of us smoked, so we refused.

After he paid the check and we were leaving the restaurant he asked us if we were curious as to why he wanted to pay for our dinner. Of course we all answered in unison that indeed we were wondering why he was so kind to us.

It was then that he explained that he was president of the company who made "SPAM" and that this was his way to thank us for all the SPAM we ate in the service.

We continued our liberty that night feeling good that someone felt good and tried to help service men. I guess we all enjoyed our SPAM sandwiches more after that incident and I guess we retold the story to everyone on every midwatch we stood.

CHOICE SEATING FOR SAILORS

FREDERICK "FRITZ" ENGLER, Saginaw, MI   USS STANLEY

While on liberty in San Diego with my three buddies; Dodge, Gus, and Red, we all learned a few lessons in life. As young sailors we were often lead astray or taken advantage of by con- men, hustlers of all kinds and shysters. Here is one story.

As we walked down this one street we were attracted to a lighted sign atop a theater-type building which advertised "Girlie Show, nude dancers" so since none of us had ever been to a "girlie show" before, we all decided to enter and see what it was all about. Needless to say, we were all thrilled in anticipation of what we were about to see.

At the ticket booth a sign noted; Admission 2.50, Choice Seats 5.00. We all decided, what the heck, its our first "girlie show" lets go for the choice seats.

We paid our 5.00 each and walked inside. Wow! The place was packed with very few seats empty. In fact the only empty seats were in the clear back row, so being disappointed and dismayed at this we approached the usher and told him that we had paid for "choice seats."

He looked at us and said "Yea, I know! So go ahead make your choice!"

What a ripoff! We stayed a little while but since we were so far back from the stage and the "girlies" only looked to be about a half-inch tall from that distance, we could not enjoy the show. So we left the theater really disappointed.

That was our first experience with a "girlie show" and another lesson in life. Another situation where a young sailor had been taken advantage of.

THREE ADMIRAL STORIES

AUTHOR/CONTRIBUTOR UNKNOWN

#1. Admiral Halsey aboard the USS ENTERPRISE: Two white hats were walking down a passageway when one turned to the other and said: "Halsey may be a bastard to work for, but I would follow the old Son-of-a-bitch to hell and back." The other sailor concurred but neither was aware that Admiral Halsey was only a few paces behind them in the passageway and had overheard their conversation, quickening his pace, he tapped them on the shoulder and said: "boys, I am not so Old!" A Lt(jg) had told me that Halsey had told this story to several of his aids, he among them, and that while he could not be sure, he felt that Halsey was secretly proud of what the white hats had said, except for them calling him "old!"

#2. Admiral Halsey on Guadalcanal: Halsey had just relieved Admiral Ghormley as ComSoPac and was making an unexpected and unannounced tour of the front lines on Guadalcanal when a young Marine Second Lieutenant platoon leader spied him coming toward his platoon with his binoculars, turned to the man next to him and said: "Go alert the platoon and tell them to stand at attention, for we are about to be inspected by a four star admiral." The young Marine walked back to where the platoon was sitting and resting, for they had been in a fire fight and he bellowed out; "OK you muthus, get off youah asses, for heah comes a fo star!" the Lt(j.g.) told me that since Halsey's party could hear the boy, Admiral Halsey turned to them and said: "I'll bet that boy is from the South!"

#3 Admiral Nimitz on Guadalcanal: Ninitz was on an inspection tour of the island and was visiting with General Vandegrift when the General asked him if he would consider awarding some well deserved medals to some Marines. Of course Admiral Nimitz said yes. The men were all lined up in one file. A certain Marine Pfc. was to be awarded the Purple Heart and The Silver Star for his quite conspicuous gallantry. He had been separated from the rest of his platoon when he heard the sounds of a Jap tank approaching and soon it became visible with eight Jap soldiers following the tank. The Pfc. killed five of the enemy soldiers and the rest scattered. The Pfc. had taken a rifle bullet in his right thigh but non-the-less, he jumped up on the tank and rapped with the butt of his rifle on the hatch, which surprisingly opened and into which the Pfc. lobbed a grenade inside, killing the tank crew.

This action was seen by one of his buddies who, when hearing the rifle fire, had joined him. Admiral Nimitz proceeded down the line presenting the medals while the LT.(j.g.) (telling this story) would read the citation, after which the admiral would pin the medal on the Marine. The admiral had just pinned the medal on the Marine next to this one when he, this brave Marine, fainted dead away. Several, including the aide, quite solicitous of his welfare, thought that this Marines wound had gotten the better of him, they gathered around the fallen Marine and brought him back to consciousness and asked him what was the matter? Was he in pain?

The aide said that for awhile the Pfc. just looked at him then in a quiet, small, voice said: "Whoee, I ain't ever been that close to an Admiral in my whole life!"

SAGA OF THE RESTUFFED MATTRESS

RICHARD S. SCHATZ, Greenfield, Mass.   **USS LSM 279**

After beaching on Okinawa 2 April 1945, we unloading troops and flame-throwing tanks of the Tenth Army, our main duties consisted of going to general quarters, making smoke, patrolling on the radar picket line, riding out storms, doing nothing a big part of the time, and ferrying supplies of all kinds from the AK, AKA, and AP cargo ships at anchor in Buckner Bay to the beaches. Early on, there were no docking facilities, but as the war progressed pontoon docks were built.

While alongside the ships loading cargo an announcement was frequently heard over our PA system. "Now hear this, now hear this, there will be no pillaging or pilfering of the cargo." To my knowledge there was no inventory of what was loaded or off-loaded. As I recall, because of war time conditions, there was a thirty percent cargo loss allowance ship to shore.

Soon after the command, "let go all lines fore and aft," the crew was all over the cargo like a pack of ants looking for treasures. The one exception was when we carried beer. There was an armed guard added aboard, but losses were sustained despite the precautions.

After a few weeks of this duty, almost everyone aboard "owned" extra pairs of boondocker shoes, Army clothing, towels, blankets, etc. We used one of the ballast tanks for a store room. No one washed clothes. When something got soiled it was thrown overboard, and you went to your stash and broke out a new whatever.

My inventory included blankets, pants, shirts, and shoes. As the war was drawing to an end I kept thinking that it would be great to get some of this gear home. At that time rumors were rampant that packages being mailed home were "zapped" by a machine at the post office, and that all booty and souvenirs were confiscated. Mailing was out of the question. Then, I had a great idea!

At that time we all owned our mattresses and hammocks. When transferred you rolled up the mattress inside the hammock, lashed it with half-hitches using your hammock lines, placed your full seabag on the hammock and wrapped the hammock-mattress around the seabag lashing them together. This made a neat one hundred pound package to wrestle around.

I measured my mattress, then folded, and refolded an Army blanket until it was the exact size of the mattress. I then sewed the edges of the blanket so that it could not move. I did the same with ten shirts. The folded shirts had to be the exact size as the blanket with no overlap or lump. I then sewed the shirts to the blanket so they could not shift. I repeated the process with another blanket and ten pairs of pants. The two blankets were then sewed together. The finished product was the exact size as the mattress stuffing which I then removed and inserted my masterpiece.

I was now ready to go home, and had foiled the system. There would be no zapping of my treasures. In the meantime there were a couple of problems. We had to air bedding periodically. This meant carrying the mattress topside and hanging it over the lifelines. It was so heavy that I needed help. The new mattress was so hard that sleeping was not comfortable. This problem was solved by "requisitioning an Army mattress from another of our cargos.

Everything was great, and then disaster struck. A new Navy regulation, from this date forward, all hands will no longer own their mattress. When transferred you will not take your mattress, and another will be supplied at your new duty station. All hands were aware of my project, and had a great laugh.

But, there was a happy ending. Some months later we returned to the states, and the LSM 279 tied up at a civilian shipyard in San Diego. I removed most of the stitches, packed my treasures in a couple of boxes, went to a civilian post office and mailed them home.

S.P.'S THE TERROR OF THE SAILOR ON LIBERTY

BERNARD E. CASE, Midwest City, OKlahoma   *USS LST 972*

With all of the problems of the U.S.Navy during WW2 one of the greatest to the sailor on liberty was the S.P.(Shore Patrol)

A common joke was "hey, is your brother in the Navy? Naw, he's a Shore Patrolman."

A frequent shout heard from a passing SP jeep was "Sailor, square that hat and roll down those cuffs." I swear if the Navy had done away with hats and cuffs, half the SP force could have been let go.

I recall in early 1946 while we were at anchor in the Los Angeles Harbor after unloading our cargo at Seal Beach Ammo. Depot, I decided to make a short visit to a former crew member name of Benny Beems who lived in Santa Ana. He had recieved an early discharge on points as soon as the war ended being as he had a wife and four kids. How did he ever get into the Navy?

After arriving in Santa Ana and waiting for Benny to pick me up I figured there would be no SP"s in this little town so I had my hat on the back of my head and my jumper cuffs rolled up. I turned a corner and "BINGO" there stood two MP"s with pencils sharpened and pads out! They checked my ID and did their duty as they saw it. No mercy. So I decided to disappear into a nearby bar.

As I was only nineteen at the time I had to show the bartender my ID card. I showed him a fudged one. He said he could not make out my age on it and I told him it had got soaked during a typhoon off Okinawa and I did not have any time since then to get a new one. So he bought me a drink.

I thought that is the last I will see of those bothersome MP's, I'm sure they have better things to do than hassle me. So I pushed my hat back on my head, rolled up my sleeves, and took a good swig of my drink. I happened to look into a mirror that was behind the bar and dog-gone it, there came those same two SP's walking into the bar.

I figured I had better show them my good ID as I had just shown it to them a few minites ago. Although most SP's are not too bright, they just might remember me. Out with the pencils and pad again! I must have been the only sailor on liberty in Santa Ana.

**Bernard E. Case,
USS LST 972**

About that time Benny showed up and I spent a few hours at his house while his wife tried to pump me about Benny's sexual exploits when he was in the Navy. Benny, who was sitting right next to her, kept making signs at me to keep quiet. I tried to assure that Benny was a good sailor who only spent his libertys sight seeing and visiting museums and such.

After I left Benny's I caught a red car back to Long Beach then jumped into a water taxi and returned to my LST 972.

I figured what the heck, by the time that SP report gets to my ship, we will be long gone. Wrong again! By the next morning the Executive Officer called me up to his stateroom. (My mail today should be that fast!). He suggested that I spend a few days on the ship without liberty, and I agreed.

Right after that J.J. Pilat conned me into taking his place on a transfer to the LCS 35 which was leaving for New Orleans.

THE BOATSWAIN'S MATE

CARL PATFIELD, Las Vegas, Nevada   USS HOLDER DD819

The Boatswains Mate got mad at the new sailor's lack of picking up the new and required needed Navy language, the Bosn got so mad when the recruit called the deck the floor, the Bosn yelled at him;

"THAT IS NOT A FLOOR, IT IS A DECK!"

The Bosn pointed up,

"THAT IS NOT A CEILING, IT IS THE OVERHEAD!"

The Bosn pointed at the porthole,

THE NEXT TIME YOU MAKE A STUPID MISTAKE LIKE THAT, I'M GOING TO THROW YOU OUT THAT LITTLE WINDOW!

ICE CREAM AND ICEBERGS

STANLEY MISIEWICZ, Shrewsbury, MA.   USS WICHITA CA-45

I was serving aboard the USS WICHITA. CA-45, a heavy cruiser, from December 1941 through January 1943. In 1942 we were based in Iceland and spent most of our time patrolling between Iceland and Great Britain, or Iceland and Greenland.

On one of these first patrols I remember, at about 0200, the shrill sound of the bosns pipe blared from the ships loud-speaker, "Now hear this; If anyone would like to see an iceberg go topside now as a large one is abeam of our ship!"

Since most of us had never seen an iceberg close-up before, and it was still very light outside at that hour in that part of the world, about half of the crew rushed topside to see it.

Four days later, about the same hour of the night, the same message came over the loud speaker waking us all up. You should have heard the uproar. The men in my compartment were all yelling, "Shut the hell up! We are trying to get some sleep!" I guess the old adage "if you have seen one, you have seen them all" applied here.

In January of 1943 I was transferred, actually I volunteered, from the USS Wichita to the 33rd SeaBees who sent out a need for manpower at that time. In two weeks a transport landed me on Guadalcanal with the SeaBees.

For a week we saw a lot of Japanese prisoners as we rebuilt the airstrip. I was most impressed by a hospital corpsman I met who said they treated Marines, Navy personnel, and natives. He had a lot of interesting stories to tell.

One story that brought a smile to our lips was the one about when he gave a bowl of ice cream to a native boy. This child had never seen, nor heard, of ice cream and did not know what it was. The boy looked puzzled at the bowl of ice cream, slowly put a spoonful to his mouth and said, "SOUP COLD!"

This was a very funny story to me at that time.

WHEN NATURE CALLS

ROBERT REED, Commerce City, Colorado USS LST 530

According to the old proverb, "when duty calls you ought to go" as in "greetings" from the draft board or Uncle Sam saying "I want you" on the famous James Montgomery Flagg recruiting station poster. But "when nature calls, you must go!" The logistics of "doing" that, have changed over the years—which is a part of our history.

In the beginning of time a tree or bush was OK; but civil- ization made it more complicated. It wasn't long before mankind had sepate buildings or rooms which they gave names like; the restroom, the john, the lew, toilet, water closet, crapper,the throne room,the out-house, the reading room,bathroom,et cetera.

Construction of the early outdoor facilities was pretty basic; dig a pit and a simple shelter with a seat that has a hole cut in it. Naturally neighbor Jones soon built a bigger and better one, with more holes and made of better material. (we have all heard of the expression "built like a brick shit-house.") An up to date privy always had an old issue of a mail order catalog, which served a dual purpose. Some of us boys learned all there is to know about a women while sitting, thinking, and looking through Sears or Wards wish book.

By the 1940's our country needed all its young men to fight a war. So, after surviving a depression, most of us went off to battle. The military was a new experience with new names to learn like "the head" or "latrine" and there was no such thing as privacy. At the crack of dawn a couple of hundred guys had to "S,S, and S" with only twenty sets of fixtures. Then, at sea, the sinks and mirrors and all, wouldn't "hold still" making things even more difficult.

At least in the World War II era on board U.S.Navy landing craft there was no such thing as a waste water filtration plant. Sewage disposal meant "overboard" by the shortest pipe possible. Pumps provided salt water to the heads (as well as to fire hoses). On LSM's and Liberty ships the "flush" consisted of a constant stream of saltwater flowing down a trough which had a few boards across it to sit on. A constant prank aboard these ships was to sit a piece of paper on fire "upstream" and then wake up a shipmate who had fallen asleep on the throne "downstream"! On LCT's you had to operate a hand pump in order to "rinse". Of course, it was easy to pee over the side, but you had to check the wind direction. Small boat crews had that down to a science as there were no "comfort stations" on an invasion beach.

If there was an Environmental Protection Agency back then, they would have had a fit. Imagine Subic Bay with hundreds of amphibious vessels all dumping stuff over the side and yet sailors were going in swimming to cool off in that tropic heat of the Philippines.

Speaking of our bureaucratic mess and its quest for a cleaner world, the USA is taking on a rich and powerful nation of over a billion people by demanding enviromental requirements by China. Over there, they still conside human wastes as their main fertilizer—far better than chemicals. A recent report said the Chinese were a hundred years behind us, with most folks still using outhouses, and they are not interested in our modern Western ways. How dare they think like that? They also accuse us Americans of trying to dump our foul smelling garbage abroad.

Closer to home, for a typical sail or power boat enthusiast I hear that there are big books for the "care and maintenance of the head" on their twenty-five foot crafts. Under the Department of Defense, the Department of Justice, and the Surgeon General, there are pages and pages of rules of what you can, and can't do "when nature calls."

Often, in cases of stopped up, or inoperative "sanitary equipment" it may be better to scuttle the ship. Perhaps Davy Jones' locker is getting too full and that might violate the Geneva Convention.

Life used to be so much simpler!

ALL ABOARD—THERE'S A WAR TO WIN

ROBERT REED, Commerce City, Colorado   **USS LST 530**

A trip to a transportation museum can sure bring back lots of memories from World War II. Never before in the history of warfare were the battlefields so spread out all over the world with invasion beaches dotting the globe. So the fighting machines, loaded with their millions of tons of supplies, had to be transported long distances over land and water. People were on the move—soldiers and sailors on troop trains—plus war workers relocating.

The railroads were the lifeblood of America then and the staggering volume of goods to be moved required every piece of equipment available. Some of this rolling stock was already antique, owners should have gotten rich because all the contracts were all cost plus. Safety and convenience were ignored. The passengers were packed aboard, often twice as many folks as there were seats. Remember, what was important to GI families: that "extra" moment of togetherness.

By 1940 the "power of the future" was diesel. Many of the railroads had set speed records using it on their long distance luxry train routes, such as the Denver to Chicago Zepher on its overnight run to the 1933 Worlds Fair.

General Motors pioneered the "jimmie" in the transportation field. Therefore when the war came along, the company was called on to supply the "whats under the hood" in the alphabet of landing craft of the U.S.Navy. Their old, and freshly, constructed, manufacturing plants at GM's Detroit Diesel, Cleveland Engine, and Electromotive Divisions, went to work. Elegant in its simlicity, a tried and tested design for railroad locomotives was adapted to be the main propulsion unit for LST;s. A pair of 12-567 2-cycle engines turning two screws in opposite directions. The Detroit Diesel Division was also swamped with orders for for motors used in smaller amphibious craft used by our Navy and most of our allies. The proven GM-6-71 automotive engine was employed to power the thousands of LCVP "Higgens Boats". LCMS boats used two of them— LCT's had a trio plus a two cylinder generator plant. The LSI was equipped with two sets of "twins" with one reduction gear and a propellor, that is; two "quads" on two screws. the beauty of this whole 71 series was that all of these machines used the same parts no matter if used on land or on sea.

At the Smithsonian Museum of American History in Washington D.C., there is a big, old, steam train on display- complete with recordings of the sound it makes as it prepares to get underway. If you close your eyes and open up your imagination, you can visualize the smells, the smoke, and the steam, as well as the ear shattering noises as the powerful black monster gets ready to move out. Those were the good old days—ask any train buff.

During the World War II era most towns had a train depot they were very proud of. One such stop was North Platte, Nebraska, which became famous for its hospitality. Many a serviceman took advantage of the home cooked meals served by pretty farmers daughters. there are lots of first hand sea stories, and love stories, that are told about these times when you attend todays ship reunions. Denvers own Union Terminal was an unbelievable beehive of travelers; mostly in uniform. Who could forget the New York City Grand Central Station. It was the crossroads of a million private lives. The gigantic stage on which played a thousand dramas daily.

MUSIC AND ROMANCE

ROBERT REED, Commerce City, Colorado   USS LST 530

While at a recent LST 530 ships party ole Chief Reed (thats me), in a genuine sailor suit, complete with Shore Patrol gear, "raided the joint". On a clipboard containing the "order of the day" there was a romantic sea story that the LST 530 folks all appreciated. It read: "In all of our memories there is a picture of a sailor in his tailor-made dress blues jiterbugging with a good looking woman in a red dress to a tune by Glenn Miller." Since all hands liked the story line, an article on the big band era seemed like a good idea. All of us people who lived through the forties were so lucky to have been around when such things as adventure, travel, and romance were more important than making money and "saving the planet".

Fortunately all of us World War II veterans that are still around were good looking servicemen (and women) who had survived the depression only to have to face an all out war. Our dangerous new world offered no guaranteed tomorrows so each moment became precious. Putting on a uniform kind of made us "heroes"—a sailor couldn't hardly pay for a drink in a good liberty town. He also couldn't find a drink to buy in some of those overseas boon- docks. So our lifestyle was a cheerful one with close friendships and the best music in history creating a wild and happy atmosphere. At least that is what we remember today—the good parts of our "good" war.

The music industry was a factor in final victory—and really advanced in numbers and quality during this national emergency. The five cent jukebox with its 78 RPM recordings became a fixture in every place where folks gathered: Be it beer joints, soda fountains, night clubs, or rollar rinks—even "dance halls in a tent". this "canned entertainment" was slowed down a bit by a musicians strike against the recording companies which lasted from August 1942 to September 1943. The result was the same tunes stayed popular for longer periods of time and we all had favorites that got played over and over again. Glenn Miller, Harry James, Tommy and Jimmy Dorsey, Artie Shaw, Sachamo, and the Duke—Wow! There was a great bunch of bands in those days. Those wonderful crowd pleasing shows followed the boys as USO tours, even when it meant traveling to the far shores and being in harms way. When word was passed that Bob Hope was "here" a guy knew that there were beautiful American women singers to feast your eyes on, "a little piece of home". Also military installations often had their own bands notably Glenn Millers 8th Air Force Orchestra in the European theatre of operations.

The hit songs of the forties sure helped the morale of the troops. Besides the public address systems on ships and bases playing our favorite recordings, we had "Toyko Rose", "Axis Sally" and "Bullshit Bessie" giving us the very latest in pop music from the states. "Lily Marlene" was a German tourch song but the Allied soldiers picked it up as their own and it soon became popular around the world. the propaganda hurt our ears back in the war years—in the 1990's its the noise!! A lot of GI's suffered permanent hearing loss from the guns of World War II. The kids today are bound to have hearing trouble later on after all that rock and rap crap of today. Us older folks are very lucky to have had all of our wonderful, soothing, beautiful music in our memories—with the youthful romance and love that went along with it all.

THE SAFE, AND MORE

TOM TUCKHORN, Cherry Hill, N.J. USS LST 760 USS LST 789

While serving TAD as a yoeman at the Amphib Base in Panama City, Florida back in 1944 I witnessed this incident: A brand new large safe was delivered to the office where I was working. The truck driver gave the O.O.D. instructions that had been passed on to him, that the combination of the safe was to be memorized, not written down, and the note was to be destroyed for security reasons. So the O.O.D. passed this note on to his relief, who in turn passed it on to the Commander who was in charge of our office and ultimately, in charge of the safe. The Commander took the note, looked at it, then uttered "humph" and handed it to a Chief and said, "destroy this!" Which the Chief did by tearing it into very small pieces and placing it in the burn bag.

The very next day the base Commander, a Captain, came to our office and wanted to see the new safe. He asked to see the inside of the safe. To everyone's amazement, no one had memorized the combination as instructed. This posed a dilemma! When the Chief came up with the idea of calling the base brig to see if anyone there could open a locked safe. Luckily there was a sailor locked up on disorderly conduct charges who said he used to be a safe cracker.

The Marines marched this man down to our office in cuffs and with a six man armed guard. After ten minutes the safe was open, and the problem solved. The sailor was marched back to the brig where, for his effort, he was released and returned to duty.

The base Commander wrote the combination down on a piece of paper, told the officers to memorize it and put the paper in a safe place. Where upon it was put into the safe, and the dial spun.

The right way, the wrong way, and the Navy way!!!!!

END OF STORY

In New York Harbor I saw a British ship loaded with locomotives, sitting on tracks, aboard ship set to head out to sea bound for England where the locomotives were badly needed. What was odd was, the ship only had one foot of freeboard, that is the distance between the main deck and the water.

While our LST 789 was beached at Iwo Jima, our Captain had the ships cooks make up gallons of beef stew and of cocoa then sent us crew members ashore where we filled the canteens and mess kits of Marines in the foxholes who had not had a hot meal in days. We all worked together during the war!

THANKS FOR THE MEMORIES

THE FORGOTTEN SHIPS OF THE NAVY

VIC "POP" GIANDANA, Coconut Creek, FL   **USS LST 278**

At the LST Convention in Orlando, our ship, LST 278, was invited to attend the graduation parade and exercises for two companies completing their boot training. This was a ceremony that was not a part of my graduation more than half a century ago. Then we went to service school, or outgoing unit, to be assigned to ships. I remember those who were selected for the armed guard. This ceremony that we were witnessing was a new experience for most of us sitting in the reviewing stand. It was a most impressive sight watching these young people perform in the highest tradition of the U.S.Navy.

Assigned to look after, and herd us veterans around the base, were a young able seaman and his counterpart, a young lady. We were allowed to have mess with them, going through the chow line, as we had done so many years ago. The food was the same! One difference was the serving of dessert. we were waited on. We, as old salts, found, to our amazement, that these sailors had no knowledge of the lingo we used, many years ago. But what was also very evident, they had no idea of what an LST was, what its function was, or had any idea of the part this ship played in World War II. They could give us chapter and verse on carriers, battleships, cruisers, submarines, and destroyers and the part they played, but nothing on the Amphibs. Can you believe that?

Over the ensuing years I have seen stories unfold on the movie screen about all classes of ships of the line, but not one about an LST. Remarkable! Can anyone recall seeing any documentary of an invasion without LST's or any other amphibous ship or small boat predominantly in the front line of the invasion? I doubt that! Could it be that we, as a ship, are not sleek and fast? That we do not fit that old cliche, "Greyhounds of the sea?" If the Navy insists on canine comparison, why not call LST's "PIT BULLS?" That would denote tenaciousness and intent. How about it Navy historians. Why not tell the true story. That these ships had a small complement of men, mostly teenagers, given on the job training, led by ensigns fresh out of officers school with possible one or two officers who had previous sea experience.

Tell them of the Marines that the LST's put on the shores of islands that became household words in America. And, of the coxswain, unprotected, hitting the beach with his cargo of men and supplies. And, then taking the wounded to ships that might save their lives.

This, slow, flat bottomed, least maneuverable, ugly duckling, did what no other ship did. It went on the beach, was able to retract, and do it many times over! They deserve to be more than a footnote in Naval History!

My ship, LST 278, was composed, like many others, of teenagers. I saw young boys become men. Their conduct and ability to do the job forever smashed that old saying; "Don't send a boy to do a mans job." They, and the others in the amphibious branch, did their job well!

Over the years I kept in touch with a few of the officers and men of our crew. Distance made meeting difficult. One day, reading the VFW magazine, I spotted in the reunions column, LST 278, New Orleans, contact Jim Wilkins. Jim had been one of our radiomen, so I contacted him. He gave me a great deal of information, and told me that there was a National LST Association. I joined that association, attended its reunions, and after fifty years was reunited with many of our crew.

Since that time my wife and I have enjoyed many friendships and memories. There is no doubt in my mind that LST sailors are a breed unto themselves. The lists of reunions held by each ship, solidifies in my mind, that we now "the old salts", still remember what we did back in those good old Navy days. When I meet I meet the wives and children of these men who served with me I know that they have heard the exploits of their LST sailor dad or husband and of the experiences he lived. Thats how it must be! We, who were there, must pass along the experiences we went through. No one else can do it!

I was thirty-four years old when I first met these men who were to become an important part of my life. Naturally, as the oldest man, I was dubbed "Pop". Now when we meet I am still Pop. I am also fortunate to celebrate my birthdays with them as my natal day usually falls during our convention period. I enjoy being with my old buddies and their families telling stories that will never be forgotten!

I will exercise my right to be curmudgeon! What singed my posterior was the absolute non ceremonial VJ Day! Very little in recogniton of all who fought, and died, defeating Japan. A few ceremonies, mostly by local military groups, perhaps a token speech by a politician who was not even born during our war. Our theatre of war was extensive. Names of places named Saipan, Kwajalein, Enewetok, Tinian, Pelilieu, Iwo Jima, and Okinawa, were all household words. To me, the lack of recognition was an insult to the fallen, and their families. The final straw that broke my back was the cavalier message by a prominent disk jockey who practically apologized for our actions in the war. That did it for me!

Again, I reiterate, pass your history down to your children your friends, tell shipmates who are not members of the ship reunion associations to join them, and help keep our history alive. No one else is going to do it! Remember, many of us go down to Davey Jones Locker each year. We have to stay on the ball if we do not want to be forgotten!

To all you old Navy men who read this book, TARE, VICTOR, GEORGE, from an old skivvey waver.

"JOE" AN UNFORGOTTEN FRIEND
(a satire)

CHARLES J. ADAMS JR., Reading, Pa.   **USS LST 281**

Joe was never what I would call a good friend. He was just another one of my many shipmates on the LST.

Joe couldn't make friends, but somehow, he and I kept touch over the years.

Joe wrote many letters to me over the years, enabling me to paint a pretty good picture of his peculiarities and idio-syncrasies. The gist of his personality was humorous.

Joe never had one dull moment in his life—they were continous. Joe has the first dollar he ever made—nothing else, just the dollar.

Joe used to be a go-getter, now he makes two trips.

Joe is smarter than he looks—he almost has to be. He has grand delusions of adeguacy.

Joe doesn't have ulcers—he gives them. He doesn't have an enemy in the world, ther're all dead.

Joe lacks average intelligence, but he makes up for it with unenlightened ignorance. He's as smart as he can be unfortunately.

Joe got rich by a lucky stroke—his wealthy uncle had one.

Joe has reached the age where the only thing that gets steamed anymore are his glasses.

Joe and I met on my LST back in the big war. He was my coxswain. He won a swab jockey rate the hard way—he started out as an Ensign.

Joe managed to get a medal in the war. He saved two women—one for the skipper, and one for the Exec.

Joe got caught gold-bricking. The CPO asked where he was? "Aft" says Joe. Then the Chief asked him, "OK, which way will you be going when I send you to the bow?" "Aft backwards" says Joe.

Joe said he had a lot to do with the Navy's alphabet system. He got a Captains Mast for going A.W.O.L.—the verdict B.R.I.G.

Joe was so dumb he thought a blood vessel was the hospital ship. He once told me that "doc" our pill-pusher told him he has a floating kidney, so Joe had an anchor tattooed on his back.

Joe said he joined the Navy "to let the world see him." He wound up on a submarine. His job? He held its nose when it had to dive. He was transferred to an LST just in time.

Joe bragged about what he was going to do after his discharge— "The same as on the LST, as little as possible."

Joe says he hasn't gotten bald, he just has a long face. (actually Joe wears a toupee that makes him look ten years sillier.)

Joe tried on his old Tailor-mades and said he only had to let out the neckerchief.

Joe claims he was a jack-of-all-trades and he is now retired from all of them.

Joe and I stopped corresponding a couple of years ago. I don't even have his old address anymore.

Joe, you know who you are, if you are still out there, send me E-mail, (thats cyber talk Joe for V-mail) Give me an update on your life and what you are doing now.

A LETTER FROM HOME
(a satire)

CHARLES J. ADAMS, JR., Reading, Pa.   **USS LST 281**

Dear Editor; Enclosed is a typical letter from my mom while I was in the U.S.Navy fighting in the big war. Doesn't she write funny though?

Dear Junior;

I'm writing this letter real slow because you don't read fast. We don't live where we did when you left home. Your pop read in the paper that most accidents happen within twenty miles of home, so we moved. I can't send you the new address because the last renters that lived here took the house numbers when they moved so they wouldn't have to change their address.

This place is very nice. It's got a neat washing machine. I'm not so sure it works so good though. I put in a load and pulled the chain and ain't seen them since. The weather isn't too bad lately, it only rained twice last week. The first time it rained for three days and the second time for four days.

About sending you that pea-coat that you forgot—your pop said it would be too heavy to send in the mail with all them buttons on, so I cut them off and stuck them in a pocket.

Your kid brother locked his keys in pops car yesterday. we were really worried because it took him two hours to get me and pop out.

Your sister had a baby early this morning, but I haven't found out what it is yet, so I don't know if you are an aunt or an uncle.

Your uncle fell into a whiskey vat up on the farm. Some of his helpers tried to pull him out, but he was so loaded he fought them off and drowned.

Three of your friends drove off a bridge in a pick-up truck. The driver pulled down the window and swam to safety; your other two buddies were in the back. They drowned because they couldn't get the tailgate open.

Your aunt has the mumps. She's so fat, though, it was two weeks before she knew it.

Your cousin was with the FBI for awhile—they caught him in Chicago. He's going to Penn State—or is it State Pen?

Your grandma and grandpop are doing fine. Grandma had her hair bobbed and colored. She don't look like an old lady anymore. She looks like an old man.

Grandpop got himself stuck in the up escalator at the mall when the power went off.

Not much has changed around here. Life has been pretty dull since you left for the war.

Love, Mom

KEEPING THE WHITE UNIFORM, "WHITE"!!!

ROBERT REED, Commerce City, CO   ***USS LST 530 & 75***

Part of the gear stowed in a sailors seabag included a couple of white uniforms. When Spring "sprung" and the weather got warm, the U.S.Navy ordered its men to switch to its Summer wardrobe for on deck duties and "public appearances." (the regulation in the Bluejacket Manual was a bit comical in its specificity: "In time of war Navy men are not allowed to wear civilian clothing ashore, except when taking exercises, or at home when less than three guests are present.") After a seventy-two hour pass to New York City on one of those beat-up, old, trains of the war years, those white Navy uniforms were a battleship gray at best.

One time the shore leave party off the LST 75 was stuck ashore for several days in their white uniforms. We were stranded by a hurricane at Key West, Florida. We slept fully clothed on the mess tables at the Naval Base. those white uniforms got ruined! When we finally got back to our ship, we tried washing our clothes in our customary way, using saltwater and GI soap, which did nothing! We even tried some of those "Rinso white" newfangled suds which didn't help either. We finally ended up throwing those whites away and buying new ones as nothing would get them clean'

One of the secrets to looking sharp was to put aside special "inspection clothes, including shoes, and clean underwear". The secret to keeping them clean was by not wearing them.

Another memory of those days was when we were anchored off Panama City and headed for liberty ashore in an LCPR when the engine died. It seemed that some swabby hosing down the deck had gotten water into the tank. Someone aboard had to clean out the fuel system before we could move. Being the only man aboard who knew how to do it, I was volunteered!

I stripped down to my skivvies, not wanting to get my clean white uniform dirty. I carefully placed it in a clean, dry spot and proceeded to "stand on my head" while working in the bilges. At that moment a group of college girls, in a boat, came alongside to see if we needed any help. Boy! was I ever "em-bare-assed" while those girls saw the sights they probably had never seen before. However, when we finally made it ashore, my uniform was still clean and white.

One thing LST people learned was what modern housewives call household drudgery. While some LST's had washing machines with men assigned to them as duty, too many men with too much dirty clothes often sent all hands back to using a bucket of water and a bar of soap. If you had a supply of hot water this worked pretty good, but when all you had was cold, salty, seawater, it was pretty hard, on both the sailor and the uniform. Some men simply soaped them up, tied a line to them, and tossed then overboard for the "rinse cycle" hoping that some fish did not mistake them for bait, or that the ship did not do a "full steam astern" and shred everything, which did occasionally happen.

Most young folks who served in Uncle Sams Navy soon learned how to take care of themselves because "mother" wasn't there to do everything for them. LST's and many other fighting ships were not designed for crew comfort, as they are today. Sailors had to make-do with what was available. No bottles of Tide, Pride, or Joy, cleaners were available. Those marvelous modern detergents would sure have helped us wash our clothes and clean our mess trays, but the real pride and joy was, and still is, in our hearts with fond memories of those "good, old, Navy days!"

MEMORIES FROM THE CREW OF LST 47

DONALD K. EDWARDS,ship historian   USS LST 47
Cincinnatti, Ohio

Memory # 1 from Paul Schuck

We were always having trouble with our anchors. Once we hooked into, and brought up, the International Communications Cable in the English Channel. Another time we went into a beach on top of our forward anchor and tore a hole in the bottom of the ship. We had it repaired in drydock in Plymouth, England. The time that took the cake was when the stern anchor wasn't dropped when we were beaching and we had to load it into an LCVP, carry it out and drop it. The weight was almost too much for that small boat.

Memory # 2 from Linwood Nutting

While in the Philippines we nicknamed the ship the U.S.S. BE NO —. Be no this, be no that, be no beer, be no liberty, be no nothing!!!

Memory # 3 from Paul Schuck

Some days in the Pacific it was so hot we had to run sea water throught the hand rails to cool them down enough so that we could touch them.

Memory # 4 from Don Edwards

Standing in the conning tower near the stern looking forward toward the bow while heading into the wind and big waves, you could actually see the middle of the ship bending and flexing.

Memory # 5 from Howard May

A seaman, Bob Roser, who came from Beaver Falls, Pennsylvania as did another famous person, Joe Namath, slipped into the ships freezer one time to try out some of the officers ice cream. When the ship rolled the door slammed shut, and locked! He finally got out but after that incident he was known as "Frosty."

Memory # 6 from Milford Boyett

While anchored in the Philippines, a ship-fitter was doing some welding on the fantail. Some sparks landed in a bucket of rags and started smoking. Tom Chappelle came by, saw the smoking bucket, and attempted to stomp it out using his big Texas coyboy boot. His foot got stuck in the bucket and flames started shooting up. He didn't know there was cleaning fluid in the bottom of the bucket. He was dancing all over the place with flames shooting all the way up to his butt. He finally jumped overboard! We sounded the "man overboard" alarm and when brought back aboard he was asked why he jumped overboard and he replied: "I knew that water was always used to fight fires, the nearest water was twenty-five feet straight down, so I went for it!" We never did get the bucket back.

Memory # 7 from Don Edwards

We were in Naples, Italy and some of us had come upon a large cask of wine that weighted a ton and we wanted to take it back aboard our ship. We handled it pretty well having gotten it down to a pier where we had a rowboat waiting to take it out to the ship.

We decided to roll the cask off the dock into the rowboat, the rowboat was in the water about five feet lower than the dock. When the wine cask landed in the boat, they both sank immediately! and we never saw either of them again.

I don't remember how we had planned on getting that wine aboard ship, or where we were going to hide it. Just another one of those things that the officers never knew, or found out about.

Memory # 8 from Don Flaherty

One night while our ship was in port somewhere, the Bos'ns Mate woke me up (it was around midnight) and said that we had an emergency in the laundry room. It was an unbelievable situation! R.J. Dolan and "Pappy" Bowen had come back from liberty all sauced up and had made a bet that R.J. could not get into the washer. Well, R.J. not only got inside but when I arrived on the scene, he had been spun around a couple of times. "Pappy" couldn't get the door open and you could hear Dolan inside the washer expressing his desire to be relaesed plus a couple of other desires he was wishing for "Pappy."

I was able to get the door open and he got out. His legs were a little wobbly but he was all sobered up. He was also as white as a ghost. I was always glad that "Pappy" had not pressed the button which let the hot water into the washer.

Memory # 9 from Dick Winterroth

Going from New Orleans to New York we learned why Cape Hatteras was nicknamed the "graveyard of the Atlantic". We hit a terrific storm and we rolled to firty-three degrees. We had heard that an LST would capsize at forty-four degrees. The waves were about twenty feet high and I wondered if we were going to make it. I also wondered why the hell I hadn't joined the Army.

Memory # 10 from Don Edwards

Upon our return back to the states from Europe we were at the Brookyly Navy Yard. A few of us were looking to have some fresh food, we were tired of powered eggs and milk plus the Captain had ordered the cooks to serve us some C and K rations that we had remaining onboard. No liberty was allowed.

Some of us jumped ship and went to the cafeteria that was on the docks and we gorged ourselves on fresh milk, eggs, ice cream, and other goodies. You can bet your sweet bippy that our officers weren't eating C and K rations so neither were we.

THE LIGHTER SIDE REMEMBERED

WALTER SCOTT, East Aurora, N.Y.   *USS LST 1061*

While daily life aboard ship was usually routine and serious, there were exceptional moments, and most Navy ships regardless of class, or size of personnel, had their memorable episodes.

LST 1061 was no exception, these are some of my recollections of some of those moments.

While underweigh, we often had a baited line trailing off the fantail in hopes of catching some fresh edible fish. One night at sea, someone reported seeing a light off our stern. The skipper made an evasive turn—so did the light. We zig zagged—so did the light. After much apprehension, we discovered it was a battle lantern, (they are waterproof), someone had attached to our fishing line trying to attract fish to the bait.

One thing that happened to many a swabby—we had one shipmate who had the bright idea of dragging his clothes astern to get them clean. He put his dirty clothes in a seabag and tossed it overboard with a line tied to a stancion. In the morning when he checked his clothes and pulled in the line, all that was left were the grommets from the seabag still fastened to the line.

For "Ripleys believe it or not" while in Honolulu on liberty I managed to mess up my dress whites by brushing against some oily construction equipment. I headed downtown to Battleship Max Cohens' Uniform Shop. I was put in a booth, measured, and in one half hour I was handed my new dress whites and the cost was ten dollars. Can you believe that?

One time overseas we ran out of coffee. Somehow arrangements were made with another ship to trade a movie for some coffee. We both came out losers as our movie was a Shirley Temple flick, and their coffee turned out to be chicory.

Coming back from liberty one night a shipmate brought back two bottles of liquor. The O.O.D. at the quarterdeck told him to toss it overboard at the fantail and that he would be listening for the two splashes. The shipmate then headed below with two bottles of liquor but minus his two shoes.

Although everyone did not shave on a regular basis, Aqua Velva after shave lotion was one of the biggest sellers from the ships store. It seems that when mixed with Coca Cola, it served as the best "cocktail" of the day.

One of the best music programs playing all the latest hits from the states, was the "Tokyo Rose" broadcasts which the radio gang would pipe throughout the ship. While her intent was to demoralize the troops, her program actually raised our moral.

Launching a small boat was usually routine in calm seas as long as the bow and stern hook were released simultaneously. On one particular day when the sea was especially rough we were ordered to make a run. Our crew jumped in at the davit and when we hit the water, the boathook released the bow snap on the swell but I failed to get the stern snap off. When the swell passed, the bow went down and the stern hung up in the air. The boat hook, the coxswain, and I, almost ended up in the water! On the next swell I managed to get the stern snap off and we made our run with no further incident.

Lastly, being young, adventurous, and curious, our LCVP boat hook and I, although we had been adviced not to, decided to check out one of the a Japanese caves overlooking the bay at Okinawa. Upon entering the cave we were surprised to see how much paraphernalia was still laying around. Books, dishes, letters, and papers, cluttered up the place. We took a number of souvenirs that day but the only thing I have left is a Japanese Navy postcard from one brother just entering the service to another that evidently had been in the service for some time. I had it transleted years ago and keep it in my World War II scrapbook.

Yes, memories last a life time!

LET THERE BE LIGHT

GEORGE DAWSON, Wantagh, N.Y.   *USS YANCEY AKA 93*

During the Korean War I was a radioman on the USS Yancy, AKA 93, making many trips between Oakland, California and ports in Korea and Japan. One bitter cold night we were anchored in Yokosuka Bay, Japan. The signalman on duty was a sailor named Johnson. He was given a long message to send by signal light to a ship at the other side of the bay. It was the longest message I had ever seen and Johnson was unhappy about having to send it. Actually, it would have been easier and quicker to deliver the message by boat, but "orders are orders," so Johnson reluctantly went to work by turning on the light.

He held the several pages of the message in his left hand and manipulated the signal light with his right hand. He would transmit one word and then look up to see if the other ship had received that word, which would be indicated by a quick blink of the other ships signal light. Things seemed to be going smoothly, for every time Johnson looked up hr would see the blink that meant the word was received. It took over an hour to send the message, without a hitch, even though Johnsons hands and feet were nearly frozen by the cold.

After completing the message, Johnson looked toward the other ship expecting to see the final "roger" or confirmation that the entire message had been received. However, all he saw was a light that kept blinking—blink—blink—blink. He then realized that he was seeing a blinking buoy. Johnson used every dirty word in the English language, and some that had not been invented yet. But at least he holds the record for having sent the longest message in history to a blinking buoy.

SO LONG AND DON'T COME BACK!

GEORGE DAWSON, Wantagh, N.Y.   *USS KYNE DE*

After the end of World War II and before the Korean War began, the USS Kyne and USS Snyder, destroyer escorts, were used to take Navy Reservists on training cruises. I was on the USS Kyne in the Spring of 1950 when she, along with the Snyder, went on a cruise to Quebec, Canada.

The trip North was uneventful, as we dropped depth charges (killing nothing but fish), fired our guns at targets, and had rescue drills. Everyone was looking forward to our arrival at Quebec City, and a few days of liberty. The Canadian newspapers treated our visit with enthusiastic interest. Pretty French-Canadian girls stood on the wharf as we docked, and we provided guided tours of the ships for the Canadian citizens.

But, "boys will be boys" and "sailors will be sailors" the world over. The first incident occurred when one of the Gunners Mates pointed a three-inch gun at a gentlemen walking along a nearby

"But, Daddy, you know there's a shortage of hotel rooms—we can't put him out."

street. Where ever he went the gun followed him, which made him feel very uncomfortable and engendered some negative reactions towards our heroic crew. Next, some of our sailors met some Canadian sailors and became instant drinking buddies. One of the Canadian chaps who had been treated too generously to Canadian Club and other libations by one of our sailors kindly agreed to let his American counterpart borrow a Canadian Navy jeep. This speed merchant came careening down towards the wharf, couldn't stop in time, and plunged into the river.

SCRATCH ONE CANADIAN NAVY JEEP!!!

The hearty welcome we had received at first began to weaken, as I and a shipmate discovered when we went to the grand dining room of the prestigious Chateau Frontenac Hotel with our ladies, and were told to "go to the coffee shop."

Just one more event was needed to put the finishing touches on our "good will visit" to our friendly neighbors to the North. As we were leaving the pier for our return trip, the USS Snyder was moving too rapidly and turned to Port too sharply. Her stern ripped off a large section of the pier, leaving another impressive souvenir of the U.S. Navys visit to Quebec. I suspect that some Canadians were rather pleased when the Korean War erupted soon after this, requiring the U.S. Navy to turn its attention towards the Pacific.

Van Watts, USS ENTERPRISE

VAN WATTS
THE WHITE HAT'S PHILOSOPHER

"ONE TIME CPO REMOLDED NAVY WITH AN IDEA AND A PHILOSOPY ACQUIRED COMING UP THROUGH THE RANKS" captioned his biographical sketch in a recently released history of chief petty officers.

But before he was a "one time" CPO Van Watts was a "one-time" WHITE HAT—a WHITE HAT who one day would implement throughout the Navy—not with a book but with programs that do anything but gather dust on a shelf—the ideas and philosophy he had acquired living among WHITE HATS!

Today, celebrated throughout the Navy, that one-time WHITE HAT is perhaps honored most when, in our Nation's Capital, this year and every year, an ALL-NAVY Sailor Of The Year Event climaxes his monumental work—the U.S. Navy's worldwide Sailor Of The Week, Month, Quarter and Year Programs.

Of them a LIFE editor would phone Watts, "I know what these programs mean to the Navy! I just completed a Reserve Officer's tour aboard a carrier!"

And of them OUR NAVY would editorialize "To hometowns that never see a ship come into port, to millions who never see the sea, his programs have become a means of sparking interest in the Navy and its importance to the freedom-loving world!

Such comments are typical of countless others concerning programs with which this naval philosopher from the ranks—this WHITE HATS' PHILOSOPHER—would spark morale, leadership, incentive and recruiting, with which he would improve both command-crew and community-Navy relations, with which he would publicize the sea service in every state in the Union, and with which he would celebrate and dignify the Navy's enlisted men and women.

For sixty years this great man has served his Navy and his country surpassingly well. I am honored to present to you some of his poems and other writings which, along with his worldwide programs, have made him famous, and now spark "WHITE HATS OF THE NAVY!"

BETWEEN BATTLE STARS

VAN WATTS, Fulllerton, CA.   **USS MACKINAC**

In 1943 I returned from the South Pacific with my first battle star, having been a member of the crew of the USS MACKINAC. Charged off in advance as part of the price for Guadalcanal, according to her official history, at Malaita, sixty miles North of there, the little seaplane tender had survived "the most advanced post assigned" in World War II's famous First Offensive, the combined land, sea and air reconquest of the Solomons.

Now, ordered to report to a naval advance base outfit, I was on my way back to the South Pacific to earn another star in the Battle of New Guinea. Aboard a Greyhound bus bound from Seattle to San Francisco I was about to learn something concerning the perils of travel other than by ship. For in the wee hours of the morning I would awake, too cramped to move—having slept most of the night cuddled up on my left side—to find myself staring into the wide open eyes of a darling young lady cuddled up on her right and who too was now awake, her eyes, only inches away, staring into mine!

Blinking her own pretty blinkers, she startled me with "you have such beautiful eyelashes !"

Hoping she was flirting—my male ego—in Bremerton I had just said goodby to another darling young lady—my wife!

I would soon learn that, in Portland, my traveling companion had boarded the Greyhound in anticipation of rejoining in San Francisco, a waiting husband!

If anything more was needed to deflate my male ego I would also learn that this darling young lady had cuddled up with me for the night only because the seat next to mine was the only one available! But more deflating would come with the realization that her observations had been purely scientific and technical—she was a taxidermist! Her husband was a taxidermist! And together they operated a taxidermy!

"Why You—you- you just wanted to stuff me!" I stuttered—while she laughed so uproariously everyone else aboard the bus awoke! Well, it was nearly morning anyway! And who was going to complain to a serviceman on his way back to earn a second battle star— or who knows—maybe his 22nd!

SAILOR'S MOMENT

VAN WATTS, Fullerton California   USS ENTERPRISE CV 6

I'm going up to watch the sea again,
To watch the waves break 'gainst the side,
To watch the ship the ocean ride.

It's great ! To stand there by the rail
In exhilaration to inhale,
The breath of the heaving ocean
And to worship there—in somber devotion.

The sailor views the endless pain
And marvels at Neptune's domain.
The waves are breaking miles around.
Foam and caps everywhere abound.

The expanse is everywhere the same -
Uniformly the waves do claim
Each and every a sister part to be
To form the magic oblivion of sea.

He wonders why—he does not know,
Why the spacious blue enchants him so.
He knows only that its grand to be
Held in the spell of the magic sea!

EVITA

VAN WATTS, Fullerton, California   **USS ALBANY**

Evita Duarte wed Juan Peron October 18, 1945. She became
First Lady when Peron was elected President of Argentina in 1946.
She was already world famous when my ship, the USS ALBANY,
visited Buenos Aires in January 1948. She was twenty-nine in that
year and a very beautiful lady, much more beautiful than any of
those representing her on stage, or in the movies.

Argentina's first couple would inspect our crew at quarters,
escorted from division to division by Vice Admiral Lynde D.
McCormick and Captain John Ocker. I was the S1 Division Chief
and so delivered the salute for the division as Evita, Juan Peron,
the admiral, and the Captain paraded past. Evita was closest, no
more than four or five feet away, as I saluted.

While our honored guests were given a guided tour of the ship,
the crew would remain at quarters, the only exceptions being officers and enlisted men expected to stand by and present spaces included in the tour. Asked if there were any parts of the ship she
would particularly like to see, Evita's only specific request was to
see the bakery—to my delight! For the bake shop was part of my
domain as Commissary Chief!

Of course I rushed below to catch more glimpses of Evita while
she was glimpsing my bake shop! Unfortunately, my boss, the Supply Officer, whose bulk suggested altogether too many previous
visits to the bakery, crowded between me and Evita and the other
dignitaries! Well, as they say, rank has its privileges and I never
again got as close to the internationally famous beauty as I had
when I delivered my division's salute!

Evita would die only four years later, July 26, 1952. She was
only thirty-three years old. For more details, see the movie!

UP FRONT WITH JAMES MICHENER

VAN WATTS, Fullerton, California   **USS MACKINAC**

We would take him on what may have been, I guess, the ride of
his life, picking him up, and leaving him, two weeks later, at our

rear base, the New Hebrides Island of Espiritu Santo. It was there, during the next eighteen months, he would write his first novel. In it, he would have his narrator say in his only partly fictionalized work; I "I never saw a battleship except from a distance. I never saw a carrier, or a cruiser, or a destroyer. I never saw a submarine."

But—old shipmates remind me—Michener did sail on at least one naval vessel in the first of her narrow escapes from the Solomons—the little seaplane tender we called the MIGHTY MAC. When we didn't call her that, we called her by the number on her bow—the LUCKY THIRTEEN! She was lucky all right! Lucky enough to survive, with Michener aboard, "the most advanced post" in World War II's famous "First Offensive."

Strange—but not so strange—that modest fellow never seems to have mentioned it. But if you ever wondered where he was the day the action began, he was with us—up front—way up front—at an island shown on military maps behind enemy lines—refueling planes under the very noses of the enemy.

For, on August 7, 1942, the day of the landings on Guadalcanal, sixty miles North of there, at Malaita, THE USS MACKINAC would be refueling the planes that scouted the enemy. The success of one of the wars most daring exploits would depend completely on lack of detection. But, charged off in advance as part of the price of Guadalcanal, there was no question of her eventually being discovered. The only question was who got to her first, enemy subs or planes or, from the landward side, their demolition experts.

An over-aged destroyer converted into a seaplane tender and sent into the area to refuel scouting planes in advance of our landings in the southern Solomons had been gambled and lost. No one could have honestly expected the MACKINAC to return. Within four days all but one of the nine big PBY's in her first assigned squadron had been shot down by the huge Japanese fleet which, history says, "roamed the area at random."

But, on the fifth day, with still a bare chance of her survival, the MACKINAC would be ordered to evacuate "the most advanced post." As we upped anchor and sailed, the last of her PBY's flew over to warn that forty Japanese bombers had been sighted headed her way. Either they were after bigger game—or didn't see the speck below that was us.

For tailing far behind a departing fleet that had deposited Marines on Guadalcanal and, in the face of superior enemy forces, retired as fast as it could go, the MIGHTY—and mighty lucky little -MAC escaped with Michener and company!

Eight days later we would head South to set-up another base in Ndeni, leaving him at our rear base, Espiritu Santo. We never

USS ENTERPRISE

saw him again but, years later, would read in the press that he "retreated to a jungle shack and began writing the stories that were to appear in TALES OF THE SOUTH PACIFIC.

CHRISTMAS IN THE SOUTH SEAS

VAN WATTS, Fullerton, California   *USS ENTERPRISE CV 6*

A POEM
'Tis Christmas in the South Seas;
  Yet we hear no sleigh bells jingling.
Here in Honolulu Harbor,
  There are naught but boat bells ringing.
We have a tree on board our ship,
  The best pine that could grow
On a coral strand from thirsty sand -
  But we haven't any snow!

And myriad lamps are twinkling
  On our South Seas Christmas tree;
Bunting and crystal tassels
  Make it a pretty sight to see.

Songs echo across the water -
  'Twould seem like Christmas night;
But is Santa Claus a-coming? -
  How the darn mosquitoes bite.

We have waited past endurance;
  Where, O where can Santa be?
Does he know it's eighty-nine
  In the shade of this Christmas tree?

SCARLET EVENING

VAN WATTS, Fullerton, California   *USS ENTERPRISE CV 6*

A POEM
O Scarlet Evening, lay o'er the main—
Over the ocean, pray gather again,
Bring to the sailor in thy returning,
Meaning of purpose and strength to dream;
Sooth his hearts longing, ease his yearning.
Go, limping Sun God, o'er the ocean's rim -
Leave the Scarlet Evening alone with him.

ON THE BEACH AT WAIKIKI WITH DOROTHY LAMOUR

VAN WATTS, Fullerton, California

During World War II, like other glamorous movie stars, Dorothy Lamour would work at the fabled Hollywood Canteen. Renamed the Bob Hope Hollywood USO. it was there that I would later be honored by the Navy Leagues Hollywood Council

But lets go back to 1941 when Life Magazine would name Dorothy the GI's NO.1 Pin Up Girl. For that was the year in which one of those GI's (namely me) would encounter her on the beach. It could have been a perfect ending for a short story I was living that day as I explored Hawaii by air, land, and sea—having already been up in a Piper Cub before bicycling to Waikiki.

An illustration from an anthology Van Watt, at age 19, Published in Seattle.

It could have been a perfect ending, I say, except for two six foot-four Kanaki guards, one on each side of a beach blanket on which lay Dorothy Lamour, the queen of the South Seas basking in the sun.. But such was not to be and escaping out to sea, from a surfboard I would safely contemplate the Armed Forces NO. 1 Pin Up Girl.

Who, then, could have imagined that thirty-two years later, as a resident of Toluca Lake and member of its Chamber. I would vote to make Dorothy our Honorary Mayor, and that, in THE TOLACAN, both she and the sailor she had encountered at Waikiki would make front page.

And I, at least, could not have imagined that still later—and another 23 years after that occurrence—I would be planning to attend Dorothy's funeral in North Hollywood's St. Charles Borromeo Church. But who would show up that very day, September 26, 1996, but a charming lady from down under, Dawn Valk, who for the last several years had served as a liaison between ANZAC units and GI's commemorating such World War II events as the BATTLES OF GUADALCANAL and the CORAL SEA. One of those GI's would meet her at LAX and, with his lady friend, accompany her to my studio. And was I surprised if I had not been—they were all ardent Dorothy fans—when with collective voices they insisted that instead of canceling my plans we would all attend Dorothys funeral.

At 93 and tottering, teary-eyed Bob Hope would be there, of course. So was much of Hollywood. Giving the eulogy was an old timer from Paramont who had known Dorothy since those "road" pictures with Bob and Bing. A son, reminiscing, would bring all to tears—if Dawn Valk, that vivacious lady from Australia, would cry all through the services, but it was George Suber, my GI friend who had met Dawn at the airport, had nudged me towards the register. "Sign it, Van," he whispered, "You're the only one of us who knew Dorothy."

We would all sign, Dawn Valk exclaiming softly, "They will be so proud down under that they were represented at the funeral of a celebrity as much a legend there, as here.

Some attending had written after their names tender little messages like. "I love you Dorothy," or "God bless you Dorothy." In signing, it occurred to me how appropriate it was that, here to represent them symbolically were two of those millions of GI's who would have loved to have had even such a fleeting encounter with their NO. 1 PIN UP GIRL as I had told about in HAWAIIAN RHAPSODY after my signature I wrote impulsively "REMEMBER WAIKIKI!"

AMAZONS AND SHOW BUSINESS DOWN UNDER

VAN WATTS, Fullerton, California   USS ENTERPRISE CV 6

It was my last night in Brisbane and, seated front and center in an audience of Australian and American servicemen, what possible harm could befall a Yank who wished nothing more that to get safely back to his duty station? But, in the grand finale, a chorus line danced and sang in support of a dazzling redhead who swirled in a red skirt to the very edge of the stage to toss a rose in my lap!

And while I sat there, mesmerized, thunderously applauding Yanks and Aussies were yelling, "she wants you!"—"Go backstage!"—and nudging me in that direction—"You have to!"

And so I did! Fumbling all the way with the rose that entitled me to escort the star of the show to her hotel! A hotel that happened to also be the one in which I awaited travel orders! And, in blackened-out Brisbane with it wartime curfew, what else was there to do but to entertain her in turn with an account of my Brisbane experiences?

Only two days earlier I had arrived by rail from Sydney to await ship transportation back to the New Guinea battlefront. It was a couple of days that began, innocently enough, in a restaurant where the Australian wife of a U.S. Navy Lieutenant had inquired concerning his ships where abouts and, in return for no help at all, offered me a guided tour of the city. It would include a visit to a theater where a teen sister, prettily adorned with gold cap and blue uniform, ushered us into a movie and, when we left, left with us.

And thus escorted with a lovely lady on each side, I would be paraded through streets thronged with military—"How do you do it,Yank?"—to a restaurant where a third sister, no less lovely than the two who had strong-armed me into the place, would wait on our table.

Now the first sister was married as indicated. The waitress had been introduced as the wife of an Assie Airman. These facts were known, it would develop, to a young U.S. Navy man who seeing us together, concluded that I must be dating the only unwed sister of a blonde, blue-eyed, and beautiful trio. And having entered the restaurant, all of a sudden this young man loomed over our table, recognized by the sisters but to me a total stranger yelling, "I'll kill you!"

Raging on that the usherette was his fiancee, "Don't think you can take her away from me just because you're an officer!" he screamed. Then, lowering his voice, he repeated as if it were a solemn oath, "I'll kill you!"

But, suddenly, three furious sisters were between me and the threatening fellow who fled before their flailing purses!

Yes, the youngest sister had been engaged to the shore-based Navy man but provoked by his behavior, broke the engagement. Fair enough! But conscious of the seriousness of a public altercation, I would leave the restaurant now escorted by a trio of sisters who, by taxi, would rush me to the presumed safety of their suburban home. I say presumed for dawn would reveal my assailant only partially concealed across the street where he waited in hope, apparently, of catching me departing alone—as I would well understand—having seen the sisters in action!

"But shouldn't I explain to him—?

But the sisters wouldn't hear of it! For if he had believed that I was courting the usherette before spending the night in their home— they were right—now he would be convinced of it!

So—a hasty breakfast and another taxi to speed me and my

**Van Watts,
USS ENTERPRISE**

protecting Amazons back to town! There a whirlwind tour would end when our pursuer had pursued us into a trap of his own making. Absent without leave, his apprehension by the shore patrol would free the lieutenants wife to return to her search for her husband, the waitress to her restaurant, and the usherette to her theater—and me to unwind from a tour that had left my head in a spin!

And what better way to unwind than a show presented in honor of members of the armed forces?

I hardly expected of course to escort to her hotel and mine the glamorous redhead who so spectacularly climaxed the event! And whom I would thank for what had to be my greatest moment "Down Under"!

I can hear them now—the yells of a thousand Yanks and Assies—not one of whom would not have taken my place as I tucked her into a taxi!

But a tale that had kept you awake would put her asleep! The little darling of the armed forces had given her all! And it seemed cruel to awaken her then or in early morn when a Yank who had been threatened with death one evening and thunderously costarred the next would head North to the relative calm of his battle station!

"SIE KANN ESSEN MIT DER HUND!"

VAN WATTS, Fullerton, California   USS ALCHIBA AKA 6

From May 4, 1943 to June 4, 1943, a period of thirty-one days, I was transported from the New Hebrides to San Francisco in the USS ALCHIBA. A Chief at the time, I subsisted in the CPO mess which had adopted a stray mongrel as the ships mascot. Through the Chiefs randomly throwing him scraps, in general his care was entrusted to their one mess cook. he was a Berlin-born sailor who had only recently been sworn in as a United States citizen by our ambassador in New Zealand and who sill spoke English with a considerable accent.

Since I had studied German some, even translated a volume of German folk tales into English, he and I had an agreement that for the thirty-one days that it took to get back to San Francisco we would speak to each other only in German. Because he had a sense of humor I could say things like, "Sie kann essen mit der hund!"

This would result in uproarious laughter, first his, then mine, then that of the entire Chiefs mess! Though they did not understand what was said, the Chiefs thought it must have been funny. Why, even the hound was barking!

"But he always barks," explained the mess cook, "when he hears bad grammar—and a worse accent!"

A MERMAID

VAN WATTS, Fullerton, California *USS ENTERPRISE CV 6*

O sailors learn!
And mermaids spurn!
A mermaid rose up from the sea
To make a tragic wit of me.
Upon my heart she yearned to seize
And lured me with enticing pleas.
She coaxed me with the sweetest bribes,
Taunted me with scornful jibes.
She charmed me with her beauty's wealth
While in my heart love crept with stealth.
Enchantment bore me into sin
To lose a love I could not win.
I breathed the fragrance of her breath
And dove into the Arms Of Death

DOES CUPID GO TO SEA?

VAN WATTS, Fullerton, California *USS ENTERPRISE CV 6*

Of woeful sailor who thinks to marry!
How he must tinker, linger and tarry
On thoughts of the girl he left at home,
The awe-filled seas of the world to roam.

Van Watts, USS ENTERPRISE

Would an inland girl contented be
By the watching shores of a fateful sea?
Or will mother's plea and fathers's frown
Discourage the girl from the inland town?

Now this is the problem's complexity,
If gentle Cupid disdains the sea -
With the love of his soul will a sailor part
For the worldly love of his earthly heart?

THE ANCHOR CHAIN CATASTROPHE

VAN WATTS, Fullerton, California   *CV 6*

In the dull lives of seamen "twas a great event -
To narrate it blithely is my faithful intent.
A couple of sailors was put over the side;
Of our aircraft carrier in a punt to ride.
Close to the ship's eyes which rust had so tainted;
The Captain decreed that they should be painted.
So he chose these two seamen who, always haughty;
Were oft times to be overly naughty.
Though just returned from a weekend spree,
they suffered a nausea of the salty sea.
Nevertheless they were placed in that double-ended boat.

USS ENTERPRISE CV-6

Van Watts Studio

With a barrel of paint and two brushes to tote
To the forward end of our sleek gray bark
And under the bow to commence their work,
To paint the color back in the eyes so stark;
Where the swinging anchor chain was wont to mark.
The sailors could find no ring nor spar to which
Their double-end punt they could readily hitch.
In haughty contempt of trivial things with destain,
They fastened their punt to the anchor chain.
Neath the overhanging fo'cas'le they went to work.
Dreamed of eight bells, never stopped to shirk.
The paint flew thick and plastered the bow -
I'll make this brief—were shame to tell how;
So bent on their jobs completion,
They worked with a zeal just short of devotion,
And were well succeeded with lavish motion,
To paint the bow of this pride of the ocean.
They were unaware of the great commotion
Above on the fo'cas'le caused by the boatswain.
So, lost in their work, they forgot ship and meer,
The boatswain about then decided to veer,
That is, let out a little more anchor chain -
Which suddenly shot down into the main.
Hauling punt and painters into the deep,
Full six fathoms; But—why weep?
Mid a burst of bubbles and a splotch of paint
Which covered the water with a milky gray taint.
Up come the sailors to the surface anew,
Astonished, bewildered and a bit peeved too!
When they remembered how, in disdain'
They hitched their punt to the anchor chain!

A LEMON IN THE CROWD

VAN WATTS, Fullerton, California   **USS SIERRA**

Aboard our destroyer tender Captain Paul deVoe had just relieved Captain Charles Mauro.

Feeling pretty good about his new command, our new skipper
called all SIERRA officers together in the wardroom and told them:
"I never have seen a finer group of officers, there isn't a lemon in
the crowd!"

But there was!

All but the new skipper were casting glances at an officer also newly reported aboard!

Lieutenant Lemon was taking it with a grin and even chuckled a bit, when the wardroom exploded into a laugh!

Said our slightly embarrassed new skipper "Well, I certainly didn't intend to offend anyone!"

I don't think he did!

EMERGENCY APPENDECTOMY OPERATION
A Human Interest Story

FLOYD H. BAKER, Esse, N.Y.   *USS SCHENCK DD 159*

The date was March 15, 1943 and the USS SCHENCK had been at sea eight days out of Algiers, North Africa, with another eight or more days to go before reaching their home port in Boston, Massachusetts, U.S.A. when Floyd Baker came down with a case of acute appendicitis and the Pharmacist Mate onboard thought it may have already burst which would mean that if Floyd was not operated on immediately, he might die.

With no doctor nor medical instruments onboard a tough decision had to be made. Actually, there was no choice! The ships pharmacist and an assistant had to operate!

The operation was a success with Floyd spending the next eight days in the Captains bunk, in his cabin. Upon arrival in Boston Floyd spent some time in the hospital and recovered completely.

Floyd does not remember the name of the Pharmacist Mate who operated on him, so if any former shipmates, or that Pharmacist Mate, read this story can help, please contact Floyd, or George Sharrow the author of this book.

MEMORIES

JOHN RINALDI, Lodi, N.J.   *USS YMS 458*

Reading some sea stories I too remember sweeping flying fish off the decks of our minesweeper. I also used the sea as my washing machine, one time losing a set and never seeing those clothes again. Here are a few of my memories of Navy life.

Returning from liberty on one of the Marianas Islands one of my shipmates brought a small monkey onboard thinking we needed a ships mascot. After just two days the whole ship was being crapped on by this monkey, and his favorite spot was our galley. We saw the cook chase the monkey with a meat cleaver in his hand and I remember eating a beef stew that night that did not taste anything like beef.

Another time while in convoy with several other minesweepers off Okinawa we ran into a typhoon. The sea was very rough and I got really seasick. I was manning the helm and really had to heave, I told the sailor who was manning the engine order telegraph to take the helm as I dived out the starboard hatch and manned the rail. Watching me made my shipmate sick so he abandoned the helm and dove out the hatch on the port side heading for the rail. With no one at the helm that minesweeper did a complete circle before the O.O.D. realized what was happening. He rushed to the pilot house, grabbed the helm, then managed to get back on course and in formation. He saved the ship from certain disaster that day.

Soon after World War II we had liberty in Kobe, Japan so two buddies and I decided to tour the area. They had a small bus, so we climbed onboard not caring where it was going. After about a mile the bus stopped and the driver went to the rear of the bus and to our amazement commenced putting wood into what looked like a small stove located there. It turned out that the bus was powered by steam and he was stoking the fire.

War was hell, and at times very rough on us, but now we can look back and laugh.

HELP! WE ARE SINKING

DONALD C. THESSEN,　　　　　**USS MERIWETHER AKA 203**
Albion, Nebraska

With all the training that had taken place in the states upon arrival in Pearl Harbor training started all over again. One morning we weighed anchor and sailed with a number of other APA's, AKA's, and escorts. We were headed for the island of Maul for invasion landing exercises. The orders were passed, the landing craft were lowered over the side, the cargo nets were hung over the sides of the ship, and the beach party loaded into the landing craft. The invasion of Maui was underweigh. I do not know how deep the Pacific Ocean was in this area but understood it was quite a long way to the bottom.

Somewhere, possibly about half way to shore, we began to see traces of water coming up through the flooring of the boat which alerted the boat crew to the situation. Someone had forgotten to put the drain plug into the bottom of the boat and we were taking on sea water. There was a mad scramble to get the flooring up, locate the plug, and get it back in place. You must understand that a landing craft is quit a heavy piece of equipment, plus add the weight of another twenty men and equipment that were onboard. The pressure of the water coming in through the drain hole made it difficult to get the plug screwed in and there were some anxious moments before we were able to the threads started and the plug tightened.

I do not think anyone had thoughts about it until we were ashore when the remark was made; "I wonder how deep the water was out there?" Thank God we will never know!

A DIRTY LETTER

FRANKLIN HAGEN, Longview, Texas   *USS BLACK DD*

While serving aboard the destroyer USS BLACK we were doing lifeline duty for the aircraft carrier USS ORISKENY CV31 in the Tonkin Gulf during the Viet Nam Conflict, it had been a long time between mail calls when we received word that the carrier had just received a sack of mail for us.

A chopper was dispatched from the carrier which dropped the mail right on our main deck. That is called air mail! Along with the mail they gave us a couple of good movies in appreciation for us providing life line service for them.

Life line service is when a smaller ship steams alongside and aft of an aircraft carrier in case any of its aircraft when landing or taking off has to ditch into the sea. The life line ship then picks up the pilot. If such a mishap occurs and you pick up a pilot, when you return him to the aircraft carrier, they in turn must give you five gallons of icecream for each one.

In the mail I received a letter from my kid brother back home in the states. I carried it around in my dungaree shirt pocket for awhile when a friend, CM3 Albertson, wanted me to open my letter. I guess he had not received any mail and wanted to read mine. A thing we did quite often in the Navy, especially a letter from a girl friend. So I opened the envelope, and when I extracted the letter, a piece of toilet paper fell out and onto the deck. Upon picking it up I was shocked. It looked like someone had taken a crap and wiped their butt with this piece of toilet paper.

The letter read: "Big brother, I bet you can't guess what I was doing when I thought of you!"

It did not take long before everyone onboard ship knew about my letter and its contents. Everyday someone would ask if I received anymore mail from my brother. Everyone got a good laugh from this.

I wrote my brother a letter back and told him not to express his feelings on paper anymore.

BEACH PARTY

DONALD C. THESSEN,   **USS MERIWETHER APA 203**
Albion, Nebraska

This story took place during one of the most serious under takings of the Second World War. The invasion of Okinawa and the Kamikazi attacks. It was April 1, 1945, some April fools day!

Come time to go into the beach we off loaded into the landing craft and made it ashore without too many problems. We tried to find a sheltered place to put up a tent for the radio equipment but the shelling and dive bombers had pretty well taken care of any trees that were standing. We finally set up near a deep shell hole that looked like it might come in handy if we needed some shelter from an enemy air attack.

The area just outside our communications tent seemed to be the gathering place for officers from both Army and Navy who were making the decisions about what was to come ashore on this particular beach head. A stub of a tree nearby had two wraps of wire around it with hand grenades hanging from the wire. Generally we felt things in our area were pretty well under control. I believe it was about the third day we began to hear reports on the TBS radio of destroyers on picket duty starting to take hits from Kamikazi's. The entire beach head had been operating under a condition red which meant no aircraft belonging to anyone were supposed to be flying in our area.

This day seemed like it was going to be just like all the rest. Our commanding officer and an Army Colonel were visiting. I had my ear glued to the radio when I heard something said about aircraft overhead. About this time all the landing ships along the beach opened fire! You have heard the saying "He who is a slow starter ends up in last place?" That was usually me, but not this time. All I could think of was that big shell hole in front of our tent and wondering if it was going to be a bomb or strafing attack. By the time I cleared the tent, it was too late. The shell hole was filled completely to ground level and I do not remember if I layed down or ran back into the tent. When the all clear sounded and people started coming out of the shell hole, low and behold, the Army Colonel was one of the last ones out and he was mad as heck.

I guess he had considered that shell hole to be his private air raid shelter.

SEA LAUNDRY

ROBERT R. MADSEN, Lena, Wisconsin   ***USS LSM 317***

Many ships in the U.S.Navy such as LST's, LSM's, DD's, APD's, and others having a low freeboard, that is, the distance from the ships main deck to the water is only five to ten feet, or less. Sailing aboard one of these ships is entirely different from a cruise aboard an aircraft carrier or one of the larger ships of the line whose main deck could be as much as twenty or more feet above the water. I jokingly call men on these larger ships "hotel sailors."

If you have not enjoyed the thrill of riding out a storm at sea on a small ship, especially one with a flat bottom, you have missed something. The chore of clearing the decks of flying fish that came aboard during the night, or the thrill of standing watch on an open bridge when the ship does a thirty degree roll and the sea comes up and slaps you in the face. The task of trying to take a leak in the forward head when a swell drops the ship out from under you. What a thrill! Trying to take a crap under these conditions is even more thrilling, especially on one of those open-trough commodes with the bubbling, gurgling, sea water rushing through the trough and washing your butt each time the ship pitches or yawls in the sea.

Having a low freeboard offers some advantages also: Good fishing when the ship is at anchor. Being able to use the sea as your washing machine during times of water rationing. While underweigh we would take an old halyard, toss a few half-hitches on a mop handle, toss the mop overboard to bobb along in the ships wake a few minutes and you get a clean mop.

When the LSM 317 was in the Leyte Gulf of the Philippine Sea back during the "Big War" fresh water was hard to come by and water rationing was a "must" no fresh water was to be used for laundry or showers.

The crew got around the "no showers bit" by taking "quickie" or "at sea" showers. We would take a shower every other day by using the last digit of your serial number to decide your day. It went like this: One man would step under the shower spray just long enough to get wet, then step aside. He would then lather up with soap while a second sailor would be under the shower getting wet. Than a jump back into the spray to rinse off. Using this maneuver a sailor could take a shower in thirty seconds or less and use only a quart or so of water per man.

The skipper knew what was going on with the showers but overlooked it as he knew the crew needed its showers. However, doing laundry using fresh water during a rationing period was strictly forbidden.

One seaman, Joe Smith, could no longer stand the smell of his dirty clothes and decided to do something about it. He took all his clothes except what he was wearing, and using a long rope and clothes-stops, tied them all together and tossed them overboard to wash in the ships wake as we did our mops.

As he lighted a cigarette and tied the end of his rope to a nearby stanchion he watched as his clothes bounced around in the bubbling white of the ships wake.

Then it happened! The line broke and seaman Smiths' clothes drifted away into Davey Jones Locker. Stupefied and mad at himself for putting all of his clothes on one line, Smith spent the next few days trying to borrow clothes from friends figuring he would never see his old clothes again.

As fate would dictate, a week later another LSM anchored in this same area off the Leyte Gulf, and when pulling its anchor from the bottom one morning found it to be afoul with a bundle of clothing.

Knowing how precious and hard to get navy dungarees were at that time, a caring boatswains mate noted the name stenciled on the clothing and decided to send out news of his find to other ships in the area. Tell Joe Smith we found his clothes!

The radioman on duty aboard our LSM 317 received the message and in a few days seaman Joe Smith was reunited with his lost clothing all fresh, clean, and folded.

THE SHIP'S PARTY

FRANKLIN HAGEN, Longview, Texas   *USS DIXIE AD 14*

It was the year 1963, we were in Yokosuka, Japan and we were about to have a ships party in honor of our ships Captain, then Commander, Beckmeyer who was about to be promoted to Captain.

Commander Beckmeyer had come up through the enlisted ranks, in Navy language, he was termed a "mustang." It is exceptional and unusual for a mustang to achieve any rank above Commander. In recognition of his achievement the crew of the USS DIXIE decided to honor him with a party.

Our supply division was to be in charge of the party and I was assigned the job of set-up and preparation of the hall where the party was to be held. On the chosen day of the party, around 1100 hours, I departed the ship along with three seaman to assist me so we headed for the rented hall where the party was to be held to set up tables, bar, etc.

By 1500 we had the tables set-up, the hall decorated, the food all prepared and refrigerated, and the bar set up and well stocked. We were all set for the party which was to begin around 1800 hours.

Here we were, four sailors ashore with three hours to kill with a well stocked bar at our disposal. To us it was one hell of a temptation and a dream come true as we all loved to drink. Naturally, we succumbed to the temptation.

The drinking got heavy, the bull shit started, the bragging began, then came the dares. I kept telling the men what a brave and bold bastard I was, and soon they dared me to prove it.

"If you are such a brave ass," Seaman Wilcox said. "When the old man walks in the door I want to see you step right up and give him a big kiss!"

"Yeah," Seaman Aboto chimed in, "if your such a bad ass you just prove it to us!"

"Yeah," Seaman Crowden added his two cents. "Prove it! Prove it!"

We continued to drink and they continued chiding me and pushing me to prove myself to them. I guess I got pretty drunk and stupid for when the rest of the crew arrived they found out about my "dare" and the pressure for me to do it was intensified!

Long about 1830 when the newly ranked Captain Beckmeyer walked into the hall and joined the party a loud applause erupted and in the spirit of the moment I stepped right up to the Captain and planted a big, juicy, kiss on his cheek saying: "Captain, baby, you have got the sweetest cheeks in the whole Navy!"

Holy shit! All hell broke loose! Everyone was embarrassed and shocked that I would really do such a thing. Everyone, that is, except for three seamen; Wilcox, Aboto, and Crowden who were standing together laughing and exchanging high-fives enjoying every minute of the situation I had created.

Me? I was too drunk to realize what I had done. Immediately my Chief Commissaryman and Ensign Sholly grabbed me, escorted me out of the hall and had me taken back to the ship where, in my bunk, I fell fast asleep,

The next day aboard ship I was working at my cleaning station below decks when I saw the Captain coming down the ladder into my compartment.

I snapped to attention and saluted, then told the Captain, "Captain Beckmeyer Sir, I am truly sorry for my actions at the party last night and I humbly apologize!"

The Captain returned my salute and said: "That's alright Hagen, I have been in the Navy thirty years and this is the first time anything happened to me that I could write home and tell my grandkids about."

I am sure glad that Captain Beckmeyer had a sense of humor as I could have been in deep trouble for pulling that stunt.

"Alls well, that ends well!" Nuff said.

A PLEASURE CRUISE

JOHN McGROGAN,   *Shore Duty, Polermo, Sicily*
Union Beach, N.J.

Germany had surrendered, I, like most of the sailors stationed in and around Palermo, were getting ready to close down the Naval Base in our area. We were still at war with Japan so most of us were just waiting for reassignment. During a lull in duty, which was not too often, a few of us used to spend some time down at the seaport area. One day, we spotted a sailboat, about 35 to 45 feet long, just sitting there apparently with no one watching it. We were later to learn that the boat was taken from the Germans and was being used by some top Navy brass. We had in our group a carpenters mate second class. He also was from New Jersey. He claimed to have sailed before the war, so he was to be our captain. There were two other sailors besides me and him, their names escape me at this time.

On a day that had a good weather forecast we decided to do a little sailing out in the Mediterranean Sea. Everything was going great; good wind, good wine, and calm seas. That was soon to change. We started to encounter some increase in the wind and seas. By this time I realized that just because I came from the Jersey shore, I was not much of a sailboat sailor. We tried several times to tack into the wind but did not have much success at that. Each time we tried, we got further and further away from land. After about an hour or so, we lost sight of land completely. I should mention that we had no radio, no auxiliary engine, and no compass. We did have a couple of life preservers. We were completely lost. Our appointed captain had no idea which direction we were headed.

By this time, we were taking on water and had lost some of our sail. I guess we were al pretty scared. Here we had survived the war and now we were all going to drown playing around with a sailboat. Suddenly on the horizon, a mountain or a large piece of land appeared. Our general direction, with some rowing, could get us to safety. The only problem was that the wind had increased to a full blown gale. It is hard to remember just what we were doing at this time. We drank what little wine we had left and it gave us a little false courage. we decided to go down with the ship. Then from out of nowhere we spotted what looked like driftwood. To our amazement they were three small fishing boats. Some Sicilian fishermen had spotted our boat from a distance. It took quite a while to climb from our boat to their small fishing boats. As bad as the weather conditions were, these fishermen seemed at ease in the rough seas.

As we approached their town it seemed that everyone in town was there to meet us. The mayor of the town hugged us and made some kind of speech. we were so tired and wet, we really did not know what was going on. They fed us, dried our clothes, and treated us like some kind of heros. It took the four of us a full day to get back to our base in Palermo. we rode on various types of transportation; wagons, carts, and trucks. When we finally arrived at our base, we were put on report with a variety of charges. We were accused of selling the boat and its contents to the black market, which at that time was doing a land mark business in that area. After pleading our case and explaining the reason we could not return the boat or its equipment, the officer in charge gave us permission to search for the boat. We drove back to the town where we were picked up. We did find the boat, or what was left of it. It had crashed against that mountain I had mentioned earlier.

Had it not been for those Sicilian fishermen, I guess we would have went down with our ship. We brought back some of the smashed parts of the boat to the base with us. I don't think the officer in charge believed our story. there were words mentioned like black market, activities that could land us all in the federal penitentiary at Levinworth. The good ending to this story and our acquittal of all charges ended when the mayor of that town, came to Palermo and wanted the Navy to award him and his town with a medal for saving the lives of four United States sailors.

I was shipped to Naples, Italy. I do not know where the other three sailors were shipped to, and to this day I do not know if the mayor, or his town, ever received a medal.

BEST * ONE * LINE * STORY
THE RADIOGRAM

JACK WESSEL,   **USS ROBERT A. OWENS DDK 827**
Nineveh, Indiana

While serving aboard the destroyer, ROBERT A. OWENS, during the Korean police action, in the Atlantic Ocean. I received a radio transmission from my mother it read:

"Your sister gave birth to her baby. Pats features, Georges fixtures!"

HITCH HIKING

TERRANCE BROWN, Chandler, Arizona

During the years 1950 through 1970 hitch-hiking was a common way for servicemen to travel. At that time the pay scale for servicemen and women was very low. Few sailors had cars, busses were very slow, trains inconvenient, and air travel too expensive. The general publics attitude was different back then, people were more trustworthy, plus they knew of the servicemens plight. There must have been far less kooks, perverts, and bad people, on the roads hitch hiking during that period as you never heard of car jackings, muggings, murders, that sort of thing being done by hitch hikers. Today, it is different, even I, tell my wife and daughters they should never pick up a hitch hiker because they could be asking for trouble. Times certainly have changed!

All sailors looked forward to the weekends when in port as it usually meant that two-thirds of the crew would be going on liberty. It usually went like this: One third of the crew had the duty. One third had what we called "a short weekend." Which was a forty-eight hour period starting at 0900 Saturday, ending at 0900 on Monday. The other third had "a long weekend." This was seventy-two hours long, usually commencing at 1600 Friday and expiring onboard at 0900 Monday. Everyone looked forward to those long weekends and you would be surprised at how far from their home port some sailors would travel on a long weekend.

On Friday afternoons and Saturday mornings the roads just outside the Navy base would be lined with sailors looking for rides. A lot of them held signs indicating their destinations, while others read "will pay" meaning they would help contribute gas money to the driver.

Even when going home on leave, when they had much more time to travel, most sailors would hit the road with their thumbs out. Actually, it was an adventure too. You never knew who would be offering you a ride, or how long it might take you to reach your destination. Many time I got soaked to the skin from an unexpected rain shower, stranded in the middle of no where on a dark night, or picked up by someone you did not care to ride with. You were young and took many chances. It was the lowest cost, and fastest way, to get where you were going.

I came from a large family of eight boys and two girls, we were all very close and missed each others company when we were separated for long periods of time. Seven of us were in the service scattered all over the country and world. We knew our family worried about us and missed us so whenever the opportunity presented itself we headed back home for a visit. Home at that time was Detroit, Michigan, which was a long way from my home port in Norfolk, Virginia.

One hitch hiking incident I remember well took place on a cold Winters morning. I had left Norfolk when my liberty commenced at 1600 hours the previous day. It was now about 0800 the next day and I had made it as far as Toledo, Ohio. I was tired, cold, and disgusted, as it seemed like hours since I had seen a car. It really was probably only a half-hour as I had made pretty good time getting this far, so fast.

Finally a car stopped! Freezing and tired I jumped into the car and flopped into the back seat. I noticed that the driver was a fellow sailor and a woman sat beside him. He explained that his mother had picked him up at his base and they too, were heading for their home in Detroit. Wow! What a blessing to be picked up by them. I had also noticed two other men in the back seat but payed them little mind as I was concentrating at getting warm and comfortable.

From the other side of the back seat came a voice I immediately recognized. "Hey Terry, don't you know your own brother?" I leaned forward and looked to my right and there sat one of my older brothers who was also in the service and stationed in Boston, Mass. He too, was on his way home on leave.

Needless to say, everyone in the car was joyful and amazed that such a coincidence could happen. The conversation in the car became cheerful and lively all the way to Detroit. They drove us right to our home and then drove away. What a great trip it had turned out to be. However, when it was time for me to return to Norfolk my mother packed me a lunch and insisted I take a train.

How many families can boast seven sons in the Navy? All served aboard ships and sailed the seven seas and a lot of oceans. Our service time totaled thirty years. We are all life members in the Veterans Of Foreign Wars where we go to reminisce those times gone by.

THE SHELLBACK INITIATION

by GEORGE SHARROW

Every member of the U.S.Navy, be he officer or enlisted, is considered to be a "Pollywog" until he is aboard a ship of the line that crosses the Equator and is initiated into the "Loyal Order Of Shellbacks.

Once a ship crosses the Equator, King Neptune and his court take over the ship and the rite begins. The Captain actually turns the ship over to King Neptune. Many times the Captain, himself, is a "Pollywog" and must undergo the initiation.

Captain of Enterprise Turning Ship Over To King Neptune

Van Watts Studio

Many have crossed the Equator aboard a small ship or in an aircraft but you are not an official "Shellback" until you have undergone the initiation rites and received your certification. It does not matter if you are a sailor, soldier, marine, or airman: If you happen to be aboard a ship of the U.S.Navy when it crosses the Equator "LOOK OUT!" If you are a "Pollywog" you cannot hide! You will be initiated into "The Loyal Order Of Shellbacks!"

You realize that something strange is about to happen when you notice that a pirates flag, "the skull and crossbones," has been raised to the yardarm and you see groups of "old salts" gathered about the ship planning something and when you walk past they seem to snicker at you.

The shrill sound of the bosns pipe over the ships loud speaker commands, "All hands report to the main deck! The uniform of the day is the oldest clothes in your seabag!"

All "Pollywogs" are gathered from their hiding places aboard ship. These "Shellbacks" are all dressed as pirates. They are very rough, ugly, and armed to the teeth with rubber knives and small sandbags which they use to keep you in line. On the main deck you notice all sorts of weird contraptions scattered about. Things like an electric chair, a black coffin, a four-feet deep pool of water with a

King Neptunes Court

Van Watts Studio

chair rigged over it, a yellow target-sieve secured like a tunnel to the deck, and a platform garbed like a throne with three large, ornate chairs, and red carpet. Other weird things are also noticed.

When the entire crew is assembled in front of this make-shift throne the bosns pipe sounds again. "Now hear this! His royal majesty King Neptune has arrived!"

The senior "Shellback" aboard has been dressed up like King Neptune complete with crown, royal robe, and all the trimmings. King Neptune takes his place on the throne along with his court, a proclamation is read to the crew by "Davy Jones" and the festivities begin!

The "Pollywogs" are put into groups of four or five, presented before King Neptune, charges read, and their punishment passed into the hands of "Shellbacks" who will lead them through several stages of the initiation.

You may be forced to kiss the greased belly of a fat bosns mate, you are then spattered with grease, egg goo, or paint, perhaps even feathers are a possibility—then you are led to the electric chair, the dunking stool, run the gauntlet, face the barber, or some other fun activity. Read the Van Watts story "Mascot Of The Big E" in this book for a good description of this ceremony.

Pollywogs Suffered Many Indignities

Van Watts Studio

Finally, all "Pollywogs" are sent through the yellow target-sieve (which is about three feet in diameter) on their hands and knees with a stream of sea water behind them to make their passage slippery and hasten them along. Meanwhile a group of "Shellbacks" have positioned themselves around this tube armed with sand filled weapons they use to hit at you as you pass through this tunnel-like tube. As you emerge from this target-sieve you are hosed down with sea water and then welcomed into "THE LOYAL ORDER OF SHELLBACKS!"

It has been a memorable experience and a lot of fun. After the initiation all hands enjoy a feast prepared by the ships cooks and a holiday atmosphere prevails throughout the ship.

Sadly, the "Shellback" is fast becoming an endangered species as we have fewer ships in our fleet and they seldom leisurely cross the Equator. Then again, it seems to me that men and women of todays Navy know little, and care less, about our great Navy and its time honored traditions.

It must also be noted that the ceremony described in this story usually takes place aboard larger ships. During war time and aboard smaller ships this ceremony may differ or be much less extravagant due to circumstances.

If you are a "Shellback" and desire to keep the knowledge of this great tradition alive and preserved for history please contact: Philip Perlmutter, The Shellback Association, 57 Parcot Ave., New Rochelle, N.Y. 10801. He will send you information of the organization and per-

George Sharrow,
USS MT. OLYMPUS AGC 8

haps a copy of their newsletter, "The Shellback Reporter" and tell you how you can join this fine organization.

POLLYWOG TO SHELLBACK

GEORGE SHARROW, Dauphin, Pa.   *USS Mt. Olympus AGC 8*

As a poet I am naught,
  but, of this story you must be taught.
Before crossing the Equator you are a pollywog,
  after iniation you will be a seadog.

Traditions in the Navy must be upheld,
  so with the tolling of the ships bell;
King Neptune took over the ship,
  he would make this a memorable trip.
So when the Boatswains whistle blew,
  we knew we would be in the stew.
After this day we would no longer a pollywog be,
  to this all the old salts onboard would see.
We all took part in the fun,
  for there was no place to run.
They lined us all up like ducks, in diapers
  then we danced to the tune of the piper.
As the salt water hoses on us did spray,
  we did roll and stumble in disaray.
From an old air target they made a tunnel,
  and into it we did funnel.
Using canvas bags filled with sand,
  they did all fill their hands;
Then clobber us using this, they did,
  every officer, and enlisted, Sam, Mike, and Sid.
We all went into the dunking tank,
  again, no matter what our rate or rank.
Although it seemed quite silly,
  we did all kiss the fat boatswains belly.
When it was over we all testified,
  this fun, frolic, and mayhem was justified,
For after all this turmoil, torture, and flack,
  WE WERE NOW A NAVY SHELLBACK!

MASCOT OF THE BIG "E"

VAN WATTS, Fullerton, California   *USS ENTERPRISE CV 6*

At chow time ruffians from R divisions would swoop across
the deck to scoop me up and deposit me at the head of their line,
whereupon a team from S division would come battling to my rescue with a bowling over all.

Moreover, I would be dispatched daily to the galley to test hot
pastries fresh from the oven—someone had to do it. I was told!
Nobody had to do it! But a plot to double my size would be discovered only when the chief cook was overheard telling the baker; We'll
stuff him with ice cream and pastries!"

"Boy Wonder," "Boy Scout," "Cabin Boy," "Jim Hawkins," and
"the kid with the Camay complection," by these and other nick-
names, in bootcamp I would be known!

And aboard my first ship; "The Mascot of the Big E" would take hold.

But a mascot gets to eat at the head of the line. To enjoy, on icecream days, a bowl full! to watch ships divisions battle for his custody! To be paraded about like a hard won trophy! And to be inspired by all this—and more!

For how do you get a mascot across the line?

Arrested on my way to boot camp by a police officer who thought that, "at most," I might be twelve years old. Only months later this old sailor's first crossing of the Equator would occur August 20, 1938, enroute from Norfolk to Rio.

But "How can we get our mascot across the line" as one old sailor put it—"without killing him?" to which another replied mercilessly. "We'll make him the Princess."

But, in the shellback committee dealing with such matters, an old China sailor, who in the Far East had acquired some uncanny wisdom, vetoed my selection.

"A young sailor who looks like a girl is always picked for these rites," the tattooed and wrinkled old salt confided, "but you—you look too much like a girl!"

"The kid with the Camay complexion" barely could restrain from striking the ancient shellback—This rage in time would melt into gratitude. For the role of King Neptunes daughter was not one I could have expected to—or even cared to—survive!

But the problem of getting "the mascot of The Big E" across the Line had remained to perplex Shellbacks meeting in committee. A solution would be sought with the help of the giant Huck.

"Even a mascots qualification as a Shellback must look fairly authentic," the biggest man on the ship would explain to the smallest.

"I have talked with the Chief Master-at-arms. He will be Davy Jones. It is Davey who will be in charge. He promises to personally conduct you through the area of the torture instruments.

"You should arrive safely at a platform on which you will see a couple of chairs and several barbers. I will be in the tank below. I'll tell the barbers to make it look a bit real but to take it easy on you. I'm hoping they will just flip the hinged chair in which you will be seated and flop you into the pool.

"In the pool will be other Shellbacks. I won't let them give you a second ducking. If you swallow a bit of salt water I'll shake it out of you. I'll get you out of the tank alive. Then all you have to do is run that gauntlet."

Concluding, Huck tried to sound on the optimistic side, "I'll talk to everyone I know who will be in those lines. The only think that really troubles me is possible last minute changes. All I can tell you is—run for your life!"

And, so instructed, I waited anxiously for the day King Neptune and his Royal Court would appear out of the equatorial mists

From the forward part of our carriers flight deck our Captain would escort His Majesty and Her Royal Highness to a viewing stand amidships.

A thousand pusillanimous Pollywogs had been herded into line. With the reading by Davy Jones of a proclamation by His Majesty, the initiation would begin. Those Pollywogs ahead of me being sent on—this one to the guillotine, that one to the coffin, this one to the electric chair, that one into surgery—and so on. I turned my eyes to Davy Jones for salvation.

Would he remember? Could he remember? Beyond, I could see the giant towering over all inside a tank erected from timber and canvas. Huck was just below the platform on which barbers savaged their victims, one cutting paths through their hair while another, with a brush and a one gallon shaving mug, slopped paint into the mouth of each complaining victim.

But —

It was rumored that the worst of the initiation was the gauntlet! That in the electric chair all a Pollywog got was a jolt! That in the guillotine what fell on ones neck was only a piece of plywood'

Pollywog Entering A Coffin

Van Watts Studio

**Davy Jones Reading
Proclamation**

Van Watts Studio

That a Pollywog had actually been seen getting out of a coffin! Well, sometimes one just doesn't know what to believe!

But "Hear Ye!" Hear Ye!" thundered Davy Jones, and, tucking me under his arm, he would carry me through an area of devilish-looking instruments to toss me upon the platform. Davy was keeping his promise and, at the same time, making it appear to a thousand other Pollywogs that he was at least roughing me up!

But seized and thrust into a chair, snip, snip, snip, with his clippers went one of the barbers while into my mouth another plunged a brushful of paint.

They're making it look real enough, thought I, as the hinged chair was flipped over backwards somersaulting the ships mascot head over heels into the tank!

Down, down, down, I went!

But somewhere in the water below huge hands located me, lifted me up and out, carried me to the edge of the tank, and let me slide gently down onto a steel deck cushioned with layers of canvas!

And there I lay, looking up at Shellbacks with bludgeons raised when a familiar voice commanded; "HOLD!"

Huck was giving orders to everyone within range of his voice, "TAKE IT EASY NOW!"

It was all he could do in the presence of other Pollywogs to whom no mercy at all was being shown. It was enough to signal the Shellbacks with whom he had conspired that the ships mascot was coming through!

In that gauntlet I had caught glimpses of Pollywogs propelled by the stings of water-soaked canvas bludgeons, reaching speeds I had thought unattainable. But seeing others fall and, on hands and knees, crawl to the ends of those lines. I found it necessary to reassure myself that Huck had gotten the word to most of those Shellbacks flailing away!

But I had run a gauntlet before! While others were encouraged to join the Navy, well-meaning persons had tried to turn me back. A childless couple had told an arresting officer, if I really was a runaway they would adopt me, and a lawman had released

Pollywogs Running the Gauntlet

Van Watts Studio

me to continue my dash to the sea, afraid he said to think of me defending the country! The mascot of the Big E gritted his teeth and charged!

On and on he went!

On and on through those awesome lines of the gauntlet!

But the bludgeons that should have bruised him, instead saluted!

"You're a spoiled brat!"

"You're a spoiled brat!"

"You're a spoiled brat!"

Those dreaded Shellbacks yelled, "and look who's spoiling you—US!"

LIBERTY IN MONTE CARLO

JACK CROSWELL, Cripple Creek, Va.   *USS PICKING DD 685*

It was in the Fall of 1952, I had only been in the Navy a short time serving aboard the destroyer USS PICKING as a deck hand when the ship was enjoying a cruise in the Mediterranean Sea as part of the United States Sixth Fleet.

We had the Commodore of our squadron, Captain Lyman, aboard our ship so I guess that is how we rated Monte Carlo as our liberty port. RHIP, rank has its privileges!

The country of Monaco is the tourist capital of the Mediterranean. It was also the choicest liberty port in the Mediterranean.

Some of the worlds finest hotels, clubs, restaurants, and beaches are located there, Some of the worlds most beautiful women go there on vacation. All this plus the large gambling casinos made this port the best liberty available on the Riviera.

As we lined up for inspection in our dress whites before being allowed to go ashore our division officer gave us this warning: "Gentlemen, you are not only guests of this country, you are all personal ambassadors of the United States Of America and I expect you all to conduct yourselves as such. I want no fighting, heavy drinking, nor getting into trouble of any kind. Do I make myself perfectly clear?"

"Yes Sir!" We all shouted back at him.

Then the Ensign looked directly at me and said: "Especially you Crosswell. If you get into any trouble your ass will be grass and I will be the lawn mower!"

"Aye, Aye, Sir!" I replied in a most sincere, honest, respectful sort of way. I had been known to drink and get into fights so I guess that is why he singled me out.

Desiring to be on my best good behavior I went ashore with a friend, a second class radioman who was married, drank very little, and never got into any trouble. We planned on having a good dinner, just a few drinks, then perhaps a little gambling at one of the casinos.

Separating ourselves from the main body of sailors who were heading for the more unsophisticated areas of Port LaCondamine, where we were tied up, We headed for the town of Monte Carlo.

Upon arrival in Monte Carlo we were impressed by the cleanliness and beauty of the town. The shops and restaurants were over whelming. What really caught our eye was one fancy restaurant with tables out side on the sidewalk.

"That's it!" I told my buddy. "We can't get into any trouble in a place like this." The waiter placed us at a table near a large party of mature civilians who seemed to be really enjoying themselves. They even had a strolling musician playing a violin.

After awhile the violin player came close to our table and I hailed him. "I used to play a pretty good fiddle." I told him. "Could I play a tune on yours?"

Without hesitation he handed me the violin and said to me: "Please do!"

I got up and with great confidence and began playing that well known tune from back home; "Turkey In The Straw." I played the song through three times while strolling around the party table."

To my amazement everyone started clapping their hands in time to the music. When I finally stopped playing and handed the violin back to the musician, everyone applauded loudly.

The musician introduced himself to us. He was Jeffery Hobday, conductor of the Monaco Symphony Orchestra.

I about fell off my chair!

Mr. Hobday invited us to join his party at their table, which we did. We drank their wine, ate their food, and had a real good time. The next thing that happened was, they moved their party to a private club a few miles away and took my buddy and I along with them.

Sometime during the course of the evenings events my buddy and I both succumbed to all the drinking and excitement and we passed out. I do not remember a thing after that.

I later learned from shipmates aboard the USS PICKING that some during the night a large yacht had pulled up alongside our ship and they had carried myself and my buddy aboard and we had been put in our bunks fully clothed.

The next morning I returned to my job, I was assigned to chip and paint the side of our ship. I had one hell of a hangover.

About eleven hundred hours I heard the shrill sound of the boatswains pipe coming over the ships loud speaker followed by: "Seaman Crosswell report to the quarterdeck immediately!"

"Holy shit!" I was wondering. "What did I do now?"

Upon reporting to the officer of the deck on the quarterdeck he took one hard look at me and said: "Crosswell, you look like hell! Get out of those dungarees, put on your dress whites, and report to the Commodores cabin."

Bemused and befuddled I replied: "Aye, Aye, Sir!" went below, changed into my dress whites, inspection shoes and all, then went directly to the Commodores cabin as ordered. Not knowing what to expect once I got there. I was one scared sailor.

I had never been in, or near, the Commodores quarters so I was both excited and nervous as I approached the area...there was chief quartermaster in his dress whites standing at the door, as if guarding it. He was a member of the Commodores staff.

"Hi Chief," I offered a greeting. "I'm Crosswell, and I was told to report to the Commodores Cabin."

Without saying a word to me, the chief knocked on the cabin door, opened it and said; "Sir, Seaman Crosswell is here."

"Send him in!" A voice came from within the cabin.

As I entered the Commodores living area I was over whelmed. I sure do not know why they call it a cabin when it was actually a small apartment. I never expected this. There were two sofas, several upholstered chairs, lamps, cocktail tables, a large wooden table in the center of the room loaded with food, and the port holes even had fancy drapes over them. Everything was elegant in Navy blue and gold.

Commodore Lyman was the first to greet me. Extending his hand for me to shake he said: "Good morning Crosswell. Some friends of your have come aboard to visit you and tour our ship." with that, he gestured towards the other men in the room.

Immediately I was surrounded by the group of men I had met last night and partied with. Jeff Hobday greeted me warmly, followed by the other five members of his party, all of whom I remembered from the previous night. To my surprise, three of these men were direct ambassadors of Prince Rainier III, President Of Monaco. The other two, who were dressed as generals, were military advisors to the Prince.

Words cannot express the feelings that overcame me at that moment. One glance at the Commodore told me that he was over whelmed also.

After lunch with the Commodore, we toured the ship with the Commodore leading the party while explaining all the workings and purposes of our ship. I was lost in the crowd of dignitaries, bull shitting all the way, and actually enjoying myself with the thrill of the moment.

Each time we passed an officer, a sailor, or a work party, they all snapped to attention and saluted. That memory alone, will last a life time.

Caught by surprise by their arrival, the Officer Of The Deck now had six side boys and a boatswains mate lined up at the gangway awaiting their departure.

As they prepared to leave the ship, Hobday and the entire party not only shaked my hand, but gave me a warm manly embrace, as is their custom. Their remarks to the Commodore were:

"It was a great visit. Thank you Commodore."

"See you later Jack!" One said to me, much to the Commodores surprise.

"The USS PICKING is the best ship in the Sixth Fleet, just as you said it was Jack."

"See you Jack Old man!"

Everyone aboard ship was still all smiles and in a good mood as the visitors cleared the gangway and entered their waiting limousines.

Then it came in a loud, clear, voice. "Crosswell, please join me in my cabin." This was an order, not a request. It was spoken to me by the Commodore.

Back inside the cabin I stood at attention as directly in front of me stood, the Commodore, the ships Captain, and the executive officer.

They all seemed to speak at once:

"Crosswell, how could you?"

"What the hell did you do last night?"

"I can't believe this all happened!"

The Commodore asked me to tell my story, which I did in full detail up until the moment I passed out.

"Well," the Commodore said. "You were apparently bragging about how the USS PICKING was the best ship in the Sixth Fleet and just how great the United States Navy was, and you invited them aboard this ship to prove it to them."

"I did that Sir?" I asked quite feebly. I had not remembered doing that.

"You certainly did!" The Commodore did all the talking while everyone else listened. "I am real proud that you love the USS PICKING and the United States Navy the way you do, but, the next time you go ashore please know the people you are drinking with." He really did not seem mad at me, just a little upset. "It is very embarrassing when the personal envoy of the President of a foreign country is going to pay you a visit and you are unawares of it."

"Yes Sir!" I said meekly. I felt that I had to say something.

"They just drove onto the pier, got out of their limousines, and walked onboard." The Captain was visibly shaken.

"I am proud of the way it all turned out." The Commodore added. "By the way Crosswell, you are restricted to the ship until we leave Monaco."

"Aye, Aye, Sir!" I acknowledged with a sigh of relief.

"That will be all Crosswell." The exec finally said something. "You may return to your duties."

Another now snappy; "Aye, Aye, Sir!" I exited the cabin.

I was like a hero to the rest of the crew for the rest of the cruise except to my radioman buddy who never went on liberty with me again.

The story does not end here!

Years later, after leaving the Navy, I became an agent for the United States Treasury Department serving four Presidents: Nixon, Carter, Ford, and Reagan. It was during my time with the Treasurer Department that I ran into now Admiral Lyman, and Conductor Hobday and we renewed our acquaintance. Then a year or so later I ran into the Ambassador Of Monaco and his staff at a social function and we had a great time recalling this incident.

Today I am retired from the government and most of the world living on a small farm in Virginia where I enjoy recalling all the great memories and experiences while serving our great nation.

FRENCH WAVES

GEORGE DAWSON, Wantaugh, New York

During part of World War II I was a radioman at the U.S.Navy Base in Oran, Algeria (North Africa). Our radio shack was on the Eastern side of the city, while the French Navy's radio station was on the West side a few miles away.

One day I was manning the teletype machine connected to the French Navy's station. After completing the official messages, I started a friendly conversation with the French operator. All of the French operators were Navy women, or "French Waves," as we called them. This woman seemed to be very personable, and I thought that I might be able to get a date with her. I suggested that we meet somewhere.

She agreed, and it was decided that we would meet at a popular bar and restaurant in the heart of the city. We would meet at the restaurants side-walk cafe. "How will I recognize you?" I asked.

"I will be wearing my uniform," she replied. "I will be sitting at one of the small tables. I will have a magazine in my left hand and a glass of white wine in my right hand."

At the appointed time, I appeared at the side-walk cafe, eager to meet my new friend. However, there were at least twelve "French

Waves" sitting at small tables, holding a magazine in their left hand and a glass of white wine in their right hand! I realized that I had been the victim of a very cleaver and well-planned practical joke. Who says the French have no sense of humor?

OFF LIMITS LIBERTY

WALTER E. HOFFMAN, Greenville, Pa.   USS HAMBLETON

While the USS HAMBLETON was having the torpedo damage repaired in Casablanca harbor there were many escapades taking place among some of the crew.

One of these was an unofficial weekend liberty I took to an area called the "New Medina." It was enclosed by a high wall and encompassed a very large area of many city blocks. It was sort of a detention area and was off-limits to military personnel. It was patrolled on the inside by Military Police and the Shore Patrol. the front entrance was guarded by French Gendarmes. Entrance had to be gained by scaling the back wall, which was lined with Arab shops and stalls which necessitated entering after curfew.

This particular weekend, after having dinner with this one family of French/Arabs they wanted to take me on a tour of this "New Medina."So in order to be able to roam about freely they dressed me in an Arab womans dress, which covered all but my eyes. This of course was necessary because of all the patrols. They also made me take off my Navy shoes and put on slippers, otherwise, they said my Navy shoes would be a dead give away. . So arm in arm, with a girl on each side of me we went on our walk through the "New Medina." there were a good many Military Police and some Shore Patrol. At times we received some funny looks from the Military police due to the way the girls

**Walter E. Hoffman,
USS HAMBLETON**

were giggling. I also got a few odd looks, probably because I wasn't too good at walking like a woman.

I guess the highlight was when we passed a Shore Patrol from the USS HAMBLETON. It was Lt. Defour with two enlisted men. I gave the Lt. a wave, but he just ignore it. This time I was able to return to the ship without incident. Many, many, escapades later I paid the piper at a Captains mast!

Some time later, back on the ship, Lt. Dufour came up to me with a snapshot of myself that he said he took off the wall of a room in the "New Medina." I, of course, professed great innocence, and he just grinned.

LET'S FIND A BETTER NEIGHBORHOOD

GEORGE DAWSON, WATAUGH, NEW YORK

When I joined the Navy shortly after Pear Harbor, I was hoping for duty on a destroyer. I didn't get it! After graduating from radio school as an RM Third Class I was sent to an Army camp (Camp Crowder, Missouri) along with about two hundred other Navy men. In addition to the radio operators there men who could speak various foreign languages, such as French or Spanish. There were also many Navy officers. we had no idea of why we had been sent to an Army facility.

We were given much the same training that many Army Signal Corps men received, along with instruction in firing rifles, carbines, pistols, and the like. We went on field maneuvers, received commando-type training, and went through the "overhead" fire course.This involved crawling on our stomachs one rainy night while live machine-gun bullets were being fired about eighteen inches over our backs. we were also taught how to recognize various poison gases, such as mustard gas and phosgene gas. Then we were all assigned to "communications teams." My unit was Spanish Team # 3, which was made up of about twenty men; radio operators, Spanish speaking sailors and a few officers.

Equipped with rifles, gas masks, helmets, and Army-type clothing, we were considered ready for some sort of action. When we asked for explanations we were told only that "When you come back, if you come back, you will be covered with medals." We thought we would be invading Spain, and that our task would be to go ashore with the invading force and set up field radio stations to communicate with ships off shore, with our allies, and possibly with underground freedom fighters.

At Norfolk, Virginia, we boarded a Liberty Ship and were quartered in a cargo hold that had been converted for carrying troops. It was dark, dismal, poorly ventilated, and stank of fuel. There were no showers, and the food was vile. Half way across the Atlantic the engine failed and we bobbed around in the ocean while the rest of our convoy slowly disappeared over the horizon. Fortunately, repairs were made and we managed to catch up with the convoy just before dark. The only other excitement was a u-boat scare, but the escorts took care of that efficiently.

When the Rock Of Gibralter came into view we were convinced that indeed an invasion of Spain was imminent. However, we passed right by the Rock and ended somewhere off the coast of North Africa. The ship anchored way off shore one night, and we Navy men were ordered to go ashore in landing craft. as I climbed down the rope ladder the landing craft was plunging up and down violently, and all I could think of was that I would break my leg trying to get into it. I managed to get into the boat safely, but not until I lost my helmet overboard. It was a long trip to the beach, and we maneuvered in and around the masts of sunken ships. We landed without incident and awaited the arrival of our officers, but then were told that the officers would not come in until the next morning.

We did not know where we were or what we were supposed to do, so we scouted around until we found a spot that seemed to be safe, secure, and quiet. We dined on K-rations, sentries were posted then huddled together in our little tents we tried to sleep. In the morning we awoke and started to examine our surroundings in the daylight. To our great discomfort, we found that we had settled down in a French Navy ammunition depot. There were hugh shells and cases of gun powder all around. We were at least grateful that our efforts to start small fires the night before had failed. It can be very cold at night in North Africa. We quickly moved to another neighborhood!

We never did learn why we had landed at this spot, and our officers knew less than we did. After several days of hanging around doing nothing, we took off for another site. We landed in Oran, Algeria, and spent eighteen months there manning a radio station. Returning to the U.S.A. we were not covered with medals, as promised, but at least we were still alive!

FAMILY

JOHN A. ANDERSON, Mechanicsburg, Pa.   **USS LST 392**

A family is planned when a boy meets a girl
    Their thoughts of affection abound.
Courtship soon follows with heads all awhirl;
    Commitment is on solid ground,

A marriage proposal, accepted with love
  And plans for a wedding in June;
The blessing of Angels who watch from above;
  Two hearts who are singing one tune.

A gathering of sailors—the crew of a ship
  Create a family, too,
And whether on shore or on a long trip,
  Each man has his own job to do.
In Naval tradition your ship is your home
  While you are a part of a ships crew;
Regardless of where in the world you may roam
  Or what you are required to do.

They called us together to form a new crew,
  Our loved ones we left behind.
They gave us a ship—the Three Ninety-Two
  Our billets were promptly assigned.
We shared our sorrows as well as our joys
  While we were fighting a war;
A wounded shipmate—one of the boys,
  Or some realization ashore.

A heart warming episode took place one day
  As we landed on Sicilys shore,
One shipmate could think of no other way
  Than to leave, forgetting the war.
So off into town with his buddy he went.
  His grandmother lived down the street!
To return the same day was his honest intent,
  But the ship had a schedule to meet.

A day or two later the Three Ninety-Two
  Returned to the same landing site,
And there on the beach stood the rest of her crew,
  Both waving, awaiting their plight.
It was odd that our landing site took us so near,
  It was odd that we went there again,
But stranger than fiction are tales that you hear
  When you listen to many a man.

We sat on the French River Seine one cold night
  Awaiting to leave the next day
To cross o'er the sand bar by morn's early light,
  But it snowed that night, causing delay.

Some GI's aboard had to challenge the crew,
  To them, we were the foe.
No battle stars earned for the Three Ninety-Two
  We lost—We ran out of snow!

Not only onboard the Three Ninety-Two
  But after we'd left her as well
Some friendships continued to thrive and some grew,
  Some have a great story to tell,
Such as the two sailors whose friendship began
  When they met as a part of the drew.
At the alter the one was the others best man!
  Greater friendship no one ever knew.

Since Euclid, Ohio, in Seventy-nine,
  Reunions are part of our lives.
We meet for a weekend of mem'ries divine;
  Old shipmates, along with our wives.
We'll never forget the friends that we made,
  Our "family," forever so true,
We're proud of the friendships which never will fade,
  We're proud of the Three Ninety-Two!

THE PEE TEES

HALSTEAD ELLISON   *courtesy of PT Boats, Inc.*
                                     Museum and Library

Have you ever been the combat zone
  Holding a new beach-head,
With the enemy there in the jungle,
  And the enemy overhead?

And out on the angry sea behind,
  They say there's a heavy force,
Of enemy coming behind your back,
  To wipe you out, of course?

Now, if you have, you'll really know,
  As does each poor Marine,
The thrill, the joy—to hear,
  "We have a Pee Tee screen!"

At setting sun we hear them start;
  That husky, deep-throat, roar,

We count each motor, note each craft
Departing from the shore!

They say condition now is "Black,"
One wonders what may hap?
For we have taken islands that
Were treasured by the Jap!

Now daylight breaks, the boats come in,
We count them, one by one.
You'd think each sailor in those crews
Were, each—our only son!

And then, marines can settle down
To fight 'til setting sun!
The Navy saw us through the night -
Our work has just begun!

SEA FERRETS
by Edward E. Cole

JOHN ALLEN, Olympia, WA   from Our Navy Magazine 1947

Can you sit serene, on a brone that's mean
Or stay on a plunging steer?
Can you calmly flop in a boiler shop
And peacefully pound your ear?
Can you keep your feet on a sheet of sleet
In a wind that'll freeze you thru?
Then you, maybe, mate, have the stuff to rate
A berth with a P.T. crew.

Swoop like a gull and dive like a plover
Turn on a dime, with a nickel over,
Racing whippet and jumping goat,
Leaping Lena, the P.T. boat.

You'll practice poise with the P.T. boys
By swimming a waterfall.
You'll learn to trek on a canted deck
Where a cockroach couldn't crawl.
And when they feel you are hard as steel
And tough as a rubber sole.
They may admit you are almost fit
To go where the P.T.'s roll.

Maybe you'll do for the craft
  That's quickest,
That gets its hell
  Where the hell is thickest.
And tackles anything that is afloat;
  They're all the one size to the P.T. boat.

You'll handle guns that are bathed in tone
  Of thundering ocean water.
You'll launch your fish in the whee and whish,
  Of shells that are packed with slaughter.
You'll dash and drive at the subs that dive,
  Or the heavies whose salvoes flame,
Through your sides are frail as Salomes' vail.
  You'll battle'em just the same!

You play hopscotch with the ocean dragons,
  With subs, destroyers, and battlewagons,
Through the odds are great and the chance remote
  You'll take on a fleet with a P.T.Boat.

EDDIE RICKENBACKER RESCUE

EDWARD A. GREEN,   *Ron 20 courtesy PT Boats Inc.*
                           Museum and Library

For the men of PT Ron,1, Div 2, stationed at the South Pacific atoll of Funafuti in the Ellice Islands, Thursday November 12th, 1942 began just like any other day with a beautiful sunrise, blue sea, and clear sky. Toward evening a radio report from a Navy patrol plane indicated a raft about ten miles from the island. PT 22 with LT(jg) Al Cluster USN as skipper went out to investigate and pick up Capt. Walter Cherry USAF, pilot of the U.S. Air Force B-17 which with Eddie Rickenbacker and seven others had crashed in the Pacific 23 days before. Cherry said that two rafts with other survivors were in the area. At first dawn on Friday, November 13th, the Div of four PT boats (22, 23, 25, 26) along with their tender, the USS HILO, and with four patrol planes began a search of the Pacific for the two rafts with the six other survivors.

The day passed with no result, except for eyes that ached from hours of searching an empty ocean. Just at sunset a radio message to the PT tender, the Hilo, sent by Lt. Eady USNR, pilot of a Navy patrol plane, reported that he had spotted a raft with survivors who included Rickenbacker, landed near it, and gave the bearing. The

Goony Garvey has an idea for a new Navy life raft.

Hilo relayed the message to the nearest PT, the 26- boat, with the Div commander Lt. Commander John Rice USN on board. Ensign John Weeks was skipper and Ensign Edward Green was the executive officer. We pushed up the throttles and headed on the bearing given, the boat cuttubg through the moderate swell and pancaking down after passing each wave crest. Chief Motor Mac "Tex" Feathering, along with MM1C Herman Oading and MM3C John Hornyak, had a bucket brigade going in the engine room to keep water in the Packards, for their water-jackets were leaking, and to walk between them was like getting doused in a hot shower.

The distance was about thirty-five miles and it was pitch dark when at 8 P.M. we were happy to see in the dark emptiness of the ocean the red and green wing lights of the plane dead ahead. We drew as close as we could and agreed that Col. Adanson USA, the senior officer of the group of survivors, would stay in the cockpit of the plane, since he was too ill to move. The two other survivors, Eddie Rickenbacker and E. Bartek, then paddled the raft the few feet over to the fantail of the PT. Each man of the crew jockeyed for position to be the first to help Mr. Rickenbacker aboard, so he said, "Just call me "Eddie" boys, but get me on that boat!" Helped by Chief G.M. Blozis, R.D. Nelson, Q.M.Wepner, the survivors got aboard and the boat pointed its bow toward Funafuti, 40 miles away, going slowly because the Navy patrol plane had to taxi behind, being unable to take off in the moderate swell that was running. Of the two survivors on board Bartek lay on the foredeck covered with blankets, glad to rest and sleep. We took Eddie Rickenbacker to Ensign Green's bunk and instead of sleeping he

An 80 foot Elco PT boat typical of those used in the Pacific theater. This boat is equipped with radar and has roll-off racks for the March 13 torpedos. Additionally, the boat is heavily armed with twin fifies in the turrets as well as 37 mm and 40 mm guns. Depth charges and smoke generator can be seen on the stern. Tis class PT would most likely had bave a crew of about sixteen pluss at least two officers.

PT Boats, Inc. Museum and Library

stayed sitting up and for almost two hours talked about his experiences, looking like a sunburned skeleton with his piercing blue eyes and hawk nose. The cook brought cold pineapple juice, but at the suggestion that warm soup would be better the cook obligingly got the soup.

Rickenbacker was excited about his rescue and told many details about their three and a half weeks adrift, almost all of them later recorded in his book "Seven Came Through", and in the movie that was later made about the rescue. He recounted details how they boarded the rafts with no time to get provisions after ditching the plane in the ocean, caught rain in their handkerchiefs, ate flying fish that fell into the rafts, ate raw a seagull that landed on R's head and which he grabbed by its feet and wrung its neck so they could have a feast, how one man became delirious and died. Most of all, Rickenbacker was impressed by the power of prayer. Bartek had a pocket New Testament so the men spent a few minutes each day reading aloud from it and praying. Rickenbacker encouraged this to keep alive the hope that they would be rescued and to survive. Now all his efforts and prayers to keep hope alive had been vindicated. He was a happy man, happy that his trust in God had not been misplaced.

The 26-boat arrived back at Funafuti lagoon in the early hours of the morning, Nov. 14th, and a motor launch from the base hospital met us as we anchored and transferred the survivors from the PT and plane to the hospital boat. They remained at the hospital for some days regaining strength for the flight back to the U.S. the morning of the 14th also brought news that the raft with three other survivors had been rescued by natives from a neighboring island, and a PT brought them back to Funafuti.

This is the main outline of the Rickenbacker rescue, and Friday the 13th turned out to be a good day for the seven men rescued at sea.

TRUE STORY, SO HELP ME

SKEE BOSCOSKY,   *Ron 13—courtesy PT Boats Inc.*
                                     Museum and Library

During a calm moment from kamikaze attacks, I was on the beach in the head, sitting down, naturally, when in popped an Army General, (exact rank, I can't say for sure). He sat down next to me and asked, "How goes it son?" At that moment the Army's twin 40's on the beach roared to let us know that the Japanese were on the way. Sanitation was forgotten. We grabbed our pants and away we went. Neither one of us wanted to be found in that muck. But what gets me, is how he beat me out that door, when I was the closest to it.

NAVY LINES

Author Unknown   *courtesy of PT Boats, Inc.*
                                           Museum and Library

The Navy always has its lines
No matter where one goes.
We have to stand in line to bathe
And then to see the shows.

We stand in line to get our chow;
We stand in line for pay;
We stand in line to get our mail
Or hear, "There's none today!"

They say if we're not "squared away,"
"Get back in line there,Mac."
Some day they might decide we should
Line up to hit our sack.

We stand in line for choc'late malt,
Or soda, or coke, or beer.
Half the time the line's "secured"
Whenever we get near.

I'll stand in all the Navy lines
But you can bet your life
When I get home I will not stand
In line to kiss my wife!

THE PERFECT SQUELCH

JOHN H. ALLEN, Everett, Washington   **USS SALEM CA-139**

Shortly after morning muster the Executive Officer of a cruiser which was being de-mathballed was making an unofficial tour of inspection to see how the work was progressing on the vessel.

He had just passed the after turrent when he heard a sound which caused him to stop dead in his tracks. Someone was whistling. Above the roar of chipping hammers and rivet guns he heard someone whistling a popular tune.

Fully aware of the fact that whistling is "taboo' in the Navy, the Exec leaned down a hatch and shouted, "Who is whistling down there?"

"Me sir," promptly replied an unseen voice.

"Are you a yard worker or do you belong in this ship?" bellowed the Exec.

"I'm a sailor," replied the voice.

"Well don't you know that only two people in the Navy who are allowed to whistle?" Thundered the Exec once more. There was a slight pause.

"Yes sir! Boatswains mates and damn fools," calmly said this unseen voice.

"Well, what-in-hell are you?" the now purple-faced officer asked.

"Second class boatswains mate, sir" matter-of-factly stated the still unseen voice.

A dead silence prevailed as the Exec. tactfully withdrew from the area.

THE PERFECT SQUELCH II

JOHN H. ALLEN, Everett, Washington   USS SALEM CA-139

It was shortly after midnight and the liberty launch from one of the anchored ships in the Hudson River was about ten feet out from the fleet landing. Save for the crew of three men it was empty.

Hearing a shout, the coxswain straightened up and peered into the darkness at the ramp leading down to the landing stage. In the darkness he could hear the sound of thudding feet flying across the dock.

Then into the brightly lighted area of the stage came a sailor who was obviously in a hurry. He clutched his white hat in one hand and strained for breath as he thundered down the ramp and onto the landing.

Two surprised S.P.'s made a vain dive for the hurtling figure as, never slackening speed, he took off like a broad jumper, shot across the water and landed on one oar in the bottom of the liberty launch. He lay there for a moment stunned, then arose slowly to his feet brushing off his dress blues.

"And just what were you trying to do?" said the bewildered coxswain. The sailor looked at him with a sheepish grin on his face.

"I just couldn't afford to miss the last boat and be late," he said. The coxswain broke into a howl of laughter.

"You dumb swabbie," he said to the sailor. "This boat is the last one alright but its not going. It just happens its on its way in!"

BOOT!

JOHN A. ALLEN, Olympia, Washington   OUR NAVY Magazine

The sleek, gray destroyer was ploughing her way swiftly through the turbulent waters of the angry North Atlantic. She was on a three week shake-down cruise, having taken aboard a batch of still-damp-behind-the-ears recruits at Newport, her last port of call.

For a week the weather had been threatening and the huge waves were becoming increasingly choppy. All hands aboard ship had been warned of the danger of being washed overboard during the normal course of a days work.

Forward of the torpedo tubes on the port side of the ship, a fuzzy-cheeked boot was busily, but not ambitiously turning to on what passed for a paint chipping detail. Four of his not-to-ambitious mates were eagerly engaged in a heated discussion as to how they could kill the maximum amount of time with the least amount of energy.

The fuzzy-cheeked boot was working near the life line, his foot swung precariously over the bottom strand in the same manner as his hat perched saltily on the back of his head. Suddenly the ship gave a violent roll as she made a turn and up and over the life line went the fuzzy-cheeked seaman.

"ACTUALLY, HERB WASN'T TRANSFERRED. NOBODY WOULD TAKE HIM, SO THE OLD MAN SIMPLY DROPPED HIM FROM THE MUSTER ROLLS."

Instantly his non-working cohorts raised the alarm "Man Overboard." The word was relayed to the bridge and the trim destroyer heeled over and shuddered to a stop. Quickly and efficiently the still-green crew went about their tasks. Hardly had the word been passed when the ready lifeboat was lowered into the water and the search for the missing man was underway.

For over an hour the lifeboat searched the waters. Lookouts on the ship strained their eyes as they vainly sought a bobbing object among the tossing white-caps. Finally, the search was abandoned; the man appeared to have been lost. Reluctantly the skipper ordered a muster to learn the name of the unfortunate seaman.

The word was passed to fall in at divisional quarters and a muster was held. One by one the division officers reported to the skipper on the bridge. All hands present and accounted for. The old man's brows knit in a puzzled frown. He barked a few crisp orders and a moment later four trembling young seamen stood before him. Although they jumped as he fired questions at them, they maintained that a man had gone over the side.

Still puzzled, the skipper undertook inspection of each division. All present and accounted for. On down the line until he reached the First Division.

"All present and accounted for Sir," said the young Ensign in charge of the division. The old man grunted and was about to stride on when something caught his eye. Turning, he pushed aside two men in the front rank. There, standing directly before him in the rear rank, was a fuzzy-cheeked, soaking wet young sailor, his saltier-than-ever white hat still perched on the back of his head.

"Whereinhell, have you been?" roared the skipper. The seaman withered under the blast, and although wringing wet, drew himself up to attention and saluted smartly.

"I fell over the side Sir," he said through chattering teeth.. A beet-red flush crept up the old man's neck and covered his face.

"Well, how did you get back on board then?" Bellowed the old man. The seaman defiantly stood his ground.

"I grabbed a trailing line when I went overboard and climbed up on the fantail when we slowed down," he said. The skippers mouth sagged open as the seaman continued.

"When I got back on board and heard the word being passed that there was a man overboard, I went and fell into quarters like they told us at boot camp Sir."

A hopeless look spread over the old man's face. Shaking his head slowly he turned to the division officer.

"Put this man on report for leaving the ship without permission, Mr. Jones!" And with that, he strode angrily off.

WHEN DREAMS GET TOO REAL

JOHN ALLEN, Olympia, Washington   *OUR NAVY Magazine*

Shortly before the start of the war, one of Uncle Sams new heavy cruisers was steaming slowly along on a routine patrol off the Virginia Capes.

It was a typical warm southern Summer night, complete to the faint suggestion of the moon which hung low on the distant horizon. A number of the crew, to escape the humidity below decks had taken advantage of the Captains memorandum and had brought their sacks topside.

It was a little past 0100 as the dim shape of the blacked-out cruiser swished silently through the water. High on the darkened bridge surface lookouts peered intently into the semi-blackness.

Suddenly the tow-headed young seaman on watch on the port wing of the bridge stiffened. Straining his eyes, he peered off into the darkness. In the faint light of the moon he saw a figure rise and then stand by the rail. Then, before his horrified eyes, the figure placed one foot upon the middle strand of the life line and vaulted over the side of the ship.

Instantly the lookout went into action, yelling "man overboard" at the top of his lungs. He raced to the ready life buoy and pulled it free. It slid off into space and a moment later its light marked its location on the water.

Aboard ship the general alarm began to clang and the sharp notes of a bugle cut through the quiet night. The cruiser shuddered violently as she lost speed and swung in a wide circle.

A lifeboat was quickly lowered over the side and raced back towards the lighted buoy before the cruiser had trembled to a halt.

According to the ships log, exactly three minutes had elapsed from the time of the lookouts cry to the return of the lifeboat to the ship. This was rather remarkable and spoke well for a green crew who had roused out of a sound sleep after a hard days work.

As the ship again got underway, the Captain and the Executive officer stood on the bridge waiting for the man who had gone over the side to be brought to them. A moment later one of the ships MAA"s appeared, followed by a dripping, befuddled looking sailor clad only in a pair of shorts and a skivvy shirt. The Captain immediately identified him as a young quartermaster third class.

"Well," growled the skipper."What have you got to say for yourself Harris?"

Harris stood there, shivering slightly, more from the wrath of the Captain than from the midnight plunge.

"Come on speak up," said the Captain.

Although out of uniform, but in true keeping with Navy tradition, the quartermaster came to attention, and spoke.

"Its all because of Daisy, Sir," he said. Then he explained to the Captain that Daisy was his girl and that she lived on the farm next to his fathers in Iowa. As he continued, a faint smile tugged at the corner of the old mans mouth.

"You see, Sir, I got to dreaming about Daisy tonight after I turned in. That dream seemed mighty real too. Well, to get in Daisys place I had to get across a fence that separated our farms."

The smile on the Captains face was bigger now as he looked at the dripping sailor. "Go on," he said.

"Well Sir, when I got to that fence I just naturally hurdled over it like I always used to do. Next thing I knew, I was in the water."

As he sheepishly finished, the smile on the old mans face exploded into peals of laughter.

"Yes, I guess dreams can be pretty real sometimes, son. Go get some clothes on."

FAVOR RETURNED

JOHN H. ALLEN, Olympia, washington   OUR NAVY Magazine
(This story is about an officer, but it is so good that I decided to print it.)

Captain Al Bentley, holder of the Navy Cross and six other high decorations was air sick—and how! Never during his rugged Jap patrols with the USS SILVERFIN had he felt as he did now.

He ventured a glassy-eyed and green-tinted look over the side of the cockpit and mentally vowed that if he ever set foot on terra firma again he'd never leave it. Just then the Army fighter plane spun into a violent power dive and the Navy officer gave up all hope of reaching the ground in one piece.

In the forward cockpit, deftly handling the controls, Colonel Tom Bentley was having a whale of a time. Al's younger brother was really laying it on—but thick.

Known as a "hot pilot" and loaded with combat ribbons for his destruction of twenty-eight Nazi planes, the Colonel was wringing the speedy Army fighter plane out—much to the discomfort of his older brother. He threw the plane into a series of violent barrel rolls, outside loops, wing-overs, and was now winding it up with a shuddering power dive toward the ground.

As the plane finally landed and rolled to a stop before the hangers. Tom climbed out, turned and cast an amusing grin at his shaken sickly-looking brother who was climbing out of the rear cockpit amid much difficulty.

"Still think that the Army can't fly.pal?" he laughingly asked. Al just gazed blankly at him, muttered something which sounded like "I'll settle with you later!" and headed at a staggering gait for the bar at the BOQ.

The following week Colonel Bently paid a surprise visit to the USS SILVERFIN which was tied up at a pier on the coast. He stood impatiently on the hot deck while a messenger was sent for his brother. The Captain finally hove into view with a grin that bespoke more than brotherly affection.

"Hello doggie," he said. "Your just in time to take a ride with the Navy. Care to go for a dive with us?" It took a bit of persuading but finally Al coaxed him to go along for a practice dive in the submarine.

Al led the way down through the conning tower and the hatch was clanged shut behind them. Sailors scurred to their stations at his "Prepare to get underway" and the sub began to throb as the powerful diesels roared into action.

"Prepare to take her down."—"Level off at 250 feet." the bow of the sub began to slide forward. Sweating sailors went efficiently about their tasks. Captain Bently escorted his brother throughout the boat and they interestedly watched the men working the valves, dials, and complicated mechanisms which ran the underseas craft.

Finally came the "On the bottom,Sir". The submarine trembled for a moment then settled herself on an even keel.

"Well, Tom, how does it feel to be on the bottom?" Al asked. "We're down 250 feet now. Do you notice the pressure?" The Army Colonel replied that he thought he could feel a slight pressure in his ears, but remarked that the effect at 20,000 feet was much greater than this.

The SILVERFIN's skipper continued to escort his brother on a tour of the boat, explaining the various workings of the intricate machinery as they went along. When almost an hour had passed he gave the order to "Take her up."

Sailors again hurried into action but the motors this time remained silent. The sub's skipper began to look a little worried. Just then a sweating CPO rushed up to him. Grease covered his bare shoulders and his face was filled with anxiety.

"The motors have failed Sir," he said. Immediately the Captains face became grave. Following in the wake of the Chief, he rushed aft. His brother stood there, his horrified gaze fastened on the hatch through which Al had gone.

They had been down for over an hour now. The air in the silent sub was becoming fouler by the minute and the sailors had stripped to the waist. Even the nattily-dressed Colonel Bently had removed his tie and was breathing heavily. For fifteen minutes now they had been using the oxygen tanks. Tom had almost collapsed when a sailor told him that the knocking he had heard on the subs hull was probably a diver looking for life within the boat.

Finally the sub gave a violent shudder and the motors began to hum steadily. Captain Bently returned just then and told his brother that they had finally located the trouble. He instructed one of his men to increase the output of oxygen and again gave the order to; "Take her up!"

Al motioned to the conning tower ladder and his brother started up. A few moments later he was frantically fumbling with the wheel of the escape hatch. Al lent him a more than willing hand. Finally it spun open and Tom scrambled madly through the opening. He stopped when he had emerged to the waist and, looking up at the clear blue sky, took several deep breaths.

Then a look of amazement spread over his face. Calmly seated on the grilled deck before the conning tower, two dungaree-clad sailors were busily engaged in a game of cribbage.

The look of amazement changed to a scarlet flush as the Army flyer saw the small gangway and the taut lines, fore and aft, which still moored the USS SILVERFIN securely to the dock!

SPLASH ONE

JOHN H. ALLEN, Olympia, Washington OUR NAVY MAGAZINE

One of the biggest chuckles to come out of the grimness of the war was provided by the late Major Richard Bong, one of the Army's top-ranking aces during the fighting in the Pacific. His fighter squadron operated out of Leyte shortly after the invasion of the Philippines.

A few days after the airstrip had been secured, one of the Navy's largest seaplane tenders dropped anchor in Leyte Gulf. She was carrying a flag aboard, with the result that her radio room was a maze of radio and radar gear which enabled them to keep in constant touch with the tactical aspects of the situation at all times.

Forward of the radio room was flag plot where the radiomen off duty liked gather to get "cut in" on the latest dope. the only circuit in this compartment was an Army receiver set up on the fighter wing voice frequency.

One afternoon the "grapevine" confirmed rumors of a big strike which was about to get underway. Heavy bombers were to attack Ormac, across the island and Major Bong's P-38's were escort.

The receiver in flag plot was set up and tuned to perfection. The show was about to begin. Through the open hatch the air strip clearly visible and shimmering P-38's could be seen roaring up into the sky.

Soon the entire squadron of sleek, red-tailed P-38's were in the air heading for their rendezvous with the bombers. Inside flag plot the radiomen closer to the receiver. Reception was loud and clear and crisp voices crackled from the speaker on top of the receiver.

They were almost to the rendezvous when suddenly.... "Bandits!" More tense commands from Major Bong and the men in flag plot could picture the bussing P-38's streaking into attack formation. The very air was charged with action, and they crowded closed to the receiver in flag plot.

"Stay in formation."

"I got'im Lookit'im burn!"

"Lookout! There's a Nip on your tail."

In a few moments it was all over and the squadron was ordered to return to formation. The men in flag plot relaxed with heavy sighs. Then the sound of a sputtering engine filled the compartment and they stiffened.

"What's the matter Bill?" Bongs voice was filled with anxiety.

"Gotta take her down. They got my engines."

"No chance of making it back to the strip?"

"Nope." the voice was final. The air went silent for a moment.

"Okay, Bill. Hit the water and ditch her. We'll send the boats out to pick up the pieces."

"Roger. See you later."

The men in flag plot could visualize the P-38 as it started its downward glide. Then Major Bong'g voice was heard again, crisp, with authority, but radiating American humor.

"When you ditch her, don't forget to stick around. Don't start swimming for the states, soldier."

HONEST REPLY

JOHN H. ALLEN, Olympia, Washington OUR NAVY MAGAZINE

One of the biggest problems of a supervisor in a radio shack aboard ship is keeping proper circuit discipline at all times. Especially during the long mid-watches from midnight until 0730, the boys are inclined to tap that key, ever so lightly, and shoot the breeze with a shipmate on the other end.

During peace time circuit discipline is a MUST. In war time it is even more than that, for the life and death of a ship may lie in the hands of a careless or foolish operator who disregards circuit discipline.

"I often wonder wotinell the gang on recruiting tell these peacetime rookies."

Shortly after the invasion of the Philippines had been completed, a large seaplane tender steamed into Leyte Gulf and took up her mission of tending the patrol planes for their vital flights towards Japan and the China coast.

Aboard ship was a two star admiral whose staff consisted mainly of communications personnel. Ships company radio personnel was made up of mostly of vets who had seen quite a bit of service in all theaters of the war, but the admirals staff was loaded with greenhorns who still thought that it was a great life.

Living by the book was the admirals rule. He demanded proper discipline within his communications department and he got it.

However, one night during the mid-watch an amusing incident took place which gave all hands a good laugh for many weeks after.

The tension of the campaign had eased off somewhat and things were beginning to get a little dull. Routine traffic was the order of the day as the rest of the fleet left the Philippines and headed up the road to Tokyo.

CRM Edwards was sitting at the supervisors desk in the shack keeping an apprehensive eye on a rosy cheeked RM3C who was fresh out of the states (and radio school), His circuit consisted of the tender and an Army outfit on the beach. Traffic was not very heavy and consisted mainly of a routine check every hour or so as the signal bridge was visually handling most of the load.

Along about three o'clock in the morning the Staff Duty Officer came dashing into the shack with a coded priority message destined for an Army command in the islands.

Edwards headed the message, checked it and tossed it down to the radioman on the Army circuit.

Then the fun began. Evidently a new operator had taken over on the beach for he couldn't seem to make out a thing the ships radioman was sending. The message was sent slow, then it was sent fast, But alas, the Army was unable to receive it. Priority being pretty important, Edwards finally sat down at the circuit and took over.

Even he failed. Finally, after twenty futile minutes of sending and trying to secure "Roger" from the beach. Edwards began to lose his temper. The following conversation was the cause for laughter whenever mentioned for weeks after, as procedure signals were abandoned and plain language took its place. It wasn't logged, naturally, but if it had been it would have read something like this:

Ship: "say, can't you read me at all?"
Army: IMI
SHIP: Should I send slower?"
Army: IMI
SHIP: "Put your supervisor on the circuit!"
Army:IMI
Ship: (really mad now) INT JAP?
Army: Negat WAC.

THOSE GOOD OLD NAVY DAYS

A.R.JACK BANKS, Miami, Florida   **USS ENTERPRISE**

'Twas surely a great and momentous surprise
  When told I was drafted to board ENTERPRISE,
For sea duty had escaped me so.
  Excepting those days in sunny California,
As a young swashbuckling Coronado Commando.
  Those rollicking "cruises" in Coronado Ferry,
Belied approaching duty that turned damn scary.
  But if Lady Luck smiled, turned back the clock,
To do an unscheduled repeat.
  I'd jump at the chance to pull on my blues,
As fast as a blinking heart beat—Ha! Ha!
  As fast as a blinking heart beat.

THE SIDECLEANERS LOCKER ERUPTION

A.R. JACK BANKS, Miami, Florida   **USS ENTERPRISE CV-6**

'Twas outboard the island, those air sucking in-takes
  Keeping flame in fire rooms aglow.

Jack Banks,
USS ENTERPRISE

Jack Banks,
USS ENTERPRISE

There were hushhush doings up there too,
  Privileged only to those "in the know."
Was the space where sidecleaners stowed their gear,
  Scaffolding for "dancing" o'er the brine.
A nasty thankless backbreaking chore,
  For youngsters who'd stepped out of line.
But often there's asset springing from doom,
  That task for breaking young backs.
At times at days end, there was heady reward,
  Aromatic s-w-e-e-t raisenjack.
Big E lay anchored near Mog Mog that night,
  Nearly time for taps to be blown.
When out of the gloom fuming to nostrils—
  Came bouquet which wasn't sea foam.
"Whats that I smell?" The O.D. snapped.
  Looking me straight in the eye.
"Its from the galley—the bakeshop sir!"
  "They must be baking cherry pies."
'Twas nip and tuck for our sidecleaner boys,
  Discarding that sweet smelling mess.
They had bottled their brew before its time,
  A procedure you cannot guess.
My whimsical surmise, a veiled damn lie,
  Fooled not the O.D. nor a soul.
For at 0800 next morn after "Colors,"
  A massive search did unfold.
But alls well which turns out well,
  As happened for our sidecleaning crew.
For they transferred the rest of that fermenting mess,
  To fresh-water breakers— saving their illicit brew.

NEW YORK CITY CAPER

A.R. "JACK" BANKS, MIAMI, FLORIDA USS ENTERPRISE CV 6

Less than a year after kamikaze pilot Tomi Zai made his devastating attack on the USS ENTERPRISE, she lay moored at the Bayonne Navy Yard ready for action. The "Big-E" had been overhauled the previous summer at the Bremmerton Navy Yard on Puget Sound. Leaving Bremmerton we steamed to Alameda, then to Pearl Harbor, then thru the Panama Canal to New York City where we celebrated the grandest Navy Day ever. During a short stay at the Boston Navy Yard where we were converted into a troop transport by welding sleeping bunks to the hanger deck, ENTERPRISE made two crossings, one to Southhampton, one to the Azores, bringing Army veterans back to the United States.

Happily, the war with Japan was over and much of the "Big-E" crew, both officers and enlisted men had left the ship and the Navy forever. The only enemy remaining was labeled boredom. But soon life would perk up for `men standing the 0800 quarterdeck watch that nearly forgotten day.

On "Big-E's" starboard quarterdeck was the O.D.'s duty shack. In that tiny cubicle the O.D. and others standing watch conducted ships business while in port. Located in that shack was a seldom used squawk box connected to Combat Information Center, located in the island structure of the ship. Midway through the watch a commanding voice came booming over that squawk box telling us to be on the lookout for a civilian yard worker carrying a large roll of papers, that he must not be allowed to leave the ship. The roll of papers were TOP SECRET DOCUMENTS!

The O.D. questioned all of us but no one remembered for sure if a person fitting that description had left the ship. After several of us talked it over, we felt that maybe someone did leave a few minutes before. There was a problem. No one standing watch was thinking of the task at hand, the ships security. A far cry from the "big-E's" Pacific war days. The O.D. ordered the Quartermaster to telephone the Marines at the main gate to hold such a person if they spotted him. Time was on the "fugitive's" side, the yards telephone book had been misplaced and we could not contact the Marines at the gate.

Several of us thought the O.D. should allow some of us to go after the culprit, using the ships jeep. There were Colt 45's stowed in a locker under the O.D.'s desk. After a short deliberation the officer ordered three of us to carry out our suggestion. Quickly piling into the jeep with a driver, we three "jackasses" were ready for action. A boatswains mate, the messenger, and me, the ships bugler. Some search team, huh?

Arriving at the main gate in short order, Marines waved us through the gate shouting words we took as encouragement My heart pounded as our jeep sped us to our adventure.

In short order our driver found what appeared to us to be a likely place to start our search. there were liquor bars and lounges on both sides of the street. Youthful logic dictated we start our quest there. Imagine the surprise, misbelief, and outrage shown by patrons and bartenders as three seamen "warriors" armed, and wearing undress blue uniforms began asking questions about a non-descript man carrying a large roll of papers.

As we proceeded to the next lounge, a patrol car drove up. A tough old cop crawed out, shoutingfor us to drop our guns to the sidewalk. After complying to his order he yelled; :Who the hell do you guys think you are carrying those guns?" We all knew New York City cops were tough but none could have held a candle to this brute.

After gathering up our 45's and web belts he ordered us to the rear seat of the patrol car. He yelled for our jeep driver to follow him. On the way to the police station he would have none of our explanations. He groused we'ed all go to jail for breaking the law. My first run-in with the law had me scared stiff and I believe the others were too.

At the police station we were ushered into a police captains office and were asked numerous questions. But he also allowed us to answer them. We explained that we were under orders to search for a Navy yard worker who had left our ship with unauthorized secret documents. We didn't tell him that we had stampeded an inezperrienced officer into this farce. The policecaptain lectured us, telling us how we had broken the law, carried firearms without a permit, taking civilian law into our own hands, harassing Bayonnes good citizens, and so on. Calling "Big-E's" Executive Officer (the police captain did most of the talking), we were soon released.

Back aboard the USS ENTERPRISE, not one word was ever mentioned, nor to my knowledge were the others ever questioned about our misadventure. It is as if it had never happened, happily forgotten until now. However, questions still remain for me.. were secret documents ever in jeopardy? If so, were they ever recovered? Or had this whole horseplay been a rouse perpetrated by persons bored even more than we were?

THE BLUEPRINT CAPER

WILLIAM B. CROFTON,   **USS HOBBY DD610**
Saginaw, Michigan

While riding anchor off Hollandia, New Guinea in June of 1944 I was, one morning after quarters, visited by Chief Boatswains Mate Robertson who informed me that Lt. Holcomb, the engineering officer, had an assignment for me. Being the ships yeoman anything having to do with paperwork usually landed in my lap. I was expected to know just about everything in that field.

The Chief took me aft to the crews sleeping quarters, just forward of the ships twin screws. There, using a special tool, he loosened a deck plate into a storage area called the peak tank. He advised me that Lt. Holcomb wanted all the ships blueprints that were stored in that tank to be taken out and checked for any we did not have on file in the engineering office.

I told the Chief, "OK Chief, round me up a work crew and we will get right on it!" The Chiefs reply was; "You are the work crew ! Now get right on it."

"Aye, Aye Sir!" I replied and I headed down into the hold with just enough light to see the tied up bundles of blue prints. I was surprised to see that they were dry because the deck was just above the bilge tanks. I had to monkey walk the bundles to the above deck and within minutes I was stripped down to my shorts with sweat running off me like rain drops. Shipmates passing through the area took delight in seeing me, a yeoman, working up such a sweat. Soon I had thirty-six bundles of blueprints out of the hold, and stored in and around the log room in the engineers shop.

I made up a master list of prints on file in the ships office forward and in the log room aft. This was to act as a safe guard in case the ship got hit. With sets of prints fore and aft we were bound to have one set unharmed.

Lt. Holcomb had been after me to do this task for quite some time but because I thought it to be a waste of time I had ignored his request. Once in a while when Lt. Holcomb asked for a certain print that I did not have on file I would go to a sister ship, the USS Kalb or the USS Gillespie, and pick up it up. These ships were both Fletcher class destroyers like us.

It was a hot, tedious, task that I had long put off as I knew there were only a few prints we did not have. Duty, is duty, so I applied myself to sorting out and identifying each print. Sure enough, just as I had thought, there were only three prints that we did not have on file. Lt. Holcomb was elated and said. "I knew you would find some!"

The three prints that I found were of small parts of motors and pumps that his engineers could fix blind folded. The work and effort I had put forth was worthless, but then I did not run the U.S.Navy and did as I was told.

So now I had thirty-six bundles of duplicate, triplicate, and quadplicate blueprints with no place to store them except back in that lousy peak tank, and I was determined that lousy hold would not see me in it again. As a temporary measure I stacked them on the oil pipes used for refueling at sea. These pipes were on the main deck, just aft of the quarter deck, it was a place where a lot of sailors hung out to sit and smoke or talk when they had free time. The thirty-six bundles of prints made a comfortable seat.

At morning quarters Lt. Holcomb would remind me to find suitable storage for the prints, but I never did. I respected and admired Lt. Holcomb but he and I were on different wave lengths. He fretted and worried about his job and his career while I did neither. The war was all around us and things could end in a hurry as we had often witnessed. Besides, I had other duties in the ships offices that kept me busy along with the oil kings daily requirements of fuel reports, water reports, etc. Lt. Holcomb was a "hands on" type of officer always down in the engine room working with his men. I was not as dedicated as he.

Usually when we were in port or at anchor, as we were now, we would have movies on the main deck in the evening. Most hands not on watch would be at these movies as it was our main source of entertainment. These movies would often run past taps. One night the movie was very long, I still had the next days, "plan of the day" to print up and distribute. It was after midnight when this job was finished and I was headed for my bunk and a good nights sleep.

At this hour when at anchor most hands are asleep except for the quarterdeck watch and a few others. As I walked aft on the main deck I passed the stack of troublesome blue prints. I looked around and the petty officer of the watch was standing drinking coffee with his back to me, no one else was in sight, the O.O.D. must have been in the ward room doing the same.

I was all alone, just me and the blue prints! All of a sudden I got this sudden impulse and I threw every one of those damn blue prints into the sea. I did it slowly, one bundle at a time so not much of a splashing sound could be heard. Then I hit my sack completely contented, thinking the bundles would become water logged and sink to the bottom of the sea into the domain of the fabled "Davy Jones Locker." Good riddance, I'm done with them. Or so I thought, but you know what they say about the well laid plans of mice and men?

Next morning while standing at quarters and Lt. Holcomb was calling the role, a buddy standing next to me nudged me and said, "Bill, aren't those your blue prints floating in the sea?" I looked, and sure enough, the sea was covered with those damn blue prints. It seemed the motion of the water had freed them all from the bundles and they were now awash and floating all around the ship.

A bold move was my only hope for survival and averting a court martial. I broke rank and ran passed Lt. Holcomb to the rail shouting. "Holy shit, Mr. Holcumb, some son-of-a-bitch threw my blue prints into the sea!" He turned and joined me at the rail. There they were, all thirty-six bundles, freed by the wave action, unfolded, and floating all over the anchorage. The sea was covered with them.

Lt. Holcomb said; "Oh my God, I'll be the laughing stock of the fleet. We must put a boat out and retrieve them."

"No!" I said. "They are ruined, look at one being washed against the hull, the water has made the ink run." "Thank God!"

Just then over the loud speaker came the announcement: "Now set the special sea and anchor detail. Make all preparations for getting underway." As the Captains telephone talker on the bridge on this detail, I was off and running to my station.

"All stations report to the bridge when manned and ready!"

"Engine room, manned and ready!"

"Foc'sle manned and ready!"

"Fan tail manned and ready!"

"All stations report manned and ready Sir." I reported to the Captain.

"Very well! Aweigh starboard anchor."

"Anchors aweigh Sir."

"Anchor is hosed down and onboard Sir! Request we secure from special sea detail."

"Permission granted. All ahead full, steady on course and speed."

Now the Captain walks to the side of the bridge and looks at the sea around us. "Lt. Almond! (our executive officer) What's all that debris on the water?" Almond takes his binoculars and looks. "I don't know Sir. It looks like wall paper."

"What in the world would wall paper be doing out here?"

Of course I know, but no one is asking me, and I ain't talking. I'm delighted as the ships propellers are churning up the sea and slicing the blue prints to ribbons. I'm hoping other ships will follow in our path and cut those lousy blue prints into confetti.

We are off on another strike. I stayed clear of Mr, Holcomb and the blue print caper soon became history.

****

Some twenty-five years later at our ships first reunion, Mr. Holcomb is there, and I pass him a note. "I threw those blue prints into the sea!"

The former Lt. Holcomb responds. "You son-of-a-bitch. I always knew it was you... Hope you are doing well... The USS HOBBY was a good ship and it was a good crew.

"Another good "white hat" story!

A GOOD STORY

WILLIAM B. CROFTON,   **USS HOBBY DD610**
Saginaw, Michigan

A volunteer at the Portsmouth New Hampshire Navy museum told me this story.

There was once a young man named Dutch Reuther who enlisted in the U.S.Navy and went through boot camp in San Diego,
California.

In Pearl Harbor Dutch bought a portable typewriter along with
instructions how to use it. So as a seaman he learned to type and
upon entering the submarine service became a Yeoman striker. The
war brought Dutch quick advancements while serving on submarines in the South Pacific. His mentor was a submarine Captain
named Slade Cutter who taught him how to become a dive officer
and soon qualified Dutch to stand underway Officer Of The Deck
watches. Both men became great Navy Officers with Slade Cutter
becoming much decorated. Among his decorations was the Navy
Cross with three clusters. While Dutch Reuther went on to become
a full Captain.

Fifty years later at the same place he started his Navy career,
Dutch Reuther was guest of honor at a graduation ceremonies along
with his wife. As the young sailors passed in review, little did they
know, that the Navy Captain who returned their salute from the
reviewing stand once passed in review as a young seaman recruit
as they were doing now.

Dutch often told this story of his old friend and commanding
officer Captain Slade Cutter;

One time in Pearl Harbor after having just returned from an
arduous patrol. His submarine was to be honored by a visit by Cdr,
Gene Tunney, who was boxing heavyweight champion of the world
having beaten Jack Dempsey. Due to certain circumstances, and
the war, he had become a physical fitness officer in the Navy. He
was to come aboard our submarine and inspect our crew for fitness. He found them to be fat and out of shape.

Returning to the quarter deck where Captain Slade Cutter
was standing waiting for him. Cdr. Gene Tunney informed the
Captain that his crew was in terrible shape and needed some physical fitness training and should all be put on a special diet!!!!...
Captain Cutter reached under the desk at the quarter deck and
came up with a 45 revolver, pointing it at Gene Tunney he said:
"Get off my ship you SOB before I shoot you!" Tunney became
scared and double timed it down the ships gangway and out of
our area, never to return. In pursuit Captain Cutter fired a couple
of shots into the air to confirm Tunney's suspicions that his life
was, indeed, in danger.

This is a great humorous story but I cannot guarantee its au-
thenticity as it was told to me third hand.

LADY LUCK???

WILLIAM B. CROFTON,   ***USS HOBBY DD610***
Saginaw, Michigan

This event took place aboard the USS HOBBY DD610, Desdiv 38, then attached to the Seventh Pacific Fleet, commonly know as McArthur's Navy. He had use of this fleet for all his operations in the southwest Pacific. Fleet Admiral Nimitz accommodated McArthur to keep him from pestering him for more and more support. DesDiv 38 was always busy convoying LST's and other troop and material ships in the advance towards the Philippines and to fulfill the General's promise: "I shall return." During this advance the Seventh Fleet would have safe secure anchorages in the Admiralty Islands and Hollandia Dutch New Guinea. On one occasion we did serious close in bombardment of the island of Biak in Northern New Guinea. Each DD was busy from first light until 1500 hours at general quarters responding to target calls.

That night we anchored in a good harbor and our weary crew began clean-up of all the shell casings that were all over the decks. That same afternoon a Jap Betty sneaked into our area following a flight of Air Force P-37's returning to their air field. Their IFF covered the Jap. USS Hobby, USS Gillespie and USS KALB were anchored with no underway watches set. we were following regular in-port routine to do ships work, enjoy some leisure time, and get a full nights sleep.

Suddenly the Jap Betty was above us, made a run for the USS HOBBY, then changed its course and selected the unlucky USS Kalb DD611 as its target. WHAM! BOOM! The Betty dropped a 500 pound bomb on the Kalbs torpedo tubes and the explosion blew everything forward of number two stack completely off the ship, leaving a barren deck. USS HOBBY's 40 mm guns tracked and shot down the Jap Betty who left a trail of black smoke and crashed into the jungle. Hobby and some PT-Boats got underway to assist the wounded Kalb. The PT-Boats transferred the wounded to the USS HOBBY where strong armed sailors tenderly assisted them onboard where Dr. Brownel and his Pharmacist Mates tended to their wounds in the Ward room which was quickly converted into a hospital.

The USS HOBBY tied up alongside the USS KALB where the Captains and the divisions Commodore assessed the damage and counted the casualties. there were sixty-four dead and scores of wounded. The devastation was so bad that we had to actually sweep body parts up off the Kalbs decks using shovels and put them into white sea bags which soon turned red from the blood of our dead comrade. The bags were weighted and tossed into the sea in a mass burial. It was a very gruesome, and upsetting scene. With tears in our eyes we cursed the Japs and the war.

Immediately after the USS KALB was hit her Captain came on the radio with this message: "This is Captain (unknown) of the USS KALB, we have taken a bomb hit from a Japanese aircraft. We have many casualties, both dead and wounded. KALB has number one engine operating, guns number one and two operating. KALB has steam up and is ready for action!"

But there was no one to fight! The lone aircraft was the only one that threatened us, there were soldiers in the jungle but they were being pursued by the U.S.Army. The ships had no visible enemy targets. Soon a convoy was formed with a heading 180 degrees South to Hollandia. The USS KALB trailed the convoy still showing a ten degree list to starboard.

Sailors completing their watches gathered on the fantail observing the USS KALB's progress. Each sailor thankful that it was not his ship that had been hit and praying that no more harm would befall the USS KALB.

MOONBEAM—GUIDED BOMBS AND NAVY BEAN SOUP

ROBERT G. EVERS,   **USS LST 369 & USS LST 566**
Irvington, N.J.

After remaining silent for forty-five years these two stories must be told! Both episodes took place aboard USS LST 369 in June/ July of 1943 in the Mediterranean Sea near Bizerta, Tunisia.

One night about sixty ships, including LST 369 were anchored in a cluster off shore near Bizerta. Anticipating an air raid that night by the Germans, our Captain sailed Eastward about ten miles to wait it out alone. Sure enough, the German Luftwaffle bombed the sixty other ships and we saw the fireworks from ten miles away at 2:00 a.m. In a few minutes the raid was over, but not for the LST 369! Suddenly a bright, full, moon came out, shining down on our ship like a searchlight, and with it came a drone of a single engine plane, a Stuka, preparing to dive, and dive it did! It made four passes dropping a whistling bomb each time, and when we fired not one shot in return! We fired not one shot in return. Lucky for us all the bombs missed, but not so lucky for our Captain. He was relieved from command and transferred back to the states.

Navy Bean Soup, (or Yankee Bean Soup, as it is called here in New Jersey), is still one of my favorite soups. Back then on the LST 369 our skipper didn't think so when our ships cook served this

"Outside of looking 'em all up when you get back to the states, have you any other post-war plans?"

his not-so-delicious rendition of this soup. The Captain left the officers quarters, soup bowl in hand and down to the galley he went. There he quarreled with the cook and as a result put the cook in the brig for three days on bread and water.

So the next time your wife makes bean soup if it tastes really good give her a big kiss! If it is "not-so-delicious" show her this story!

YOUNGEST CHIEF PETTY OFFICER

ROBERT G. EVERS, Irvington, N.J.   **USS LST 566**

In December, 1944 I was assigned to LST Flotilla 35 aboard the LST 566 at Brooklyn, New York on the staff of Commodore D.H. Johnson. We set sail at the head of a Flotilla of twenty ships going to Pearl Harbor via the Panama Canal. Halfway to Cuba, we were joined by a British squadron commanded by a Admiral. The Admiral sent a flag hoist signal to our Commodore, which no one on the bridge understood. Being a signalman they sent for me (I was resting in my bunk). As soon as I saw it, I knew what it said and told the Commodore the Admiral was complimenting him on his smart maneuver. I had learned the British Navy's flag code when I had visited some of their ships in England. My Commodore was impressed.

A week later, we were some where between Cuba and Panama, they woke me up in the middle of the night and told me to report to the bridge at once. The navigator had made an error when he had set the course for the night and in a few minutes the entire flotilla was about to run onto a shoal of rocks! He asked me how to signal a course by visual signal, since using the radio was prohibited. I told him I would fire one red flare and give one long blast on the ships whistle. I executed the signal successfully and all the ships turned simultaneously forty-five degrees to Port, and we avoided the dangerous shoals.

The Commodore was very pleased with my action and when we arrived in Panama he promoted me to Chief Signalman. That's how I got to be a Chief Petty Officer at the age of twenty-three. Was I the youngest Chief Signalman in the history of the Navy? Perhaps!

CLEAN NAVY

JOSEPH DOYAN,   *Navy Unit 2, Rhine River Germany*
Tigard, Oregon

The bridge across the Rhine River from Mainz to Wiesbaden was much more than the floating pontoon bridges that were built in a few hours and used just a few days with limited traffic. It was a high structure made of steel called a Bailey Bridge and would be used for a year or so until construction allowed a more permanent conveyor.

A week after the initial assault crossing the Army engineers were nearly finished with the Bailey and we all noticed an American P-47 fighter plane flying down the river course and it was just a few feet over the water. As it approached the bridge it had to gain altitude to miss the structure and as we watched, he

**Joseph Doyan, USS LST 506,
Rhine River Patrol**

laid an egg. The plane had American markings on it but was being flown by a German pilot.

As the bomb missed the bridge and shot up a geyser of water all the anti-aircraft guns on the banks of the river opened up at him, but too late! The plane left as fast as it had arrived and it escaped unscathed.

From that day on, the Army warned all the Air Force that they intended to shoot down all planes flying low over their bridges.

One last trivia in the Mainz episode. Sleeping in the same clothes for days and lacking hot water we were told one day that the Army had arranged to transport us to two different locations of our choice. One truck would deliver the men to a local house of ill repute and the second truck was headed for a building where was located a shower with hot water. I looked at the truck going to the house of ill repute and there was only five men on it. The truck headed for the hot showers had thirty sailors on it. So most of us opted for the hot shower and some clean clothes proving the point that we would rather be clean than dirty.

Somewhere I had heard that Eleanor Roosevelt, the then Presidents wife, had once made the statement that our American Navy was the cleanest physically and the dirtiest mentally. This little incident showed that she was partially right anyhow!

THE PAPER CAPER

JOSEPH DOYON, Tigard, Oregon **USS LST 506**

For most of the LSTers who served in the coastal towns of England, three things will be remembered.

First, "Stinking Chips" (fish and chips) were one of the few meals that did not require ration stamps. Of course, they were not put in a bag but instead were placed in a heap on yesterdays newspaper balled up and handed to the customer.

Second, the English bread was so hard you could slice it one-quarter inch thin. Thin enough to see through it.

Third, when we were transporting some English troops over to France, I recall sitting beside one of the soldiers in the head as he tore off one square of toilet paper, swiped, folded it in two, swiped again and folded it for a third time. By now the paper was not much bigger than a postage stamp. He was typical of the conservative British populace.

Quite different from our practice of using a full roll of paper just to clean our wash basin, one mirror, and the two faucets prior to the daily inspections.

DRUMMED OUT

JOSEPH DOYON, Tigard, Oregon   **USS LST 506**

After reading about the recent members of the Armed Forces leaving the service for misconduct my mind drifted back to 1943 when I was stationed at the Little Creek, Virginia, Amphibious Training Base.

I heard the distinct sound of drums, "bar-room-boom-boom" and saw a crowd of men coming down one of the streets. Ahead of the crowd were the drummers and in front of the drummers were several Marines with bayoneted rifles pointed at a lone man leading the procession.

This man had surrendered all his Navy clothes and was dressed in an ill-fitting suit. The sleeves came down to just below his elbows and the pant legs to just below his knees.

He was being "drummed out" of the Navy with a dishonorable discharge and these clothes were intended to make him look like a fool. The Marines marched him around the base for more than an hour and finally at the main gate a Marine threw his discharge papers along with his medical records on the ground in front of him and if he bent over to pick them up, the Marine would give him a swift kick in the butt if he could.

FORTY FOOT SHARKS

JOSEPH DOYON, Tigard, Oregon   **USS LST 506**

In Falmouth, England, harbor one afternoon in early Spring 1944, we were returning to our ship via our LCVP assult boats when we spotted a school of eight very large fish rolling on the surface. Our boat was thirty-six feet long and these fish were longer, at least forty-feet in length.

We thought they were whales so we headed for one that was on the surface and rammed into it and it just rolled across onto its back. This did not seem to bother them and they stayed near us. We had a long spear which was part of the lifeboat survival gear so we tried to drive it into the back of one of these fish as he swam alongside our boat and found it would not penetrate the tough skin.

When we got back to our ship a few of our officers had been watching us through binoculars and wanted to go see these huge fish. They brought along a rifle and found that bullets did not seem to do much harm to these fish either.

Later that day one of the crew told us that these fish were basking sharks. He had been a Navy diver in Alaska and had seen some of these species as long as sixty feet. They are not the man-eating type of shark and lived mostly on plankton.

We realized how stupid we were to ram these fish. If they had become irritated enough they could have come up under our boat, turned it over, and swallowed us up in one gulp.

PASSWORD

JOSEPH DOYON,   *Navy Unit 2,Rhine River Germany*
Tigard, Oregon

With little sleep, lots of hard work, and terrible meals, it was no wonder all the men were edgy and short tempered. This was apparent one day when our officers held muster out in the street in front of a house where we had been billeted. We all had to line up and answer roll call that the officer was shouting. We did not like this situation one bit for we were all standing at attention in an enemy land where snipers could be among the civilians in the houses all around us. When the officer called on mans name he answered with "hyoo" instead of "hear." The officer then announced, "in this outfit you answer," here." The enlisted mans reply was, "In the real Navy we answer,"hyoo." The officer retorted, "when we get back to the real Navy, you will be on report!" (Subject to disciplinary action) It was good for a laugh from all hands and this little incident broke the tension for a little while.

We had a good relationship with our Army buddies and when we mentioned that we had seen a lot of chickens at a farm house where we had just rescued some wounded solders on a little island, they suggested we go back and liberate a few of those chickens for their kitchen. When we told them the Navy would never allow us to do this, they told us that if we did, we could join them in a good chicken dinner. Needless to say, we returned to the farm and picked up some chickens.

The next night the soldiers picked us up and we did indeed join them in a feast using ten fresh baked chickens. After dinner the officer in charge stated that the password for the night would be "chicken" and that the counter sign should be "Navy."

HOUSE OF JOY

JOSEPH DOYON, Tigard, Oregon   *USS LST 506*

Our first trip to Le Harve, France was comical and eventful. As we entered the harbor through the narrow breakwater entrance, we had to do this at high tide as the Germans had sunk a ship in the channel to keep all ships out. However, at high tide, ships with a small draft like an LST could pass over the sunken ship without scraping its keel.

The beach that we landed on was rocky and very steep, when our ship finally stopped, our bow was overhanging the waterfront street.

Our officers went ashore immediately and reported to the Naval Headquarters as to the type of cargo we were carrying. Our small boat officer told Barber and me that he found a "house of joy" in town and gave us street numbers and signs that told us how to get there. Just one more thing we would have to know. Unless you say "meow" as they answer the door bell they will not let you in.

Barber and I got liberty and "high tailed" it to this house. We found it just as he told us, third house on the left, so I went up and rang the doorbell. A middle aged man opened the door and ask what I wanted. I said "meow" He looked at me kind of funny, so I figured my "meow" was not quite authentic enough. So I cleared my throat and said it again, "meow." His puzzled look made me resort to try my limited French. Is this a house of joy? He laughed as he understood my French, and called for his wife to come to the door, which she did. So the man told me to ask her, which I did. It was then that I realized I had been snookered by our officer.

Later that day in the main square of what was left of the city, we saw our first "pissery". A small enclosure the size of our bus waiting sheds back home. It was on the curb side of a wide sidewalk made for men only to urinate. The strangest thing is, anyone on the outside can see the mans head and shoulders as well as everything below his knees'

Thank God for the cars passing by to muffle any sounds.

TWO CRAPPY STORIES

JOSEPH DOYON, Tigard, Oregon   USS LST 506

In the early month of my Naval service we were sent to a Florida beach which had high winds and surf so we could learn how to handle our landing craft under those conditions. We practiced learning how to land on the beach then back off without capsizing.

Our camp was located in a very sandy area and the buildings were not of a permanent type, we lived in Army tents with a wooden platform as a floor. The toilet was a wooden building about twenty feet long and twelve feet wide, which sat over a hole in the sand which was about six feet deep.

One evening, just about dusk, the announcement came over the loud speaker that the movie would start in ten minutes at the parade field. Charlie, my friend and shipmate, was dark complected, well groomed, and very meticulous about his appearance. Before entering the service he was a former "Zoot Suiter."

It was now getting dark as we ran towards the parade ground going between the rows of tents and other buildings along with the other men. Charlie took a short cut, jumped over a low rope barrier, and disappeared!

The previous afternoon a work party of fifty men had picked up the outhouse, moved it twenty feet over a new hole, and had not filled in the old hole yet. I looked down into this hole where Charlie was standing in chest deep shit! He had been submerged so his head was dripping with human waste and toilet paper.

He took his wallet and loose change out of his pockets and threw them to me. He ripped off all his clothes and left them in the hole as he climbed out and headed for the shower room!

SECOND STORY

At our base camp in Toul we were stationed near the Moselle River where we practiced operating our landing barges. The barrack where we slept had at one time been a German military base for a cavalry division. There was no running water nor electricity available because booby-traps had been found in the system so none of it had been turned on.

There were no modern toilets so we had to use the old fashioned out houses. The most popular one was a nine-holer near the front door of our building and since diarrhea was running rampant due to the bad French water, the stalls were always filled and the smell was terrible.

One night, after dark, one of our men came running out of our barracks, flew down the front steps, ran over to the outhouse, flung open the door, pulled down his pants, sat down in the first stall and let it fly!

Now remember there were no lights in this outhouse. He found that he had sit on another mans lap and crapped all over him.

THE OPEL

JOSEPH DOYON,   *Navy Unit 2, Rhine River, Germany*
Tigard, Oregon

While with the Navy Unit 2 in Germany it was a kind of odd job type thing. We had no ship nor base that we were billeted at.

Instead, we would stay in private houses at night and at times any available shelter we could find while various tasks were being assigned to us.

Upon leaving the home we were staying at in Mainz to head for our new assignment in Bingen I decided to confiscate and take with me a very nice radio I had found in this abandoned house. It was a small table-top radio made of mahogany and it could pick-up short wave broadcasts from all over the world,a real jewel.

While we were in Bingden I met a soldier who fell in love with this radio so I kind of loaned it to him so he could sit and listen to all the short wave messages. Since he was pretty stationary and I was mobile, I decided to let him enjoy it for awhile.

Later, when that his outfit was moving out for a position closer to the front lines, I went over to his camp to try and retrieve this radio. I knew he never intended to return it to me and since I did not want to see it destroyed, I intended to barter it away from him. The reason we had to barter was because money had no value to us so we traded for things we desired, or needed.

He really wanted to keep the radio badly but did not have much to trade. Finally it came down to an old car we had seen him driving around during his stay in Bingen. It was a German made Opel with four doors but had only one drawback. Since rubber tires were impossible to come by, these soldiers had taken some steel discs and somehow made them fit the wheels of this car. Not a dream car for sure but we did trade this car for my radio. It ran good on the cement highway, but on any surface made a noise that was unbelievable.

We had to travel two miles in the dark back to where we were staying and without headlights, it was difficult. We ran into a bomb crater in the road which had been filled-in with loose stones and sand. Of course the steel wheels sank right into the sand and we got stuck! We sat there for quite some time when an Army jeep came along and since we were blocking the road he could not pass. He was lead vehicle for a convoy of trucks that were behind him so he got a dozen men and they lifter our Opel out of the bomb crater and sat it along the road so they could pass.

We eventually got pretty close to where we were working but we had to stop at a bridge because all the traffic was coming across from the other side. A soldier came to our car and told us they had heard us coming for quite some time, they thought we might be a German tank since our steel wheels were making so much noise. He was manning a gun position and they almost shot us.

He telephoned across the river to his men on the other side and told them to hold up the traffic because some crazy Navy boys wanted to cross.

The next day we scrounged the area until we found an old wrecked car that had four rubber tires still on it. We took them off this car and back to ours. Using a big hammer and a metal file we made those tires fit our Opel. We used that Opel all the time we were in Bingen then bartered it away when we had to move.

MAN OVERBOARD

WILLIAM McGUINNESS,   **USS THOMPSON DMS 38**
Oradell, N.J.

It was a cold Winter night in San Diego, California in 1949. All the store windows were decorated for Christmas so it must have been late November or December.

After a night of celebrating and drinking at the local San Diego pubs, a group of us sailors headed back to the boat landing. there we would get a water taxi back to our destroyer mine sweeper USS THOMPSON DMS 38 which was moored out in San Diego Bay.

When we arrived at the water taxi station it was crowded with other sailors. If you missed the last water taxi you were out of luck until the next morning and you would have to go back to the Navy YMCA in town for the night. If you don't have the money for a room, or if all the rooms were taken, you would have to sleep on the floor in a room adjacent to the lobby.

The water taxi was ready to leave and a whole gang of us poured onboard.

Some of the sailors were quite drunk. The water taxis were large and they were covered with canvas to protect you from the elements. You would sit down below, and inside, on rows of benches that were fastened to the deck. The water taxi coxswain sat forward, behind the steering wheel.

I was feeling no pain as I also had a few drinks. I did not want to sit inside with all those drunks yelling and singing. So as we headed out into San Diego Bay I stood up on the starboard side gunwale, just abaft the starboard beam, and held onto the frame holding the canvas covering. You were not allowed to do this but where I was standing the water taxi driver couldn't see me.

As we got out into the bay it felt great with the wind and spray blowing in my face. I was not worried if the water got rough because there were ropes holding the canvas down and if we hit some waves I would grab a rope.

As it turned out, about halfway out to the first destroyer we hit some large swells that were kicked up by a strong wind. I started to slip on the wet gunwale and I grabbed the closest rope. To my surprise, the rope was not tied to the other side. I did a back flip off the starboard side of the water taxi into the cold wintry San Diego Bay. I hit the water head first and did a complete tumblesault underwater. As I did this the propeller of the water taxi passed inches above my head. Of course if it had hit me, I would not be around to tell you this story. I would not have been the first sailor, nor the last, to drown in San Diego Bay.

The water was freezing and I became instantly sober. Luckily I was not wearing a P-coat that night or I probably would have sunk to the bottom. As I broke to the surface I still had on my Navy white hat. I turned the hat inside out and pulled it down on my head.

I couldn't believe it but the water taxi did not slow down, it continued on course, straight ahead. Several sailors were yelling: "man overboard" but the water taxi driver did not see me fall overboard and he did not believe them because they were drunk.

Not to worry, I was an excellent swimmer. I looked to shore, then to the closest destroyer to see which was closer. The nearest landfall looked too far away so I started swimming toward the nearest destroyer.

There was an eerie quiet out in the bay. There were no ships bells or loud speaker announcements as it was after midnight. I did hear car horns and police sirens coming from the city. Other than that, all I could hear were the buoy bells and the wind.

Its funny the things that go through your mind in a situation like this. As I swam I started to wonder if there were any sharks or other creatures in the bay that might seek me out. Would the Polar Bear Club of Coney Island, New York, make me an honorary member?

It was a dark night and the wind was blowing and kicking up white caps on the large swells. San Diego was all lit up and looked beautiful in the dark. the destroyers tied up to buoys loomed as large black shadows with lights here and there piercing the darkness.

The water was very cold but I guess the alcohol in me balanced that out. Only my hands, face, and neck, felt cold. I still had my shoes on and they did not give me any trouble swimming. I continued swimming on a steady course to the nearest destroyer.

In the meantime the sailors on the water taxi finally convinced the driver that there really was a man overboard. The driver put the taxi in a one hundred eighty degree turn, turned on his spotlight and headed back. Now I don't know if he had a radio onboard and alerted the harbormaster or if sailors on watch on the destroyers gangways had noticed something amiss. (I never did find out) But, about the same time as the water taxi was heading back a large searchlight on one of the destroyers was turned on and started sweeping the bay. Then a second destroyer followed suit. The first few sweeps of the searchlights missed me but then one hit me and lit up my white hat. Then all the searchlights converged on me. What a great feeling, I knew I was saved!

The water taxi reached me, came alongside, and turned off its engine. Sailors hauled me onboard. In the process of hauling me onboard, two more sailors hit the drink. They too, were quickly hauled onboard.

Once onboard I realized how cold I was and I could not stop shaking. I must have turned blue. Someone gave me their P-coat and we continued back to my destroyer. I thought the water taxi driver would be mad as hell but he was happy that I was alive.

When I got back aboard my ship I wrung the water out of my dress blues then hung them and my lucky "white hat" out to dry. I got right into my sack. I'm telling you, that sack never felt better and soon I was fast asleep.

From that night on whenever I took a water taxi, I sat down inside and stayed there until I got to shore or to my ship. Swimming in San Diego Bay in the middle of the night in Winter is not recommended by me.

THE LAUNDRY BAG

WILLIAM J. McGUINNES,   **USS THOMPSON DMS 38**
Oradell, N.J.

The laundry bag in our operations division was so big and heavy at times one man could hardly lift it off the hook. Every once in awhile we would have contests and bets to see which sailors could lift the laundry bag. One day when this, there happened to be an open deck hatch in the operations department sleeping quarters. This hatch was rarely open and you had to be very careful as it was located in the deck directly at the bottom of a dual ladder coming down from the side hatches at the main deck.

It was my turn to lift the laundry bag. It was so big you couldn't get your arms around it and it really smelled. Well I lifted it, and I was so happy about winning the bet that I forgot about the open hatch. Still holding the ladder bag I stepped back into open air and down the open hatch I went still trying to hold on to the bag. The bag pressed me against the sides of the hatch almost breaking my ribs as I went down scraping my arms, legs, and body. the bag was too big to go down the open hatch.

After all the laughter all died down my buddies lifted the bag off the hatch to see what happened to me. There I was, smashed, and bloody, on the deck ten feet below. I couldn't talk because I had the wind knocked out of me. they thought I was dead. Within about five minutes a pharmacist mate and about a dozen sailors were all down the hatch with a stretcher. the pharmacist mate carefully checked all my limbs for broken bones and moved me gently to make sure my spine was okay. then they tied me to the stretcher. I don't know how they did it, but they got me up through the hatch, then up the ladder to the main deck, then up a gangplank to a destroyer tender alongside.

Aboard the destroyer tender I was Xrayed from head to toe. Fortunately, no broken bones, but plenty of scrapes, bruises, sore ribs, and a sore rear end.

I never picked up the laundry bag again!

So all you sailors out there if you are ever going to show how strong you are and pick up a heavy laundry bag make sure there are no open deck hatches nearby.

DON'T SHOOT!

WILLIAM J. McGUINNESS,   **USS THOMPSON DD 627**
Oradell, N.J.

It was the midnight watch in the cold Spring of May 1951 aboard the USS THOMPSON DMS 38. I was a radarman second class in charge of the mid-watch in the radar shack. The Thompson conducted minesweeping during the day and at night conducted random shore bombardment of North Korean coastal towns, bridges, and roads.

As we headed North we picked up a large target on our surface radar about twenty miles South East of our ship. I reported the contact to the officer in charge on the bridge. He instructed me to keep plotting the contact and to keep him informed, which we did. The contact kept closing in on us. It was cloudy and moonless that night and our lookouts could not see anything. We began to get concerned as we were operating alone that night in enemy waters and there were no other United States Navy or United Nations ships with us.

I kept the bridge informed of the targets progress. The officer in charge told me to use the voice radio to challenge the target so I picked up the radio phone and said: "Unknown target bearing 140 range 18 miles from me, this is (censored) please identify yourself. Over!" There was no answer and the target kept closing. Our lookouts still could see nothing and since we were so close to shore we dare not use our signal lights. I challenged the target several more times to no avail. The target kept closing and would not answer us. The target was closing abaft our starboard beam from the sea and our ship was close to shore. On the targeted ships radar we probably blended in with the shore radar echoes from the North Korean mountains which rose abruptly from the beach.

We were really getting concerned as the target would not answer. We were now at general quarters with all guns manned and ready for surface engagement. the officer then told me to call the target again and tell them that we are going to fire a star shell at them. I picked up the radio phone and said: "Unknown target bearing 115 range 10 miles from me, this is (censored) Identify yourself or we will illuminate you with a star shell, over."

This brought an immediate response. The target came on the air and a young officers voice said: (censored) This is (censored) Don't Shoot! We believe we are your target. Over."

I quickly looked up the name in the code book and the target was one of our battleships. I immediately answered and said: (censored) This is (censored) Roger. Out."

Can you imagine? Here we are, all alone, an 1800 ton destroyer minesweeper with three five inch single guns challenging a 45,000 ton battleship with nine sixteen inch guns and ten five inch dual guns, in enemy water. If the battleship had not answered us that night and if we had fired a star shell at them, they may have opened fire on us and blown us out of the water. NEVER MAKE A BATTLESHIP MAD!

As it turned out, the battleship was on its way to Wonson, North Korea that night and finally picked us up on their radar and realized they were our target.

This is just another story of two ships passing in the night. We all sat down and enjoyed a good, hot, mug of Navy coffee and continued looking for other targets of opportunity on the surface search radar'

Just a note: the ships code names are censored as they were top secret!

ONE RAID—TWO ACCOUNTS

WHAT A COINCIDENCE! HERE ARE TWO DIFFERENT MEN ON TWO DIFFERENT SHIPS WITH A SIMILAR ACCOUNT ABOUT WHAT HAPPENED DURING AN AIR RAID IN THE HARBOR IN ALGIERS, NORTH AFRICA, AT AROUND 0300, AUGUST 27, 1943. IT REALLY SOUNDS LIKE AN EPISODE FROM THAT OLD TELEVISION

SHOW "MCHALES NAVY". IF YOUR SHIP WAS IN THE HARBOR IN ALGIERS DURING THAT RAID PLEASE LET US HEAR YOUR AC-COUNT OF THE ACTION.

THE CULPRIT–!

PAUL STEIN, Bayside, N.Y.   **USS VULCAN AR 5**

As I remember it, we were in the harbor at Algiers, North Africa when the British battleship HMS King George tied up alongside us. All went well during the day but then sometime during the night the alarm for general quarters sounded and all hell broke loose!

By the time I reached my battle station every gun, on every ship in the harbor, was firing away at the incoming planes. Shrapnel was falling all around us and with a pretty green bunch of sailors manning the guns, we were oblivious of what was going on around us and were intent on shooting at the enemy planes as we had been taught to do. The noise was deafening. All guns on the USS Vulcan from the five inch to the twenty millimeters had an incoming plane in their sights and could see nothing else. We just kept on firing away until the cease-fire order was sounded. I am certain that we downed at least one enemy plane. However, in the heat of battle we had not noticed that our guns had not paid attention to the nearness of the superstructure of the battleship and we had blown off the top of her main mast and put several holes in her funnel.

What we gunners did not know was that when the HMS King George realized we were shooting at, and hitting her, she trained her big guns on our ship and told us to cease fire immediately or she was going to blow us out of the water.

Once the smoke had cleared and the battle over we were credited with downing one plane, then we had to go aboard the battleship, clean it up, and make repairs to everything we had damaged.

A VICTIM

JAMES A. MARKS, Bradenton, Florida   **USS TACKLE ARS 37**

We were in the harbor, Algiers, North Africa tied up to the USS Vulcan AR 5, for repair of damages we had received from an earlier battle. It was around 0300 the morning of August 27, 1943.

We were awakened by the sound of the general quarters alarm and the noise of enemy aircraft attacking us. Normally, naval vessels try for open sea to maneuver, but this raid was unannounced and caught us not only in the inner harbor but tied up to another ship so we had no choice but to stand and fight.

Actually we were sitting ducks as were all the other ships in the harbor. Most of the ships had arrived here just after the battles for the areas just off North and South Africa. We figured that the fighting in this area was over and that the enemy was now concentrating on defending Sicily and Italy. We did not expect an air raid at this time.

Both the USS Vulcan and our ship the USS Tackle joined in the aerial barrage. The noise and excitement was intense, loud, and unbelievable. After about forty-five minutes the raid was over. We secured from general quarters and began assessing our damage.

The Vulcan being a much larger ship was higher in the water and with a green crew fresh from the states, managed to put some 40mm holes in our mainmast as well as a couple of well placed rounds through our flag storage bags on the signal bridge.

Among other ships in the harbor were a couple of British ships, HMS Prince Edward and HMS King George. They, along with other British vessels, were firing anti-aircraft devices dubbed as "bread baskets," which acted like whirling pinwheels and upon reaching a certain range, exploded into numerous shrapnel pieces, flying in all directions. I don't recall their bagging any enemy aircraft, but did shear off several newly installed "bedspring" masthead radar antennas from American destroyers in port.

As the weather already was very warm, several of us had been sleeping topside on purloined cots. At reveille and daybreak next morning, most of the cots and mattresses looked like sieves where the fallen hot shrapnel from the raid had burned through the blankets and the cots, to the steel deck where they hit and cooled off. We removed enough shrapnel that morning to fill a wheelbarrow. Fortunately, we only experienced some light casualties from that raid.

PHOSPEROUS WATER

JAMES MARKS, Bradenton, Florida   USS MERRICK, AKA 97

It was June of 1943 and I was a Machinist Mate just graduated from marine engineering at Wentworth Institute, Boston. I was assigned to the fleet oiler, USS CHICOPEE AO34 then operating out of Mirs el Kibir (Iran), North Africa. At Norfolk, Virginia,

I boarded the USS Merrick AKA 97 for transportation to North Africa.

Somewhere in mid-Atlantic we encountered a German submarine pack which proceeded to raise hell with our convoy of 380 ships before being driven off or sunk by our escorts. After this jarring introduction to the war, many of us were quite shaken by the experience and thankful that our ship had been spared.

The following evening, just after dark. I noticed this very young sailor still shaken from this experience so I attempted to comfort him in some way. After a few minutes of conversation, he told me that it was not the previous action that really worried him but, a more personal problem. He said that when urinating in our darkened head, he thought he was passing sparks.

Puzzled at first, I quickly realized his problem. I assured him that he was alright. The sparks he was seeing was due to the phosperous laden sea water in the darkened head. Our ship was passing through an area that was quite dense with phosperous and in the wartime darkened head, the toilet bowl water appeared to "spark" when he used it. He did not know that flushing water for the toilets, when at sea, was drawn from the ocean.

Reassured for now and in better spirits, he later disembarked at Mirs el Kibr for reassignment.

I missed my ship, the USS CHICOPEE, by a day and a half and learned that three days later she was torpedoed in the English Channel with heavy loss of life. Shortly thereafter, I was assigned as ships company to the USS TACKLE ARS 37, a salvage and demolition ship assigned to opening ports throughout the Mediterranean.

We were where the action was for over two years and celebrated VE Day chased into the Azores by a German submarine. I guess its crew had not yet received word of the German surrender.

CONVOY

JAMES A. MARKS, Bradenton, Florida   USS TACKLE ARS 37

Towards the latter part of World War II sometimes the ships would make the run between the states and Pearl Harbor alone, but once you left Pearl Harbor for the Western Pacific you would be in a convoy with escort vessels.

This convoy might be made up of several columns of ships in line. This particular time we were in the outside, right hand column, and for good reason, one of our cargo holds was full of 500 pound bombs. Had we been in the middle of the convoy, and took a torpedo, it would have caused damage to all the ships around us.

Considering the situation, this was a nice enjoyable day for relaxing and thinking about what ever you liked. We did not get to enjoy our thoughts for very long though. All at once one of the escort destroyers came charging thought the convoy from the far side with sirens screaming, and it started dropping depth charges about a mile, or less, off our starboard side.

I do not think the danger of the situation occurred to us as we watched all the activity. There is nothing we could have done anyhow as our ship had such a thin hull I think an armor piercing shell would have gone clear through it without exploding. Shortly, the destroyer returned to its original position in the convoy and an old Boatswains Mate standing next to me remarked quite calmly, "Well, I guess they just sunk another whale!"

Even in the face of danger an element of humor was always present.

G.Q. WALKER

JAMES A. MARKS, Bradenton, Florida   *USS TACKLE ARS 37*

While some men would bend and break, there were others like G.Q. Walker (G.Q. for General Quarters). This man was also known as an old tin-can sailor, the tin can referring to destroyers, those sleek, gray hunters of the deep. He had made many convoy crossings of the North Atlantic in mid-Winter, where destroyers would pitch and roll at forty degrees or more and the crew existed on cold sandwiches, when they could get them. Except for some special galley-rigged gimbaled pot holders, no hot foods could be prepared except coffee as pots and pans would tip over due to the extreme roll of the ship.

G.Q.Walker was a gunner on our ship and was always the first man on station when general quarters was sounded. Before lights out, he would go through his nightly routine: Sit down on his lower bunk, unloosen his shoe laces, slide his dungarees down over his shoes, like a fireman. He would pivot and lay down, then reach his left hand out to touch his life jacket while assuring his right hand that his helmet was within reach.

When general quarters sounded, in one sweeping motion, as he sat up he would pluck his helmet and life jacket from their hooks, slip into his opened shoes, button the top dungaree button as he stood up, and was gone in less time than it takes for me to tell it. You just did not get in his way. This old tin-can sailor was an ancient twenty years old.

ESCORT DUTY

JAMES BALL, Newton Square, Pa.   *USS RHIND DD404*

Late March 1942 our Destroyer USS RHIND (DD404) joined our "Tin Can" Squadron out of Norfolk, Virginia and took up stations to convoy twenty-six cargo ships loaded with jeeps, trucks, ammunition, medical supplies, and food. This was a special convoy to provide emergency aid to General Douglas MacArthur, in other words, we would now be on our way to becoming part of the Pacific Fleet, probably for the duration.

Without incident we arrived at the Panama Canal Zone. The twenty-six cargo ships were ordered through, but last minute changes from Washington, D.C. designated that our destroyer squadron was to return to the Norfolk and/or New York (Brooklyn Navy Yard) area.

Enemy submarine action all along the Atlantic Coastline was at a fever pitch. Simply put, the Navy could not spare any "Tin Cans" to Pacific Fleet. Liberty at Panama was cancelled.

Ashore, at the Officers Club, our skipper was approached by a grizzled English captain who wanted to know if our squadron would escort his ship back to New York. Our captain told him that decision would be up to the Squadron Commander.

When they were introduced, the Squadron Commander asked what ship the English skipper was referring to. The Englishman casually pointed through the surrounding club windows and indicated a ship which appeared to be the size of the Queen Mary!

When the Squadron Leader and our skipper sufficiently recovered from both their shock and surprise they asked the name of this leviathan-size ship and were told it was a H.M.S. MAURITANIA, which years earlier, was probably the largest passenger cruise ship in the world!

When our Squadron skipper explained that our "Tin Can" squadron would be cruising Northward anywhere from twenty-five to thirty knots, the undaunted English skipper explained that his ship, although now a troop carrier, was empty and that he would have no difficulty in keeping pace with us! As a matter of fact he added that if attacked by enemy subs, all we had to do was open up our convoy station ranks and he would go through under forced draft!

Still doubting the Englishmans narrative, the Squadron Commander OK'd the doubtful, Northwest journey.

Within one or two days we were somewhere off the Carolinas. It was about 1000 hours when General Quarters was sounded.

Three or four torpedoes were knifing through the calm sea on a Northeast to Southwest bearing headed for the MAURITANIA!

Our "Tin Can" Squadron opened ranks at the same time we heard the insistent horn-blowing of the English troop ship. The torpedoes were still on their way toward their target when to our utter amazement the MAURITANIA seemed to rise out of the ocean, bow rising, stern down, and appeared to all of us to take off like an outboard motorboat!

For a fraction of a few seconds I really believe no one was paying any attention to the German subs, but wide-eyed at witnessing this huge, huge, troopship burst out and forward at what appeared to be a speed of from thirty-five to forty knots! This was the most dramatic show of Forced Draft speed that any of us had ever witnessed.

The MAURITANIA continued on course same high speed for approximately fifteen miles, then slowed the resume normal, previous convoy speed. Whew! Quite a demonstration!

One or two of our "Cans" were dispatched to hunt and track down the enemy subs, but were cautioned that they could spend only an hours time in doing so. Our priority was safeguarding the MAURITANIA, plus returning as soon as possible to either the Norfolk and/or Brooklyn Navy Yard.

H.M.S. MAURITANIA made it safely to the New York area and our ship, the USS RHIND was designated to investigate a cargo ship that was dead in the water at about seven miles distant. Once we changed course we immediately spied three German subs on the surface approximately eleven miles, on the horizon, about twenty degrees to starboard of the cargo ship!

All this drama and we were only about sixty miles East of the Ambrose Lightship, off New York!

I maintain that "Tin Can" sailors probably saw more drama in World War II than sailors aboard other types of ships as witness the fact that I served aboard four different war ships and the most interesting action was aboard the "Tin Cans."

By the way, unconfirmed reported reached us that all twenty-six cargo ships which we convoyed to the Canal Zone were sunk in either the Gulf Of Mexico and the Pacific Ocean.... They had no destroyers to escort them!

A MARKED TARGET

JAMES BALL, Newton Square, Pa.   *Sub Chaser 1043*

There was this time that an Army Sergeant came aboard our Sub Chaser with a large inflated barrage balloon. He told our Captain that this balloon must be affixed to the rear of our ship as we participated in the invasion of Salerno, Italy. This was in 1943. During three days and nights of hell through bombardment, rockets, and gun fire, suddenly our ships cook who was manning a twenty-millimeter gun seemed to go berserk. He jumped away from his battle station, ran down to his galley, and emerged with a meat cleaver shouting and screaming as he ran aft. We thought for sure he had temporarily lost his mind and that he was about to kill one of our own men! Instead, he ran to the rear of the main deck and began hacking away the cable that was holding the barrage balloon fast to our ship!

The cook reasoned that most of the enemy fire we had been receiving was directed at us because of the barrage balloon. It was used to make the enemy think we were a troop ship which were their main target (most troop ships had these barrage balloons hovering from them to ward off the enemy planes from coming too close to them) since there was a large smoke screen laid all around our ships, the enemy could not really see the ships as they were under the smoke, so they directed their fire at these damn barrage balloons knowing that a good target lay underneath them.

In other words, we were actually being used as decoys to attract enemy fire away from the more important ships!

When our cook shouted all this information to our Captain and our crew, it made immediate sense. Unfortunately, neither our Army or Navy Intelligence people had informed us of this guise when they put the balloon on our ships. Once the balloon was cut loose and drifted away from our ship we had no more trouble from enemy fire. Thank God for Andy Anderson from Texas (our cook) for giving him the common sense to figure this out before we got blown out of the water.

FLOATING BORDELLO

Jim Ball, Newtown Square, Pa.   USS *AUGUSTA*

Following the major invasions of Casablanca, Oran, and Algiers, liberty was permitted only until sundown because we did not trust the local Arabs who had been thoroughly indoctrinated to be anti-American by the German forces. On one such liberty one of our sailors returned, quite unsober, carrying a large, very expensive bottle of French perfume. It was named Christmas night!

How he ever walked without falling is beyond me, and he had to navigate his way from mid-ship to personnel quarters, two decks below, and to the stern of our heavy cruiser. He managed all of the ladders and the "step-over" hatches, arriving at the entrance of our mess hall number two.

Believe it or not, as he walked across the flat, unobstructed, mess deck he lost his balance and the large bottle of perfume was smashed into a thousand pieces!

All hands were engaged... for three days and three nights... trying to get rid of the atmosphere of a bordello! We used sea water, fresh water, both hot and cold water, using scrub brushes and all. To no avail. Days, and even weeks later, visiting officers and en-listed men sensed the aroma immediately.

They re-christened our USS AUGUSTA as the only floating bordello in the entire United States Navy!

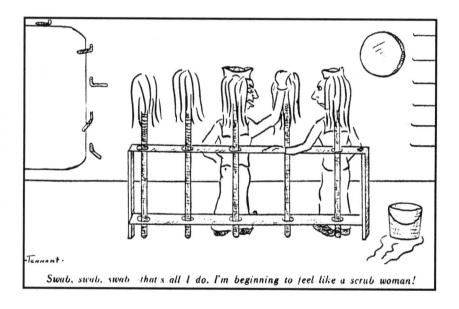

Swab, swab, swab that s all I do. I'm beginning to feel like a scrub woman!

OH, THOSE BRITISH!

JIM BALL, Newtown Square, Penna.   **USS AUGUSTA**

It was immediately following the surrender ceremony of the French held aboard our heavy cruiser and flagship, USS AUGUSTA, that we were ordered to Port Trinidad for refueling. The refueling station was a long, narrow pier that extended about a quarter mile from shore to its end out into the harbor. It was operated by the British and was named "British Fueling Station # 7" the only office on the pier was at the shore end and our ship was out at the oppo-site end.

It was a bright, sunny, warm day and the crew was taking advantage of it. All our portholes were open catching the fresh breeze, the ships band was practicing on the Well Deck, most of the crew was at a relaxed atmosphere as the British were handling the refueling process and did not want our crew to take any part in the operation. The British always seemed to have this air of superiority about them so we left them pretty much alone.

All of us, that is, except our Engineering Officer (who just happened to be a Scotchman). He was overseeing the operation, as was his job, when he noticed something was wrong. He approached the British officer in charge on the ship but got no response. So our Engineering Officer called our signal bridge and had a Quartermaster signal the British office at the end of the pier using semaphore. The message read; "You have too much pressure in fuel line. Decrease pressure!"

The British office replied; "We have been refueling ships for hundreds of years and know what we are doing." Our signalman relayed this reply to our Engineering Officer on the main deck.

Our Engineering Officer shouted to those around him who could hear; "I don't give a damn how many years you have been refueling ships!" Off he went to the bridge and the Captains office.

He made it halfway up the ladder to the bridge when.. WHAM! Bamm! The fuel line exploded! Hundreds and hundreds of gallons of the black, slimy, oil slush went high in the air, all over our ship. It went into the open portholes, covered our decks, drenched our band ruining their uniforms and instruments. Everything in sight turned black and slimy!

It took our entire crew of about a thousand men all day and night to clean up the mess. Our Engineering Officer lost all respect for the British refueling team and its leadership.

Upon our arrival back in our home port of Norfolk, Virginia we received a special cablegram from His Majesty's Oiling Station Number Seven. It was a bill for $37.50 to pay for repairs to their ruptured oil line!

Our Executive Officer, when he saw this cablegram, took all ships Yeomen and others who had seen the message aside and swore us all to secrecy that we would keep our mouths shut about this cablegram because if our Engineering Officer ever heard about it, he would take our cruiser, by force if necessary, back to Trinidad and blow His Majesty's Oiling Station Number Seven to hell using our nine 8 inch guns.

As far as I know our Engineering Officer never did find out about this cablegram.

NEGOTIATING WITH AN ARAB

JIM BALL, Newtown Square, Pa.   **USS AUGUSTA**

Being the flagship we were the first sailors on liberty in Casablanca (about Nov. 15). My friend, a red-head ships barber, and I decided to scour the town for genuine souvenirs. We were spotted from across the main street by a professional tour guide (British) who approached and offered to steer us to the best merchants of artifacts for a total sum cost of five dollars.

"Reds" bluntly stated, "Friend, I happen to know all about business and negotiating." To which the Brit replied, ever so diplomatically, "But have you ever tried negotiating with an Arab?" "Reds" gave in reluctantly. I told him I was interested in Sahara Desert Rifles. "Reds" said he was interested in buying a natural sheep or goat skin luggage bag.

The guide gave us the following instructions: "Rifles, knives, and guns you go to that Arab concession to the far left. Try to bargain as best you can, but do not buy, just get his final figure on what you wish to purchase. My arab dealer wanted something like thirty dollars for two desert guns. "Reds" reported that his dealer wanted ten dollars for a goat skin bag with leather handles.

What followed would be worthy of being on a todays television show. The guide and I went to the gun concession where I had been. The guide spoke English, Arabic, French, and Italian. He is shouting and arguing with the Arab dealer who is just as loud and gesture crazy as our guide. After about five minutes of this haranguing, the guide turned to me and said; "Give him ten dollars and that pack of American cigarettes you have in your left breast pocket!" I was dumbfounded!

The British guide explained that American cigarettes were a rarity in North Africa. What the Arab will do is cut each cigarette into four parts, sell each part for one dollar and make about eighty dollars on your sale! The rifles were magnificent. Inlaid wood, hand carved, flash pan firing, ram-rod, etc.

"Reds" quoted price for his goat skin bag was ten or fifteen dollars. The guide went through the same harahging as with the other Arab dealer then turned to "Reds" and said; "Give the dealer five dollars!"

We returned to our ship which was tied up to a pier. Just as we were about to ascend the gangway the "O.D." said over his loud speaker to us; "All right, put that stuff against the warehouse wall and forget it!" "Reds" turned to me and said, "He is talking about your stuff. Who ever heard of rifles being taken aboard ship when on liberty?" I said back to him; "What do you mean, me and the rifles, our ship is loaded with guns of every type you can name."

"For a minute I thought that line was going to part."

But, I placed the rifles against the warehouse wall and my friend "reds" with his goat skin bag in his hand, ascended the gangway.

The O.D. must have turned his head away for a few moments because when he returned our salute he barked at "Reds" ... "I was talking about you and that damn goat skin bag... do you realize that the goat skin was never properly cured and cleaned. You could contaminate the entire ship!" the he turned to me and said; "You, go get your damned rifles and bring them aboard."

Later I was offered all kinds of money for the rifles but I never sold them. I lost one when I loaned it to a friend who had it mounted over his taproom in Philadelphia and the place caught fire and burned to the ground. The second one I had loaned to a friend, he passed away several years ago and I never thought to reclaim it... and the world goes on.

GENERAL PATTON STORY

JAMES BALL, Newtown Square, Pa.   **USS AUGUSTA**

One of my shipmates and liberty partner was "Reds" our ships barber. One day I was standing-by in my yeomans office not particularly busy at the time when "Reds" phoned me to come on down to his barber shop and pretend that I was waiting for a haircut as going to cut the hair of "Blood And Guts" General George Patton who was onboard our ship, along with his staff, heading for an invasion.

This was another epic for TV... "Reds" made up in advance what he would be talking about with the General and how the invasion should go! There were two other ships barbers with whom "Reds" would banter back and forth with while he cut Pattons hair. Patton would probably be sitting there reading orders,etc.

"Some of "Reds" banter; "If I were in charge of this invasion force I would first recruit the Mafia from South Philly, then with plenty of bribe money, I would convince all the Arabs to join in and really raise hell, etc., etc.,etc. About midway through "Reds" tirade General Patton said, "Reds, shut the hell up and finish my hair cut!" That did it.. The barber shop then became as quiet as a funeral parlor.

Odd, but at the time, almost no one had ever before heard of "Blood And Guts," but they sure became acquainted with him during our trip to Africa. This guy was something else! He even bawled me out because I saluted him as we passed each other in the passageway. Patton said," Sailor, what the hell are you saluting me for?" I stood at attention (minus my hat as we never wore one while working in the office aboard ship)... I replied; "Because you are a General in the U.S.Army, Sir."

Not good enough... "Blood And Guts" must have originated the cuss word vocabulary because he was good at it. After a steady expression of expletives Patton Said; "You *#!+% people don't even salute your own officers, etc., etc." Unfortunately, General Patton wasn't familiar with Navy custom aboard ship. We simply saluted an officer in the morning because all day long you are running into them.

Patton stood about six feet tall, had tremendous shoulders and chest, with a hard bitten look about him. I believe if Patton walked into any restaurant attired in civilian clothes at least half the patrons would rise and stand at attention.

SMALL SHIP, BIG STORM

JAMES BALL, Newtown Square, Pa. *Sub Chaser 1042*

After the invasion of Southern France our Sub chaser 1042 returned to Tunisia, North Africa. We were then ordered to Marseilles, France to turn this ship over to the French Navy. We left port at 1030 and within twenty hours we ran into a furious gale which lasted about seventy-two hours. The worst storm in twenty years of Mediterranean history! It turned out to be the worst storm I would see in my four years in the Navy. On the second day into the storm we could see a U.S. Navy destroyer, about five miles away, it was looking for us, but they could not see us as our silhouette was too low in the water for them to spot us amidst the huge swells.

Half of our crew of twelve became deathly seasick. Our boatswains mate told the Captain we could only stay afloat about another eight hours. Our main lifeboat had been whisked away by the eighty mile per hour winds, there was water up to our knees in all berthing compartments, and salt water was interfering with our steering mechanism and it was hard for the helmsman to hold a straight course.

When the storm finally subsided we found ourselves off the coast of Southern Spain! When we entered the busy seaport of Marseilles, all the workers on the docks dropped everything to look at, and watch, this now vertible debris come floating up their harbor. Our guns were dangling loose from their mounts, all windows and portholes were smashed. How we ever made it I do not know to this day.

Our entire crew, including the officers, were sent to the U.S.Navy Hospital for a thorough checkup... We all came through with flying colors.

Now for the unbelievable part of this true story!

Fifteen minutes before we had contacted the signal tower and received permission to leave our safe port in North Africa unbeknown to us a messenger had entered that signal tower with a large lettered sign which read, "NO SHIP, NO VESSEL, NO CRAFT WAS TO LEAVE THE HARBOR BECAUSE A DANGEROUS GALE WAS ENTERING OUR AREA!" It seems the signal officer in the tower was in the bathroom, did not hear the messenger call out to him so the messenger left the gale warning sign right on top of the signal officers desk and he departed. Within five minutes still another, and different messenger entered the signal tower office loaded with official mail, documents, and the Base newspaper. He too hollered out to the signal tower officer and receiving no answer promptly laid his delivery right on top of the gale warning sign without noticing it. Then he also left the tower.

The signal officer then returned to his desk, was about to go through his mail, when he noticed our sub chaser signaling permission to leave port, almost immediately, he granted permission. Then he sat down to go through his official mail. Because official mail is long and tedious the officer was very much engaged for better than two hours.. then he came across the gale warning sign!

He almost died on the spot. He realized that our sub chaser traveling at about fifteen knots was already well out on the Mediterranean Sea. Immediately he declared an emergency contacting the base headquarters and everyone else but all was in vain. Our sub chaser was one hundred-ten feet long, thirteen feet abeam, and weighed about twenty-four tons. It was built of solid oak wood making it one of the most seafaring of all craft in the entire world, but unfortunately, we didn't know this at the time.

They sent a destroyer out on the double to search our designated route but by that time both ships were engulfed in the worst storm of twenty years. When the destroyer could not locate us, we were listed as missing. We found out later that we were the only craft at sea in the entire Mediterranean that day!

Officially, all hell broke loose throughout Tunisia. They launched an investigation but I still do not know if that signal officer was court martialed, or the two messengers, but the real damage had already been done.... to us! All at base headquarters in Tunisia and Marseilles were completely dumb founded that we had survived at all!

I still contend that the U.S.Navy should have issued, and permitted, our officers and entire crew to wear a special campaign ribbon because of this near disastrous event... In any case, we were all returned to the United States for a thirty day leave, then reassigned. That's when I volunteered for shore patrol duty in Memphis which, at that time, was the largest Naval Air Training Station on the East Coast. I stayed there for a whole year and really enjoyed my stay on dry land for awhile!

A TOP SECRET LEAKS OUT

JAMES BALL, Newtown Square, Pa.   *USS AUGUSTA*

It was late Spring 1942, months prior to any invasion of the European Continent. Our flagship, the heavy cruiser USS AUGUSTA had received top secret orders to rendezvous at sea with the battleship USS TEXAS, five destroyers and the aircraft carrier USS RANGER.

The USS RANGER was carrying seventy-five P-38's. All of the USS RANGER'S planes had been taken off at Norfolk, Virginia.The P-38's were to be flown off the USS RANGER by Army pilots when we reached our destination overseas, somewhere off the coast of Middle South Africa.

The Army pilots were sweeating blood because they never had experience either taking off or landing, on an aircraft carrier. They had practiced takeoffs only, on dry land with a simulater aircraft carrier deck painted on the ground! Trying this procedure on a tossing, heaving ship at sea might prove a disaster.

Our route took us over the Southeast Atlantic Ocean, just four degrees above the Equator in a neighborhood where there were none, or very little, enemy submarine sightings. That was the reason for the five destroyers, submarines held a healthy respect for our tin-cans.

Forty miles off the African coast our fighters took off from the carrier deck, shakey here and there, they all flew in wide circles until the entire seventy-five planes were in the air. Then they formed into groups of five or six, headed inland, turned North towards Tunisia, North Africa to reinforce the British General Montgomery.

Ordered to fly low the American fighters caused quite a shock to all enemy land observers. They knew they were American planes, and perhaps a major invasion had already taken place! But where?

With planes out of sight, our task force turned around and headed back to New York, Norfolk, Philadelphia, and Boston. The less observed, the better the secrecy ... except...

At this time writing letters home was under severe scrutiny, all letters had to be ok'd by your Division Officer... One brand new sailor, age 17, decided to write a letter home to his mother in Iowa. His Division Officer did not get to see it for one reason or another. His mother was so proud that she took his letter to their small town weekly newspaper. The Editor was bowled over. All the details of our task force was there word for word, line for line! He published the letter!

In this same town was a U.S.navy Recruiting Office. The Chief Yeoman in charge was having lunch in his office, picked up the newspaper, and almost chocked to death. He immediately dialed Navy Intelligence in Washington, D.C. they asked him to read the article over the telephone, after which, they told the Chief to keep his mouth shut about it and they would take care of the situation from this point on.

Within twenty-four hours, our four-stripe Captain received top secret instructions (I read the orders) to scare the hell out of this young sailor, transfer him from sea duty to permanent shore duty, but no court martial...because of his ignorance, etc.

Here is how our skipper scared the hell out of the kid. Our heavy cruiser always carried fifty fleet Marines. the next morning at five a.m. a Marine was sent to rudely awaken the kid. With this young sailor barely awake and mumbling, questioning, the Marine had been told to answer him with; "I don't know anything except it has something to do with a letter you wrote to your mother about our Top Secret trip to Africa.

When the kid reached the well deck he beheld seven Marines, with rifles, standing at attention. "My God" thought the kid, "its a firing squad!" If he had a weak heart he would have died right there on the spot. To round out the charade our Captain had a podium with a microphone, set up and a large number of the crew were standing around as witnesses.

The Captain read through the various charges for Court Martial, etc but never once used phraseology denoting use of a firing squad or jail sentence. He simply let the boy-sailor stew in his own juices of terror.

When he finished all the pronouncements our ship's Shore Patrol literally dragged the kid off to the Norfolk receiving Station to await further orders. Case closed? No, not quite! Here is the trump card:

The ships Executive Officer gathered all us Yeomen together and swore us to secrecy in saying: "The unfortunate part of this entire episode is that we are slated for two more so-called Top Secret trips to the same location. We will be carrying the same number of Army fighter planes and pilots, but with German Intelligence being as good as they are, we will probably be harassed all the way."

Fortunately, we were harassed by two German submarines but they did not attack us and kept a respectful distance astern of us. They had a great deal of rerspect for our destroyers.. but the kid-sailor had blown our cover with his letter home. Remember what they used to say "Loose lips, sink ships!"

I REMEMBER

ROY A. STAFFORD,   **USS ENTERPRISE CVAN 65**
Schoolcraft, Michigan

First some info.... before receiving orders in July 1967 to report to Hunter's Point, California to board CVAN 65 the Nav's most magnificent fighting lady USS ENTERPRISE, I spent 18 months on a NAVCOMMSTA in the Philippines called San Miguel.

We received a Navy Unit Citation with ribbon for setting up a ship to shore communications with ships off Viet Nam.

Near the end of my tour of duty in the Philippines, san Miguel was becoming more of a "McHales Navy" dream station to me, with two things at eighteen years of age, that was always on my mind, San Miguel beer and "PO" (Olongapo)!

Now, on with my story..... After our short visit with North Korea, the USS PUEBLO, and the onset of the TET Offensive in Viet Nam, we were looking for some much needed liberty.

Hong Kong, with its smells, beauty, Saki, and massage parlors and my seven new tattoos was great! Yokouska, Japan was still holding a grudge against us, besides we weren't into Snake dancing anyway!

So our Commander of the Seventh Fleet saw fit for us to partake our liberty on a base with plenty of Christian Bookstores, churches, and exciting points of interest, Subic Bay, in the Philippines "Olongapo".

Five of us out of second division (if you read this and know who you are, please drop me a line) were shinning our shoes and readying our dress whites for twelve hours of mayhem, door to door bars, women, and monkey meat on a stick!

But remember..... I had just spent eighteen months on this island that I recalled as something out of "McHales Navy."

Everyone knows that when the fleet is in town, prices on beer, food, and the other, and especially the other, goes higher than a rocket off the port side of the "Big E."

So guess what yours truly did? In a valiant effort to try and keep prices down and save his buddies some pesos?

I walked them into a Navy exchange on Subic Bay and immediately bought our civilian clothes and transformed ourselves from fleet sailors to shore based swabbies!

I led them under some bleachers on base, at a softball field, and we changed clothes. The Marine guard at the gate didn't notice our transformation from fleet to shore based, so we passed through the gates of "Heaven" into the gates of purgatory. Whoopee!"

After dinner at Papa Guayo' Restaurant, five monkey on a stick and three shoe shines, we jumped on a jitney to the other end of town and hit both sides of the street, introducing my buddies to acquaintances I knew from the previous two years.

We all had managed to crawl back to the gate as liberty was now ending, thank God, and get back to the bleachers on base to change back to our dress whites.

But guess what? Evidently some Pino base workers had watched us jettison our dress whites for the evening so they helped themselves to our uniforms. That's right, NO DRESS WHITES!

My shipmates were very concerned about my immediate health unless I mustered a plan to get us all back aboard "THE BIG E".

I led them to the pier where she was tied up and we all hid behind this big dumpster plotting our next move. I peered around the dumpster with just five minutes remaining until we would have been considered AWOL. I spotted our second division Ensign on

the gangway as J.O.O.D. He waved me aboard and said"Where is so and so, and so and so, and then, why are you in civies?" I gave him a condensed version, and after twelve hours of drinking San Miguel beer it must have boon an interesting version.

My buddies stuck their heads out from behind the dumpster and he waved them up also. He very courteously replied: "Ha, Ha, get your —"s below decks, get rid of those civies, and get your —"s in your racks!" Rack means "bed" to you non-swabbies.

It wasn't funny then, but twenty-seven years later, remembering the looks on my buddies faces.... I find it hilarious!!

I was discharged off of the USS ENTERPRISE in Bremerton, Washington the end of September 1968. A little over three months later, a fire would take some buddies and fellow shipmates of mine home to eternal rest and peace. I thank God often that I shipped out earlier and I also thank Him for caring for my shipmates. These brave men threw caution aside, stood in harm's way, fighting alongside each other the way they were trained to do! They truly were hero's and I am sincerely grateful to have had the honor to serve with them on the "BIG E!"

A LOVE STORY for the "BELIEVE IT OR NOT"

BUD RICKE, New Albany, Indiana **USS WINSLOW DD 359**

THIS IS A STORY YOU MIGHT FIND IN A RIPLEYS "BELIEVE IT OR NOT" BOOK. WAS IT A MIRACLE? OR JUST ANOTHER TRUE

"SEA STORY" THAT HAPPENED TO A "WHITE HAT" IN THE U.S.NAVY! YOU DECIDE.

From June 1942 until November 1944, I served aboard the USS WINSLOW (DD359) as a torpedoman. Day after day we patrolled the South Atlantic for German subs and keeping the convoys on their way safely through the oceans.

Sometime in late 1943, I had accumulated quite a few letters from my girl friend and since we had very little storage space, I had to dispose of some of these letters. Only, of course. after having read them over, and over, a thousand times so they were now implanted in my mind. I bundled up the oldest ones with wire and fastened a good heavy weight to them and threw them over the side. Our location at the time was somewhere East of Rio de Janeiro, Brazil.

In September 1944 a man was fishing at the New Jersey shore and thought he had caught a large fish. To his amazement, he reeled in my bundle old discarded letters. These people opened several of the letters and obtained my girl friends name and address, then mailed them to her., not knowing the fate of my ship, or me.

This lovely girl friend has been my wife for over fifty years now and we have three wonderful children. We still have the original letter from that fisherman and some of my letters as proof that this really did happen.

"Mother should have warned me about sailors."

BAD BOOZE

DONALD THESSEN,   *USS MERIWETHER APA 203*
Albion, Nebraska

After the invasion of Okinawa we were sent to Manila for some R&R which we had not had for quite some time but I am sure we had gotten more than a lot of other combat ships.

On our way the division officers started warning us about the bad alcohol that was being served in bars in Manila. I do not recall all the conversations but one was that people were going blind drinking it. Well so what? Most of us that ran together were twenty years old and thought we were tougher than old shoe leather.

Upon arrival in Manila part of the crew was given liberty and we took a landing craft to shore. The first thing we had to do was to check out those bars selling the bad booze. Anything we were told to stay away from, a twenty year old sailor had to check out for himself, especially women and liquor.

We found that the war had done a lot of damage to the buildings in this city and most of the bars were now located on the second floor. So up to the second floors we went. The first thing we saw were small round glass topped tables with barely room for four people to sit around them. Don't ask me where these tables came from because by all rights they should have been blown up when the first floors went.

"*So this is what you meant by an amusement park!*"

We ordered drinks and one sip should have been enough to make a half way smart person start thinking. We decided these were sipping drinks. Not that we were half way smart. Anyhow, after the second drink we decided to quit drinking while we could still make it back to the boat landing,

Upon our arrival at the boat landing were a few sailors who had decided to have a third and fourth drink, they were lined up side by side waiting for someone to make sure they got back to the right ships.

When we arrived back at our ship those of us who could still walk up the gangway did so, the others had to stay aboard the landing craft until it was hoisted aboard then they were carried off to their bunks, or else to sick bay depending on how bad off they were.

After that we decided playing ball on the base was the far more reasonable thing to do. So much for the great liberty parties in Manila!

NAVY HUMOR

BRUCE E. SCHORER,   **USS JOHN F. KENNEDY CVA 67**
Nicollet, Minesota

While serving aboard the USS JOHN F. KENNEDY, CVA 67, on its maiden voyage in 1968, there was a conflict in the Middle East. We were at sea for over thirty days. It was hot, and very uncomfortable. We were at battle stations and general quarters a lot of the time. I was assigned to a damage control locker. On one of these occasions, when I was suited up in fire-fighting gear, "nature called!" We had to open a hatch so I could get to a berthing area so I could go use the head.

It is quite a procedure getting in and out of one of these fire-fighting suits. While in one of the stalls, I noticed some writing way down in the right-hand corner of the door. As I leaned way over to read it, it said: "You are now shitting at a forty-five degree angle!" I found this very humorous at the time, considering the situation.

The rest of the general quarters went much better after that little humorous incident!

WHALE BOAT INCIDENT

CARL R. PATFIELD, Las Vegas, Nevada

When we could not tie up dockside, we anchored out and went ashore on a whale boat. This boat had a canvas canopy covering most of the boat; covered in bad weather, open in good weather.

Procedure was that officers got on the boat first, off the boat first. If weather was bad they may, or may not, allow enlisted men to ride under the canopy.

Coming back from liberty, the Captain was so drunk, he could hardly stand, rain was falling, along with a grand gesture, he invited the few white hats on board to join him under the canopy.

He fell asleep, waking to the realization that he had wet himself.

He had a bright thought, not wanting others to know the truth, he informed the officer of the deck, a seaman had pissed on him, and ordered the OOD to put the sailor in the brig for five days.

When he awoke, he struggled with the unfairness of his act, and called for the OOD, asking if he had put the seaman in the brig for five days, as ordered.

"No Sir," the OOD answered. "I put him in for ten days."

"WHY TEN DAYS?" the anguished Captain asked.

"Because when we undressed you for bed, we found that he had also crapped in your pants to, Sir?"

NUFF SAID !!!!

OUT OF MOTHBALLS—INTO TROUBLE
A UNITED NATIONS DEAL???

WILLIS H. BARTHOLOMEW,   *HMS ETHIOPIA AO-1*
Burlington, WA.

In 1962 when I was a first class petty officer, I was stationed at NAS Alameda, at the base hospital in the X-ray department and I received orders to an AVP Transfer Team which was being formed at the Naval Shipyard at Hunters Point, San Francisco, California. Of course no one knew what an AVP Transfer Team was, it wasn't long though before I found out.

An AVP was a small seaplane tender, the one that was at Hunters Point was the USS ORCA AVP-10. The Orca was towed down to San Francisco from Astoria, Oregon where it had been stored in the mothball fleet. The ship was going to be refitted and then given to the Ethiopian Government and would be the first large naval ship that the Ethiopian Navy would have. The AVP Transfer Team was going to be onboard the ship for six months while the ship underwent overhaul and renovation and then we were to sail with the Ethiopian crew to Ethiopia along with 20 Norwegian naval personnel. There were 20 United States and 20 Norwegian naval personnel along with about 200 Ethiopian naval personnel onboard the ship. We were to help train this Ethiopian crew on the way to Ethiopia. The commanding officer was a Commander in the Norwegian Navy. The Norwegian Navy was at that time training the Ethiopian Navy.

The Orca was renamed the HMS ETHIOPIA AO-1, which stood for His Majesties Ship, in honor of Hali Salasi, the Emperor of Ethiopia. The Orca was a diesel operated ship and required air pressure to stop and then reverse the thrust of the propeller shaft. After a couple of months the crew arrived from different bases across the United States to start their training aboard ship. On the first trip out for sea trials, we had our first really exciting event. As we proceeded under the Golden Gate Bridge the word was passed to secure the special sea and anchor detail, the Ethiopian crewmember who was on the helm immediately turned away from the helm and left the bridge, the ship started to head towards shore, our quartermaster saw what had happened and ran in from the flying bridge, took over the helm and put us back on course, it was exciting for a little while.

Later on, there was a fire in the anchor windless locker, while trying to connect the fire hoses together, the fire fighters tried to put the male ends of the fire hoses together, this of course did not work so they reversed the hoses and proceeded to try to screw the female ends together, by this time one of our transfer team had put the fire out using a CO_2 bottle. On our return to our pier at Hunters Point the wind was blowing quite a bit and our Captain was asked if he wanted to have tugs alongside to help us dock. He informed the harbor master that he would be able to handle it without tugs. As I mentioned before, air pressure was needed to stop and reverse the shaft; after about six tries and not being able to get the ship alongside the dock, the engine room informed the Captain that they only had three more starts left before they would run out of air pressure and would not be able to respond to anymore signals from the bridge. The Captain told them he would only need a couple of starts and went ahead and tried to go alongside the pier again. He used up the remaining air pressure and as we pulled in towards the pier he gave the order to reverse the engine, but there was no more air, so we rammed into the pier and destroyed half the pier pilings and took out about two hundred feet of pier. This was not the best first day of sea trials for our joint venture of hands across the sea.

During this training period, the young sailors who were assigned to the scullery proceeded to put a gallon of dishwashing concentrate in the dishwasher. It was very difficult to find them as the whole area was a mass of bubbles, they did make it out of the scullery, but they were covered with bubbles. There were bubbles coming out of the ventilator ducts all over the ship, it was a great sight, it reminded me of the movie "MR. ROBERTS!"

Sometime during the overhaul period, someone in the ship-yard work crew deliberately inserted washers between the flanges of the fill pipe for one of the fuel tanks, so that when we took on fuel, the fuel escaped into the bilge. This created a large fuel spill into the bilge of the ship, which had to be cleaned up. Not really a humorous happening, but interesting, believed to be sabotage at the time due to the give away of our tax money to foreign countries.

From the time we departed San Francisco until we arrived in Ethiopia, the crew was on water hours, they never were able to distill enough water to run the ship plus allow the crew to shower and clean-up as needed. During the night we would sometimes come to a complete stop while underway. For some unknown reason the engine room would lose all power. we would all go top-side to make sure everything was all right that we had not hit something.

When we arrived at Pearl Harbor we proceeded to dock at the Naval Base. and on the pier we had a welcoming party to meet and greet the ship. There was a Navy Band on the pier playing music. One of the young deck hands threw the monkey fist on the heaving line and hit the band leader in the back, the leader immediately stopped the band playing and loaded all the band members into their bus and left the pier. We almost lost the whole welcoming committee. Just another fun time on the HMS ETHIOPIA.

NEVER "ASSUME" ANYTHING!

ALLEN D. REGENOS, Claypool, Indiana   *American Legion*

This story was told to me by an old Army buddy who just recently passed away. We will call his name "Frank."

Frank said that after the war against Japan ended he was sta-tioned on a small island in the South Pacific when one day they had this big beach party to celebrate the ending of the war. There were Army, Navy, and Marines enjoying this party with lots of food and beer, everyone was drinking up a storm and all hands were enjoying themselves.

There were a lot of volleyball games going on all over the beach so Frank and a few friends decided to start their own game. He was getting a group together when up walked this old man dressed in sandals, shorts, and an old polo shirt who asked if he could play too. He admitted that he was not very good but added that he did like playing the game. They all said, "yea, you can play."

During the game the old man fouled up quite often, then he missed a real easy play which urged Frank to tell him: "You'r right, you ain't worth a damn!" After another bad play Frank again acousted him saying; "You really ain't worth a shit!"

After the game ended all the men playing on Franks team went their own seperate ways rejoining the party. A sailor who had been watching the game later approached Frank and said: "You Army guys sure have a lot of guts, telling the old man he wasn't worth a shit."

"Well he wasn't!" Frank told the sailor. "An old Chief like that (Frank had assumed that the old man was a Chief Petty Officer) has been in the Navy too long and rode too many waves and can't operate on dry land."

The sailor replied: "Chief, my ass, that was ADMIRAL BULL HALSEY!"

Frank said that when he heard that, he about crapped in his pants.

ITS A SCARY FEELING

WILLIAM THOMPSON, Vail Arizona   **USS HELENA CA 75**

I was serving aboard the heavy cruiser the USS HELENA when it came time for me to be discharged from the Navy. A group of us short-timers left the cruiser in Tsingtao, China and were shipped back to the states. Upon landing in San Diego, California we were taken to the Naval disembarkment area. We were corralled into this big area infront of some large buildings with lots of windows. In the center of this field was a flag pole with a large flag box at its base.

The Chief in charge began taking muster and calling out names in alphabetical order. This was a very large group of men, so I figured it would be quite a while before he ever reached Thompson which would be a long ways down on the list. I was very tired, so I climbed up on the flag box, pulled up my sea bag, and promptly fell asleep.

When I awoke, there I was with a sunburned face and the dust blowing across the field. No one, I mean not a soul, was in sight. I will never forget that feeling! I'll bet that Chief is still laughing because he had to have known I was there sleeping and just abandoned me to teach me a lesson.WHICH HE DID!

So I got down from the flag box, walked around, and located the post exchange where I bought a small suitcase that I figured I would need later. I guess I toted that suitcase and my seabag for a couple of days. I took them everywhere I went: chow lines, the head, etc. I slept where I could find an empty bunk. Then along came a Chief, seeing me wandering around and asked if my name was Thompson. "Yup!" I answered him.

"Well you had better hustle your buns because they are hollering for you out there!"

So "hustle" I did and when I came running up to the group, which was standing in formation, my Commanding Officer, a Lt. Coleman, said to me: "Thompson, where the hell have you been???"

Wow, I sure caught the devil from everyone. It seems like some good can arise even out of a bad situation. Because of my being lost and holding back my group, we got to ride to the discharge center at Great Lakes, Illinois in style on a pullman car instead of a regular troop train.

FRIENDLY FIRE

EDWIN L. METCALF, Edmonds, Washington   USS LSMR 525

In 1954 when I was serving onboard the USS LSMR 525 while operating out of San Diego, California. we sailed to an island somewhere off the coast for some gunnery exercises with our sister ship, the USS LSMR 401.

On this one occasion, the two ships were blasting away at the island with our rockets and one five-inch mount. We were closer to shore than the 401 and all of a sudden a shell landed pretty close to our ship, obviously from the 401. At least we hoped it wasn't from a cruiser or battleship from over the horizon. A few seconds later a second shell splashed into the water near us. I was the Captains "talker" with audio contact with all the departments on the ship, so I was right there on the bridge. Red faced, the Captain, a full lieutenant, turned to the quartermaster and bellowed: "send them a message> Tell them (the LSMR 401) that we are friendly, we are friendly, cease fire!"

All the personnel who witnessed this incident thought it was very humorous, even though it was very serious at that time.

A PHARMACIST MATE

LARRY W. GRIMM, Northwood, Ohio   Fleet Hospital 103

I was a Pharmacist Mate in the Navy Hospital Corps in the South Central Pacific during the second world war. MOB 3 was stationed in the American Samoas and was getting to far from the front so they broke up. They changed MOB Hospitals to Fleet Hospitals and added one hundred to their designation, thus becoming Fleet Hospital 103. A skeleton crew moved up to Espirito Santos, New Hebrides where I was stationed at the time. I was transferred to this outfit and moved up to Guam, where we, along with fifty-six SeaBees built our hospital.

The first night we were there, in our tent city, we had to stand four-hour watches on guard duty on the perimeter of our unit. The island was officially secured but there were still plenty of Japs on the island. we had riggedup a make-shift clothes line so we could wash and dry our clothes, and also a makeshift shower, both were located on the edge of our perimeter near the jungle. One night one of our men was standing guard near this area and he was heavily armed with a carbine, Colt-45 pistol, and a hunting knife. After dark one of our shipmates came out to take his clothes from the line. The guard challenged him with "SHOW A LIGHT!" The reply came back "I DON'T HAVE ONE." The guard came back with: "YOU'D BETTER GET ONE IN A DAMN QUICK HURRY!"

A couple of days later an Ensign (a ninety day wonder) made the comment that he'd like to take a shower but he hated to have to shower with the enlisted men. An "old salt" Chief Warrant Officer blared out to him: "I've been showering with the enlisted men for over thirty years and there isn't anything wrong with me yet."

After the hospital was in operation—complete with nurses, I was assigned to a surgical ward as senior corpsman on night duty. We were then considered an Armed Forces Hospital and had Army, Navy and Marine patients.

I had this one particular Army private, a Mormon from Utah. He had stepped on a land mine and lost one leg below the knee and the other one above the knee. He had also lost an arm above the elbow, and the other hand was gone except for his thumb. He would hold up that thumb and say: "Some day that's going to come in handy!" He was allowed morphine every four hours if needed. I would go and ask him "Do you need anything,Henry?" and his reply always was : Naw—go take care of the sick guys."

I received a letter from Henry a couple of weeks after he had been shipped back to the states and in it he said he expected to be walking in a couple of months—talk about guts !

A Navy patient I had about that same time had gotten tangled up with a flare of some sort and his arm was pretty well cut and burned. The doctors cut two slits in his back, removed some skin and used it as grafts on his arm. Needless to say, he could not now lay on his back. Then he had an attack of appendicitis and could not lay on his stomach either. Consequently, we kept him pretty well doped up. Then the doctors felt he was getting hooked on the drugs and cut him off. One night he came to me when I first came on duty and asked for something as he couldn't sleep due to his pain. I told him that I could not give him anything without his doctors orders. He would not take "no" for an answer and kept saying; "Come on doc you can give me something!" Finally I said "OK, you go back to your bunk and after I get the ward secured and the day people leave, I will get you something."

I went to the treatment room and filled several capsules with sugar an put them in a pill bottle. Shortly, he came back to me and asked: "have you got something for me doc?" I handed him the container and told him,"you had better only take two of these at a time as they are very potent." The next day he came up to me and said; Boy doc, that's the best nights sleep I have had in a long time." Naturally, he kept coming back for more.

A few days later we were making room for new patients from the Okinawa push. Those patients who were going to be able to return to duty in a reasonable length of time were sent to Pearl harbor, some back to the states. He came up to me this morning before being transferred and said: "Hey doc, how about giving me some of those capsules to take with me. I don't know if they will give me any at Pearl." I replied "Sure they will, just ask the senior corpsman for some sugar capsules, he will take care of you."

After a few laps around the ward and him calling me a few choice words he realized I did what I did in his best interest. He then thanked me and we parted good friends. and the whole staff had a good laugh.

TRUE CONFESSION

H.B. DEYO, Flint, Michigan   *USS LCI(G) 462*

I was onboard the LCI(G) 462 during World War II from September 16,1943 until July 1945. The 462 was a landing craft infantry but was converted to a rocket launching gunboat which went in to the beach ahead of the landing force and launched hundreds of concussion rockets into the proposed landing area.. We had a crew of three officers and seventy-three enlisted men.

After the invasion of Luzon in Lingayon Gulf, in the Philippines we went and anchored several miles off the beach head. The Admiral in charge sent word to all ships to be on the alert for possible enemy swimmers with explosives trying to blow a hole in ships that are anchored.

A buddy and myself were standing the watch from midnight until four a.m. topside, walking the decks, to watch out for these enemy swimmers. We each were armed with a forty-five caliber Thompson machine gun. Most other crew members were in their bunks sleeping.

About two in the morning we were getting pretty bored. Since we were told that the enemy swimmers would approach the ship swimming under some floating debris, I told my buddy that I was going to the fantail to get a apple crate and toss it overboard and for him to shoot at it.

When I got back to where he was standing he said that he did not believe I would do such a thing. So I walked to the bow and tossed the crate overboard then went back amid ships where my friend was standing. I reached him just about the same time as the crate was off our beam and he opened fire at it. Almost instantly, we looked up, and there standing around us was the whole crew in their shorts and T-shirts, barefooted, scared half out of their wits thinking we were being attacked.

The skipper was a young law school graduate and easy going, so we got away with our stunt, but he never put the two of us together on watch again!

I BECOME A NAVY DIVER

PAUL STEIN, Bayside, New York   **USS VULCAN AR 5**

They say you should never volunteer when in the service but I sure did!

When a notice was posted on the ships bulletin board saying that they needed divers, I volunteered! I can remember as though it were yesterday when the Chief diver was instructing us what to do and what not to do in case of an underwater emergency. The Chief decided I was to be the first new diver to be suited up. After the canvas suit is put on, the helmet is attached. As I sat on the suiting up bench watching them tightening the wing bolts with a wrench I said to myself: "You jerk, what did you get yourself into!" Trying to hide my fear I said to the Chief; "What happens if I have to take a crap while I am on the bottom?" He answered, "just crap in your pants and hope the air pressure doesn't force it into your helmet!"

Once the helmet was secured to my suit I began to sweat from fear of the unknown. Once in the suit you cannot wipe your nose, scratch your face, or any of those normal personal things. The tap on my helmet from the Chief meant that I was to stand up and walk to the gunwale of the ship. Needless to say, I weighed one hundred and thirty-eight pounds, the suit with all its weights was over two hundred pounds. I could not even pick up my leg let alone walk to the gunwale so two line tenders had to assist me in standing and walking. So there I was standing on the ladder looking over the side. I must have looked really stupid as I could see the faces of all those men standing on deck and they were laughing as they lowered me over the side and I dropped below the surface of the water.

The water was strange and cold and I could feel the fear rising up again inside me as I thought I heard the voice of my mother saying to me: "Are you crazy? Do you want to drown?" Then I felt the soft, muddy, bottom at thirty feet. I just stood there for awhile and looked around. I could just barely see two feet in front of me because of the movements I was making in the mud. It was strange standing there with the only sound that of the air rushing into my suit. Then I heard a voice over my helmet phone. "Hey kid, walk to your right about thirty feet." I realized that the Chief wanted me to practice moving around. I lifted my legs and started to walk, or so I thought. You see in order to move around down there you had to lean forward and walk on the tips of your weighted boots. After awhile I got used to this new sensation and commenced walking around like the Chief wanted me to do. I saw a jeep sitting on the bottom covered with silt. A fish came up to my face plate and started to suck on it. Then I heard the Chief say; "Don't worry kid, you have enough air in your suit to last another four minutes." I wondered what he was talking about when I realized it was kind of quiet. The air had stopped hissing into my suit. They shut off the air pumps to the suit. You could probably have heard me yelling clear back in the U.S.A. states "Get my ass off the bottom right now!" the panic had started to take over just as I felt them begin to pull me up.

As I broke to the surface a sudden calm came over me and I said to myself: "Hey! That wasn't that bad." They hoisted me back onto the deck and the two line handlers helped me move along and back to the suiting up bench where they began to undue my face plate. When I saw the Chief smiling at me I said: "Hey Chief, when can I go back down again?"

From that day on I did as much diving as I could and really enjoyed all my diving experiences.

MONKEY BUSINESS

KENNETH HERRING, Murray, Kentucky   *Unknown LCM*

I had just made Chief and was assigned the eight to twelve watch on a ship in the Far East. The last LCM from the beach came along side about midnight. All hands had to be aboard ship before I could be relieved. It was very hard to check everyone carefully, all of the ID and liberty cards, the way the men came in bunches, trying to come aboard. Finally the deck was clear and my relief came up and assumed the watch and I was free to go below and get some sleep.

The bunk felt good and I was just about asleep, when a messenger appeared in my cabin with a flashlight, shining it in my face. "Herring?" He asked. "Yes!" I answered. "The Executive Officer wants to see you in his stateroom on the double!" "Oh shit!" I thought out loud. "What have I done to deserve a trip to the Captain Quarters?" I jumped to my feet and quickly got dressed and double timed up the ladder to find out what was wrong.

"Herring!" He yelled as I entered his cabin. "You let a damned monkey aboard this ship!"

"Actually there were about a hundred of them Sir." I blurted out.

"Hell. I don't mean a sailor, damit, I mean a real monkey!" He snapped back at me.

"Look!" He yelled and pointed as I caught a glimpse of a monkey running down the passageway right there in officers country. "Do you see what I am talking about?" He asked.

"Aye,aye, Sir." I answered while looking after the monkey.

"Catch that damn monkey and get it off my ship....NOW!" He ordered me.

The rest of the night was spent running up and down passage ways with a net, chasing a monkey. Just when I thought I had it cornered, he would swing away and climb up the bulkhead, out of my reach. Success finally came just before dawn, when I had him cornered in a position where he would be caught or jump into the sea. I was finally able to net him, put him in a basket, and carry him ashore.

The boat crew took the monkey and me back to the mainland, where I tossed him out of the basket and we headed back to the ship, and I to my bunk. This story followed me for the rest of my Naval career, about the time I checked a monkey aboard my ship off the coast of Taiwan on a cold, rainy night. Now I can think back and laugh about that incident but I sure wasn't laughing that night.

I learned a valuable lesson that night. If you don't have a proper ID and liberty card, you don't come aboard my ship on my watch. I don't care what tree your ancestors are from...!

"GLORIA" THE MANNEQUIN

RAYMOND STULL, Citrus Heights, CA. _____

It was the year 1945 and we pulled into the port of New Orleans, Louisiana, for supplies and some major repairs. It was "Mardi

Gras" time and the entire city was having one big party. A carnival atmosphere prevailed with the citizens of that great city going wild and doing crazy things.

When it came time for liberty, we sailors just joined the crowd. Two buddies and I were returning to our ship after having a big night on the town and we were feeling quite good. While going down Canal Street we noticed that someone had broken the display window of a large ladies clothing store and there on the sidewalk before us lay a female mannequin. It was stripped of all its clothing and looked naked and forlorn just laying there.

Being normal sailors we could not just leave this naked lady laying there in the street, so we decided to take it back to our ship with us.

Standing on the pier we realized that getting the mannequin aboard the ship was going to be a problem, so we took it all apart. The small parts like the hands, feet and arms we concealed under our clothing as we boarded the ship. My one buddy remained on the pier, up by the bow of our ship, once we got onboard my other buddy and I tossed him a line, which we secured around the mannequins torso, and we hauled her aboard.

Safe aboard, we carried the mannequin parts to our berthing compartment where we reassembled it. With the help of some fellow crew members we came up with some fine looking ladies underwear, dressed her, stood her in a corner of the compartment and named her "Gloria." We now had a ships mascot!

Then it happened! Several weeks after returning to sea while underway in a calm ocean our Captain decided to do an unannounced compartment inspection. As soon as he saw "Gloria" he really blew his cork and ordered, "Get rid of that mannequin, right now!"

So we did, and we did it in a most unusual way. We took "Gloria" and with the help of a sail maker got a piece of canvas and sewed her up inside it along with some weights at her feet. We took her back to the fantail, where, with appropriate ceremony, with tears in our eyes, we buried her at sea. Where she will stay forever, and ever.

A "NEAR-MISS"

HOWARD BAUGHMAN.   *USS JOHN ROGERS DD574*
Severna Park, MD.

Refueling and resupplying a ship while underway at sea is, at its best, a most dangerous and hazardous situation. Both ships involved must maintain the same course and speed while keeping abreast of each other only twenty or thirty yards apart. In a rolling, tossing sea, this takes a ship's most skillful helmsman, The decks are usually awash and slippery with footing hard to maintain, The work is hard, arduous, and dangerous to all hands taking part in this great physical test of endurance. However, it is a task that must be carried out to maintain ships at sea.

We were in mid-Pacific sometime during the Second World War steaming in company with several other ships including the battleship, USS INDIANA.

Our destroyer group was ordered to replenish supplies from the battleship. One of our destroyers was steaming close along the port side of the USS INDIANA and already had lines across and supplies were being passed to her as we came along the starboard side of the battleship.

As we adjusted our speed to match that of the USS INDIANA and pulled up abeam of her, the boatswains mates aboard the battleship began tossing their heaving lines towards our main deck trying to establish physical contact with our ship.

A heaving line consists of about fifty yards of "clothesline" size line with a weighted "monkey fist" at its heaving end.. A "monkey fist" is a round metal ball about three or four inches in diameter with line tightly weaved around it. This "monkey fist" puts a good weight at the end of a heaving line making it easier to toss, gives you more distance, and a sense of direction when you toss it. In some "monkey fists" the metal ball is replaced with a wooden one.

On the decks of both ships a long line of twenty or more sailors are lined up to handle and rig the transport lines as they are passed from ship to ship. the battleship had a power winch to provide the power to move the cargo nets laden with supplies from the USS INDIANA to the destroyers. The destroyers did not have a power winch for this purpose and had to rely on sailor power while refueling or resupplying at sea. The destroyers did have power winches on the bow for raising the anchors but none amidships.

As fate would have it.......One line was heaved just aft of our beam and the heavy, lead ladened,monkey-fist just happened to hit the firing mechanism of a "K-gun" that was mounted on the port side of our main deck. This "K-gun" was loaded with a fifty pound depth charge which, when the trigger was struck, launched this depth charge high into the air towards the battleship. It sailed over the INDIANA'S number three gun torrent and luckily plunged into the sea between the battleship and the destroyer it was resupplying on its port side.

If this depth charge would have landed on the battleship much damage would have ensued. If it had landed on the main deck of the destroyer it would have caused a catastrophe as fifty or more sailors could have been killed and major damages inflicted which probably have put the destroyer out of action for quite some time.

Thank God the depth charge missed both ships landing in the sea. It did not explode, and sank to the bottom of the ocean.

All hands heaved a sigh of relief and continued the resupplying of both destroyers with out further incidents.

Just another day in the life of a sailor!

A PROUD SOUTHERNER

IRWIN J. KNAPPES, Battle Of Ormoc Bay Assn.
Middletown, N.J.   *USS MOALE DD 693*

Captain Walter M. Foster, skipper of the USS MOALE, was tough on his officers but kindly and forgiving of his mostly draftee WWII crew. Foster hailed from Alabama and like most proud Southerners of the time, still felt a bit of lingering shame over the South's loss of the Civil War, so there was somewhat of a solidarity with other "rebels".

One of his young seaman had been put on report for being asleep on watch—a serious offense. Captain Foster asked the young miscreant, "How do you plead?" "Guilty, Sir," came the reply". Detecting a Southern accent the skipper asked, "Where are you from son?" "North Carolina, Sir," came the reply. The Captain cracked a slight smile and responded, "well, thats close enough. Case dismissed!"

This is a true story and I have the name of the seaman on file but decided not to print it to protect the innocent

THE GREAT WATERMELON CAPER

HENRY F. BOHNE, Parker, Colorado

We were in port and the sonar gang was in the sonar shack doing routine maintenance and field day cleanup when I, as the senior sonarman got a call to supply one person for a work detail to bring aboard stores. Naturally, I sent the most junior seaman.

About fifteen minutes later he showed up at the door of the sonar shack with a nice sized watermelon. "Hide this quick, and don't start on it until I get back!" A reasonable request as he had obiously "liberated" it from the stores being brought aboard.

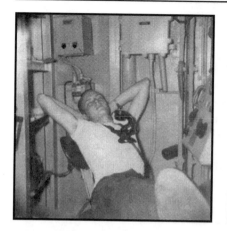

Henry Bohne, Parker Colorado,
The Watermelon Caper

Henry Bohne, Parker
Colorado, Swede

After he returned from the work detail we locked the door to the sonar shack and proceeded to share out the melon.

About halfway through the melon there came a knock on the door. Looking out through the louvers I saw a pair of brown shoes, an officer. "Yeah, who is it?"

"Mr Dye, can I come in?"

Now Mr. Dye was our Division Officer, Sonar Officer, and one of the good guys. So we opened the door, invited him in, and offered him some of our watermelon. He had a slice and completed the business he had come to transact.

A couple of days later we were at sea and standing watch when Mr. Dye came into the shack, closed the door and said he needed to talk with us. "Did the ship's mess have any watermelon recently?"

"No."

"Well, the Wardroom had some, but the portions were small. The Wardroom stores seemed to be short at least one watermelon."

With that Mr. Dye took a look around, complimented us on the good field day work and the taut watch, and left.

I told you he was one of the good guys.

A DANGEROUS TALE

JACK SPENCER, Connersville, IN   **USS KNIGHT DMS 40**

It was the Winter of 1945-46 somewhere in the Yellow Sea.

It was the mid-watch and four of us were standing our watch operating number one boiler. We had been running from a typhoon and it had chased us up into the Yellow Sea.

The sea was rough enough that a shipmate, H. Roy Glenn, had scrounged up a piece of burlap, which was about eighteen inches on a side, to stand on. Without this piece of burlap his feet would slide on the deck-plates nearly every time the USS KNIGHT would roll. She was rolling between thirty and forty degrees as regular as a clock ticking. Roy was standing his part of the watch operating the burner-front.

We, as usual, were telling sea-stories about girls we knew or wished we knew. Roy finished his coffee and decided to get some more. The coffee pot was one which some of the fire-room crew had fought their way out of a water-front beer joint with. It had been secured to a home made angle iron stand, and was heated with our two hundred-fifty psi steam line.

As the Knight rolled to starboard, Roy stepped off his burlap, slid to the coffee pot, hooked his foot around the stand, poured his coffee, put in the canned milk and some sugar. Then the Knight rolled back to port and Roy unhooked his foot and began to slide back to his work station.

At this exact moment the Knight pitched violently and tossed up the deck-plate which Roy had been standing on to operate his front burner. The deck-plate slid off toward the port side of the fire-room and Roy continued sliding toward the opening which had been left by the missing deck-plate. It must have been nearly three feet down to the Knights hull. The deck-plates were the boilers operating platform. One could not work while standing on the inside of the rounded hull. Besides, there were steam lines, water lines, etc. in the space between the deck-plates and the interior of the hull.

Roy shouted, "I'm going in the bulges!" And in he went!

He immediately stood up, and holding aloft his coffee cup, called out, "Look, I didn't spill any!"

All well and good except the Knight rolled back to starboard and the loose deck-plate came sliding across the fire-room like a damned guillotine blade! These deck-plates were about two and a half feet on a side and were about three sixteenths thick.

Roy ducked and the plate passed over him. As the Knight kept rolling, the plate kept sliding, and Roy kept ducking. We couldn't help him for quite sometime because of our laughing.

Roy never did spill any of his coffee!

Roy and I exchanged Christmas cards for many years but a couple or so years ago his card quit coming. I phoned but his phone was disconnected. I suppose that he has either gone on before me or else is disabled. Soon all of us World War II veterans will be gone. ONLY OUR STORIES WILL REMAIN!!!

C = 2 Pi r

Henry Bohne, Parker, Colorado

We were in the sonar shack on watch when one of our gang rushed in and asked how to figure the distance around one of the portholes in the bridge structure. The answer tossed back to him was "C=Pi r" with Pi being 3.14, the formula for determining the circumference of a circle.

Henry F. Bohne, SO1

Now this is not a typical topic for discussion among seamen, even one assigned to the sonar gang, so why the sudden interest in such an esoteric piece of information? Well, "Swede", one of the guartermasters, stated that he could crawl through any of the portholes surrounding the bridge.

Everybody on the ship knew Swede, knew he was big—and fat. Those of us who knew him well knew that his waistline was 52 inches.

So the problem was, could he squeeze that huge waist through one of those portholes? What was the circumference of the porthole? "C= Pi r" What was r, or better yet D, the diameter?

What ever the radius or diameter was, applying the formula gave us the information that the circumference was less than the 52 inch waist. As a matter of fact, if memory serves me right, a whole lot less.

We had been at sea for a couple of weeks, and as you all know, boredom sets in easily. So Swede's challenge quickly became a subject of discussion throughout the ship. There was much covert visiting to the bridge and surreptitious measuring of the diameter of the portholes.

Obiviously with the ship underway and the constant bridge watch, there was no way Swede could prove his contention. It was set that after we reached port he would have to put up, or shut up.

Did I mention boredom? The interest in Swede's challenge quickly became the subject of lots of small bets. Opps, gambling was not allowed. Let's just say that there were various challenges between the supporters of one side or the other, backed up by ....

After our return to port and all the hubbub of setting the in-port watch had died down, a few of us gathered on the bridge to watch Swede do his feat of passage. Of course he fit through the porthole. As a matter of fact, he went through so quickly that some of the observers missed the event. Swede had to do it a second time to placate all the losers.

What was the edge to all of us backers who knew he could accomplish the feat? Well, most of us had seen Swede "suck it up" and knew that he could pull that gut in and greatly reduce the 52 inch waist. He could "suck it up" to a point where he was in danger of losing his pants.

Henry Bohne, Parker Colorado
Rocking and Rolling North Atlantic, 1953

12 DOZEN EQUALS ONE GROSS

HENRY BOHNE, Parker, Colorado

One of the clerks in the ship's office was typing orders for supplies. One of the items being ordered was No. 2 yellow pencils.

He had been told to order 12 dozen. Now we all know that 12 dozen is a gross. The clerk decided to change the dozen designation to gross.

Yup! He forgot to change the 12 to 1 !

Of course Naval Stores filled the order exactly as written, and we received 1,728 yellow No. 2 pencils. Have you thought through this over supply problem? With about 350 men on board the destroyer that computes to 4.9 pencils per person.

The first thing we knew about this was when every division and gang was being offered a generous supply of pencils. When those requests had been filled, individuals were offered pencils.

Supply, in this case, exceeded demand.

LST 327 MESS HALL

EDWARD DECKER, Costa Mesa, Californis   **USS LST 327**

How well did you eat while in the service?

COAST GUARD BOOT CAMP ELLIS ISLAND: I learn about those inordinately endless chow lines! My first introduction to coffee. No milk or ice water about. Armored cow, one had to make-do with that god-alful, sickly sweet, condensed milk. My first bout with coffee-nerves as I was off the walls with nervous energy.

SANDY HOOK SURF STATION: What a transformation from Ellis Island to Sandy Hook, New Jersey. Meals fit for a Admiral, served family style. Cooky and his mess cooks served hugh platters of food directly on the table. Meat, potatoes, vegetables, bread, butter, and dessert. A dining room! the sailors lined up outside the chow hall awaiting Cooky's call, "chow down" sounded. Somehow I always managed to get shoved to the rear of the line or get remanded to the far end of the table. Ever hear of the term "short-stop?" The sailor seated at the center of the table short- stopped the chow until empty platters and bowls were pushed my way. Cooky got mad: Spying my empty plate he admonished the short-stopping chow hounds. No way! Cooky cussed out the multitude and invited me into his inner sanctum of the galley. What a hue and cry ensued as I, an Apprentice Seaman, exited the galley my plate piled high to its brim with eats. Cat calls followed, such as; "Hey Cooky,

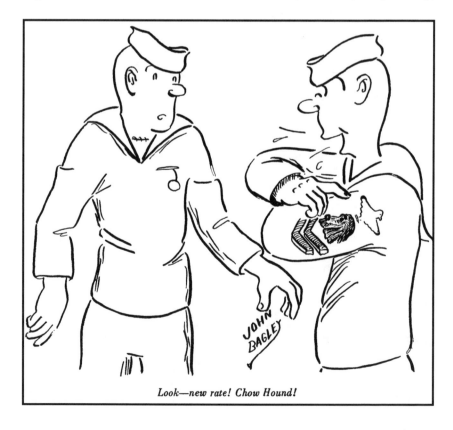

Look—new rate! Chow Hound!

is he your bung hole buddy?" My face reddened as I stuck it into the chow.

RADIO SCHOOL AT ATLANTIC CITY: Here my fattening process continued. I recall seconds, and thirds, on meat, and endless corralling of errant slices of pie. It got so bad that as graduation hastened I held off getting measured for my tailor- made dress blues with crow.

COAST GUARD RADIO STATION AT WSL: Wow! Roon and board (substance and quarters) with my CRM Adrian Kennedy and his gourmet cook, Harriet. Imagine home made baked beans simmering for all of eight hours and home made baked bread at the ready. Desserts? All home made by Harriet Kennedy. On watch: Huge sandwiches heaped high with meat and condiments. home brewed coffee served endlessly. My ample girth continued to expand. How many stones? Alim 168 at induction and now slightly passing the 200 mark.

AN LST CHOW LINE: Huge sides of beef with nary a cook to carve it up. Our ships Quartermaster, an ex-butcher, performed the task. Marvelous aroma of fresh white bread baking. Visions of dipping a slab into ones jamoke. Re: 100 percent whole wheat bread! No such animal. Some cooks were magicians turning spam and dehydrated spuds into Virginia ham with mashed potatoes.

DINING ASHORE IN PALERMO: Consumed a sweet tasty and stringy meat. Beef? No, my shipmate claims it was horsemeat. Aside: I recall an emaciated horse fall to its knees on Via Roma of Palermo as its master beat it with a whip. Eventual main course?

YOU NEVER HAD IT SO GOOD DEPARTMENT: Aboard the LST 327 we failed to realize how good we had it until GIs boarded and partook of our chow. these poor GIs had been confined to C and K rations. Modern LST: Boarded the LST 1190 in Long Beach Harbor with California LST Association. What a galley! Choice of menu, salid bar, several drink dispensers microwave ovens, and comfy mess tables with padded seats.

UNINVITED GUEST

KENNETH F. FISK, Liberty, N.Y.   *USN BARIBIZONE, France*

We were stationed at Baribizone France on our way to Berlin where we were to be part of the Naval Headquarters there.

On my birthday, the gang wanted to give me a birthday party so we all went to a small bar and made all the arrangements. The owner had some local girls brought in hostesses so we were enjoying ourselves dancing, eating, and drinking.

Then into the room, from the bar, came a quite young looking person carrying a tray and with a towel on his arm. He had on a white shirt and black tie so we thought he was a waiter. In fact, he wanted to know if we wanted any drinks from the bar, if so, he would get them for us. We were having such a good time and this waiter seemed to join right in with us so after awhile we did invite him to join us. Which he did and told several of us that he was having a swell time.

Then when it came time to go home we all picked up our P-coats and gathered around to say good nite. This young "waiter" went behind the bar to get his jacket and it was then that we noticed he was a full commander in the United States Navy with the scrambled eggs on his hat and three full stripes on his jacket!

Were we ever surprised!

After he was fully dressed he thanked us for letting him join us in having such a wonderful evening. I asked why he had disguised himself and he said that if he had worn his uniform we would have had nothing to do with him. Of course he was right.

He was a very nice person and we were pleased that he joined our party, even if he was not invited.

OOPS!!

WALTER E. HOFFMAN,   **USS HAMBLETON DMS 70**
Greenville, PA 16125

Early in 1946, the ship was moved out of drydock in Norfolk Naval Shipyard after some repairs had been made. We went to sea for less than a day and returned to Newport News for anchorage.

Already in place at the anchorage were many ships, including some aircraft carriers. Many of the crews of these larger ships were leaning over the side watching our little DMS as we approached our anchorage.

As soon as we reached our designated spot, our Captain gave the order to drop anchor. Immediately, there was the sound of the port anchor rattling through its hausepipe as it left the chain locker. The anchor disappeared over the side and splashed into the water, while the chain stayed aboard.

The sailors aboard the other ships who had been watching intently saw what happened and were soon laughing and commenting on the seamanship by the little DMS.

One of the unwritten laws of the Navy is that the Captain never loses his anchor!

The starboard anchor was dropped and held the ship firmly in its anchorage. Later that day a tug came alongside and dragged for the lost anchor, and finally brought it to the surface.

This was truly an embarrassment for the Captain and for those who failed to properly fasten the chain to the anchor.

A MARINES STORY

ALLEN D. REGENOS, Claypool Indiana   ***USMC***

As a young twenty year old Marine in civilian clothes, I was doing some bar hoping in Santa Ana, California.

I walked into a bar and as I was seating myself I made eye contact with a fellow a little older than myself seated four barstools away. I guess because of our closecroped haircuts and demeanor we both knew each other was in the military. We made eye contact again and he said "Marines?" I answered "yes" and asked "Navy?" and he nodded to the affirmative. After a short conversation he invited me to a game of pool.

As he was stacking the balls he asked: "How long you been in?" Due to the rivalry between the Navy and the Marine Corps and not wanting him to feel superior to myself, I answered; "A lot longer than you have!" Racking the balls he chuckled "I doubt that."

I boasted; "I had sea duty on Noah' Ark!" No response.

I then said; I had mess duty at the last supper!"

"Is that right?" He replied

Then I added; "Just to show you how long I have been in, when the Lord said "Let there be light!" I threw the switch."

At which point he looked me straight in the eye and said; "Heck, I,m an electricians mate and I wired that job!"

My knees buckled and I collapsed in laughter.

LIFE ABOARD LST 369

ROBERT G.EVERS. Irvington, N.J.   ***USS LST 369***

British Jeep and Corned Beef Hash

Our LST 369 was on the beach at Normandy when down from the front lines came a British Officer in a jeep. He said his men were out of ammunition and food, could we help him out? We agreed, and stacked cartons of small arms ammo on his jeep. When he saw that we were giving him cartons of corned beef hash, he said; "you can keep that stuff!" Off he went with the jeep load of ammo but no

PEEK-A-BOO

THE ENGINEER

THE COSSACK

STRICKLY REGULATION

LORD CHESTERFIELD

HARRY LANGDON

THE PIXIE

CARELESS RAPTURE

corned beef hash. To this day, I won't eat corned beef hash, even if it is made by Hormel!

E-Boat Attack In English Channel

It was the night of December 23, 1943, we were in the English Channel near Dartmouth. Together with several other LST's we were sailing Eastward from Plymouth to Southampton, guarded by one British destroyer.

About two a.m. a German E-Boat (Torpedo Boat) found us, and tried to launch an attack. I saw the boat through my binoculars and actually seeing the enemy on the surface got my adrenalin going. I was even more jumpy when the destroyer fired round after round at the enemy and missed every time. The Germans got scared too, and made a smoke screen behind which they escaped. I can still see the destroyers shells ricochet off the water in the dark like illuminated pebbles.

Carrier Pigeon Lands On Our Yardarm

One day shortly after invading Salerno, Italy I saw a carrier pigeon, with a message tied to its leg, land on the yardarm, which is the horizontal part of the ships mast. I told the Captain and suggested he shoot it with his handgun so we could read its message. Surely, I thought, it must be a German pigeon!

The Captain had a better idea. He said for me to climb up the mast, reach out, and grab the bird. I thought he was nuts, but orders are orders; besides, he was the Captain and he did have a gun, so up the mast I went!

I climbed up the ladder-like steps on the mast to the yardarm. I slowly inched my arm out to where the pigeon sat, then made a quick grad for its legs. No luck! The pigeon flew away and with it the secret of it's capsule message. I still wonder to this day, just what that message said.

Shoot Those Seagulls

The Captain of the LST 369, in the Atlantic, one afternoon ordered an anti-aircraft machine gunner to fire on a flock of seagulls because one of them had dropped some doo-doo on his hat! The gunner at first refused and the Captain repeated his order a"I said open fire!" The gunner then complied. Anytime I see a flock of seagulls to this day I recall this incident.

AN HONEST ANSWER

WILBUR SCOTT, Sacramento, CA   USS ROCKWELL APA 23

While serving aboard the USS Rockwell a friend of mine who we will call "Red" had a run in with our Division Officer "Mr. White. Red was given a Captains Mast.

At this Captains Mast one of the officers asked Red the following question: "If you were in the crows nest and you saw Mr. White standing underneath you on the deck, would you accidently drop a marlin spike on him?"

Being an honest man, Red replied: "No Sir! I would throw it at him."

Nuff said!

MY FIGHTER FRIENDS: BOB HOPE, KID CHISELL, AND ARCHIE BELL!

VAN WATTS, Hollywood, CA   *USS ENTERPRISE*

These fellows entertained servicemen throughout World War II. They had known each other since back in the 1920s when Hope and Chissell had trained in Cleveland famed Marriot's Gym which had turned out the likes of Gene Tunney. Via vaudeville and radio Hope would wind up in Hollywood and in the movies! But Chissell would beat him to it! At Great Lakes naval Training Center he would become known as Popeye The Sailor when he knocked out a professional prize fighter cold! In 1932 he would become the Navy's All-Navy Middleweight Boxing Champ and two years later would be helping Hollywood make those great fight pictures of the 1930's— and that's what he would be doing when his old friend from Cleveland, Bob Hope, arrived in Tinsel Town. Kid Chissell starred and co-starred in some of those fight movies. In others he just trained guys like Robert Taylor to look a little like fighters.

Then Bob took Chissell along on USO tours and gave him parts in his "ROAD" movies and thirty television shows, including 20 of his NBC-TV Specials.

Bob depended on the former All Navy Champ to put fighters at ease whenever he had one on his show during the four hour taping of his two hour shows. Once when they had gotten the entire cast together except for Chissell Bob had been told that he was "over at Van Watts place" And there we were telling sea stories and sipping coffee when the phone rang, but it often rang for Kid Chissell. In what must have been an endurance record, Kid would average twenty films a year for fifty years, and in the very week Bobs NBC-TV Special aired, he would also appear on the Julie Andrews Hour, and in a rerun of "To Tell The Truth!"

"Chissell!" What a name for a fighter!" Bob once said of my old friend. But how about Bell?"

Chances are that I would never have met Archie Bell had he been behaving himself and not partying in his eighties. Though to my knowledge he never held a world title, "he was some fighter!" But who could forget after his last fight at a local mall.

It seems that Archie was taking a stroll in broad daylight when a couple of young fellows jumped him. After all, he was an old white-haired man, shrunken to about five foot six. What possible trouble could he give a couple of young fellows who only wanted his wallet?

So easing around him, one was about to crush his skull with a blackjack when ringwise Archie, sensing they were up to no good, suddenly turned and his neck muscles took the impact of the weapon. Their crotches took the impact of Archies orthopedic shoes as each in turn crashed screaming to the floor of the mall, in the process one of them dropping the blackjack.

"Look at the old man beating up those two young punks," said bystanders on the mall. he pounded them into submission with their own weapon, and that was the situation when the police arrived.

When Kid Chissell passed away at age 93 back in 1987 and was interred on Veterans Day of all days. Bob Hope was in Washington presiding over Veterans Ceremonies. Much of Hollywood showed up for Chissell's funeral, the biggest bunch of flowers came from Bob Hope.

As one of Kid Chissel's closest Hollywood buddies I have told the curator of the new Great Lakes Naval Museum that, if they will do the job, I will provide the memorabilia for a permanent memorial for the Great Lakes Popeye the Sailor.

DID I KNOW MARILYN MONROE?

VAN WATTS, Hollywood, California   **USS ENTERPRISE**

When my "On The Beach With Dorothy Lamour" story appeared in several publications, I began receiving inquiries about others in Hollywood I might have known and especially about Marilyn Monroe.

Sorry, Marilyn and I missed each other—but not by much!

She passed on in Hollywood and I retired from the Navy, with plans for retiring in Hollywood, in the same year, 1962!

When I did arrive in Tinsel Town I would become quickly acquainted with Producer Bob Slatzer and Actor-columnist Kid Chissell, the Navy's 1932 ALL NAVY MIDDLE WEIGHT BOXING CHAMP—neither of whom I could have reasonably expected to get to know—much less Marilyn! The joker was that of all the people who claimed to have known her and didn't—Slatzer and Chissell really did! Slatzer enough to write a book about her!

It wasn't surprising that Slatzer and Chissell were acquainted. Both had written newspaper columns and if Slatzer was born in Ohio, Indianapolis-born Chissell had trained in Cleveland's famed mariott's Gym. And it was only an amusing coincidence that Slatzer and Marilyn were sitting next to each other in a studio waiting for an audition for parts when, back in 1946, they met

The fact that Marilyn was on hard times was nothing new. And when Slatzer and Chissell, sharing an apartment, told her they had a place for her to stay if she would make sandwiches and clean dishes, she accepted without, apparently, giving it another thought.

What followed is told pretty much in detail in Slatzer's 1974 book, "The Life And Curious Death Of Marilyn Monroe". He and Marilyn had become lovers and, as it says on the book cover, "For a brief period they were man and wife—a secret now revealed for the first time."

A likely story? Easy for you to say! I can't! Because my great Hollywood friend for many years—and one of the most honest persons I met there or anywhere, Kid Chissell—was the best man!

In brief, one weekend Slatzer, Monroe and Chissell drove down to Tiajuana—Bob and Marilyn were already live-in lovers—so it was no big deal for them to get married.

But Marilyn was finally hitting it big in one of her first movies—"NIAGARA" I guess—and back at the studio they wanted the marriage hushed up, or better yet, annulled! Afraid it might cost Marilyn her career if he didn't, Slatzer drove back in a rush to find the justice of the peace who had performed the ceremony. He was in luck! The marriage certificate had not yet even been filed! hardly a surprise! How often we hear of couples who—as much as a half century later—have discovered that their marriage certificate had not been filed!

Read all about it in Slatzers book which you can probably find a copy of in a library if not in a bookstore. My own copy was donated to a historical society because it's the only biography of Marilyn I do not consider largely fiction. To me it reads like fact, like it was written by someone who not only knew Marilyn right up to her last days but genuinely cared for her.

On the volumn's flyleaf, Bob had written "to Van and Lily Watts—May you enjoy these times that Marilyn and I shared together during those golden years of Hollywood. Best personal wishes, Your friend—/s/ Robert F. Slatzer."

But it is only fitting that I close this story with what my old Navy friend, Kid Chissell, told me about Marilyn's relationship with Bob Slatzer. "Slatzer and I have been close friends from the time we first met. And I knew Marilyn from the time she had moved in with us in 1946 until her death sixteen years later. I was best man at their 1952 Tiajuana wedding. If her studio put an end to their marriage, Marilyn remained closely attached to Bob through all the years that I knew her, often trying to contact him through me when she could not reach him direct. A telephone call from Marilyn several months before her death tells a lot about the nature of their relationship all through those years. She was in some kind of trouble and trying to reach him again. I offered her assistance which she refused saying, "I can handle it. But if I had to do it all over again, I would have stayed married to Bob. Of the whole lot of them he was the only one who understood me."

No, I never knew Marilyn. But the only two real friends she ever had were real friends of mine! Only that can explain why I have to remind myself now and then that I did not in fact know her personally. But this thought often crosses my mind—how lucky Marilyn was, for a time, to have stumbled upon a couple of real solid Midwestern fellows whom even Hollywood couldn't spoil!

DOUBLE TROUBLE

JAMES STITZER, Schuylkill Haven, Pa.   USS LSM 487

The shores, bays and harbors of Okinawa were loaded with reefs, shoals, wrecks and other hazards making navigation in these waters very difficult. In addition the difference between high and low tides could be ten feet and more at different locations. The Okinawa fishermen were very skillful at navigating these waters but at times, American sailors were not.

Our USS LSM 487 had been operating in "Nagasaki Wan" known to us as "Buckner Bay." We would anchor in a different location each day. It was my duty as a quartermaster to assist the Navigation officer to be able to safely plot our way from one anchorage to the next using our charts that I had clearly marked with the latest navigational hazards and confidential buoys. I would do a running fix using objects on shore as my guides. After being in the bay for quite some time I began to know these waters quite well.

On this one particular morning a junior officer (an ensign) had the conn and we were ordered to move to a different anchorage. He was a good officer and a likeable guy but had little knowledge about navigating in these hazardous waters.

As most of us know, when you set the "special sea and anchor detail" it sends a lookout to the bow of the ship, and one to the upper most spot on the ship, plus a boatswains mate stands by the anchor break in case the anchor needs dropped. In the case of an

LSM or LST another boatswains mate is stationed on the fantail by the stern anchor for safety reasons. (The stern anchor on these type ships is usually dropped just before the vessel is beached so it can extract itself from the beach by hauling-in on this stern anchor.)

On a fairly calm day the experienced eye can spot a shoal or reef by the ripple of the water above it. On this day the wind was up and small white-caps prevailed making this visual sighting difficult. Another problem was that our ship was not carrying a load which meant it sat high in the water making the wind act upon it as if it were a sail.

I was in the pilot house advising the deck officer as to what course and speed he should take to reach the assigned anchorage. The officer directed me to steer a course that would ground the ship. I shouted through the voice tube "sir, we will go aground on the shoals." He answered back words that I will never forget. "This tub only has a draft of about three feet."

The last order I remember him giving was, "ALL AHEAD FLANK!" I was about to shout to him over the voice tube and tell him we were headed for trouble and he must change course, when a fellow shipmate who was standing by my side shook his head and put his hand over the voice tube preventing my voice from being heard on the bridge. What had come to my mind was the "General Prudential Rule" which I had learned in Quartermaster school which I still remember almost word for word...... "In obeying and construing these rules; due regard shall be had to all hazards of navigation and special circumstances which shall render a departure from these rules".....

I am not sure if this rule applies to Quartermasters as well as officers, but I believe the action I should have taken was to have disobeyed his order. However, the shipmate on duty at the speed control obeyed the officers command and we went aground.

Wow! Did we ever go aground! The center of our ship had hit, and stuck, on a large shoal, tearing a hole in the bottom.

A tug came to our aid but could not get us off the shoal. Finally at high tide we floated high enough to get off using our own power. The hole in our bottom was no danger to our sinking because of our compartmentation but we were ordered to put into shore where a patch could be put in place.

We tied up at a dock that some Seabee Unit had just completed.

Our second stroke of trouble began when a message came over our radio that a huge typhoon was headed our way and that all ships in the Bay were to head out to sea to "ride out" the storm as is standard Navy procedure.

So as all the other ships evacuated the area we were stuck at the dock because with our hole in the bottom we were deemed unseaworthy!

The storm hit hard with several ships that were out at sea sending "SOS" messages via radio and blinker-light requesting permission to return to the pier and tie-up alongside our ship, that they were in trouble and in danger of sinking. We had no choice but to signal back "negative" because our situation was precarious.

Our LSM tied to the pier with the strongest lines that were available to us and men were stationed near each one so that when the line seemed ready to part, another would be attached. This was very dangerous duty. Most hands were ordered below decks except for those on line-watch duty.

How we ever survived that storm I will never know as several smaller vessels were washed ashore and others smashed against the shoals. The pier we were tied up to, was in shambles and I doubt they ever used it again.

Once the storm subsided we did a pretty good patching job on the hole in our bottom and we were ordered back to the Philippines for repairs and a much needed rest.

To quote from a column with a 1955 dateline... in the Pottsville, Pa. Republican Newspaper.... "50 YEARS AGO ..IN 1945...Okinawa today was a shambles... Reminiscent of it's battle ravaged litter... reduced by a 132 mpr typhoon that killed three American Navy personnel, left ten sailors missing and more than 100 Yank soldiers injured, and sank, damaged, or beached, twenty- seven naval vessels.

I dedicate this story to my valiant, patriotic shipmates who sacrificed for our great country... GOD BLESS AMERICA!

THE CUTIE TORPEDO

LADISLAV PISPECKY, Clark, N.J.   **USS COD**

After more than two years in the Navy which consisted of boot camp, radio school, submarine school, and a lot of waiting. I was finally assigned to the USS PROETEUS, a submarine tender, at Guam where I was assigned duties both in the radio shack and in the refitting of submarines returning from patrols when I finally received orders to my first duty station aboard a submarine, The USS COD.

I had to leave the USS PROETEUS in such a hurry that I left my mattress, my hammock, and half my clothes behind in the ships laundry. The USS COD was set to disembark in about an hour, it was quite a distance away, and I had to be onboard her before she got underway.

I don't know what I had anticipated, but there was no one to meet me, it were as if I wasn't expected. I walked across the gang plank, saluted the colors and went below to see where I was to go and what I was to do. It ends up that one of the radio techs I had gone to school with in New London was a member of the crew this explains why I was selected for duty on the USS COD.

I was hungry and was told that they only ate two meals a day aboard the sub and that was bad news for a growing boy like me. This did allow me some time to get squared away and check out the sub, all its compartments and equipment. Find my bunk and learn what my duties were.

My bunk? Ha!Ha! Part of the crew who commissioned the ship had their own bunks and no trespassing, no way. They had five war patrols under their belts and were not to be messed with by any stinking polywog. (read stories on Shellback Initiation and mascot of the Big E)... The rest of the crew had to hot sack it. (that means they shared a bunk with someone else) As things turned out I had to share a bunk with a gunners mate striker.

My only complaint was, why did he carry such crap around with him? He always slept in his clothes, bullets fell out of his pockets in the bunk along with other debri. I had to throw my blanket over the bunk and always sleep on the inside of the blanket. I spent 58 days doing this. I soon learned that any flat, empty space, was a good spot to sleep, such as the deck, a mess table, mess bench, or any place where there was an open bulkhead to lean on. You could not sneak into another guys bunk as they would get violent. When you got tired, any place would do, except on watch. The one exception was the deck boards as they made a big groove in your back. Most of the time aboard the boat we walked around in shorts and sandals.

The Captain of the USS COD was a Commander for this patrol, The Executive Officer was a Lieutenant.

The USS POMPOM left port with us to perform coordinated patrol and life guard operations for the Fifth Air Force in the East China Sea.

I was assigned to a watch section and my duties were to operate the radar and sound equipment and make repairs along with the other Radio Technician onboard. As you might guess, we had repair work my first day. Remember, repair work cuts down on possible sleep time. Repair work did not excuse you from standing your watch, four hours on, eight hours off.

There were very few dull moments when out at sea in a submarine as you must be always watchful, of everything that might pose a danger to the boat.

We ran through three different mine fields within a weeks time. We were bombed by an enemy plane because we did not dive soon enough to escape his wrath, destroyed several small eneny ships while surfaced using our deck guns, and had opportunity to fire on two enemy convoys but our torpedoes turned out to be duds and we sustained heavy depth charge attacks.

Then while in the Formosa Starights off the coast of Japan we came across another large enemy convoy with a lot of choice targets. We started our attack on the surface, we watched as our torpedos began broaching and diving. Obviiously these electric fish had stabilizer problems. Then we heard one torpedo hit the target but did not explode. More duds!

The escort vessels saw the torpedos and started coming after us. The faces of the crew turned ashen grey for hell was coming to greet us. The escorts were firing their deck guns at us and were zeroing in on us. Shrapnel was hitting the outside of our conning tower. In a matter of a few seconds we changed from running in and attacking the enemy to running like hell, at flank speed, to get away from him. Thats a traumatic change like winning one second and losing the next.

The water was only about 110 feet deep. Not enough depth! Too shallow for security. We were running for deep water when the order was given to "dive" and we went to "battle stations submerged" immediately. As we dived the Lt. who was in charge at the time vehemently argued with me when I told him to fire the "Cutie torpedo". Eventually he did order the "Cutie torpedo" to be fired!

The "Cutie torpedo" was a smaller torpedo which carried a smaller charge than a regular torpedo and was invented to be used in a situation such as this. This was a sound directed torpedo that would home in on the slightest sound in the area it was directed at. (A rumor was that some subs had been sunk by their own Cutie torpedos) once their guidence system was activated the slightest sound would cause the torpedos fins and rudder to move or oscillate. This type torpedo saved a lot of men and submarines in its time. It definately saved our ass this time!

The one escort was soon over us, THERE WAS NO WAY TO ESCAPE IT, It dropped four depth charges. The noise was tremendous and scared the crap out of me. It made three runs at us without a direct hit but several oil lines ruptured from the pounding and were soon fixed.

Then came a fourth run, and a fifth. I became a veteran fast! You have to have a tight asshole so you don't shit yourself and hold onto your testicles so you don't get ruptured! We braced ourselves as four more depth charges rain down on us. The shock waves from this barrage threw me against a bulkhead.

On the sonar we hear him slowly fade to the 1600 yard mark, the same familiar pattern. Now he turns and listens and whoops, he smelled blood again and begins his sixth run at us. He is on us again and the horror of all horrors is unleashed as the depth charges go off again. We don't have rubber bones and stretchable joints although these chiropractic charges try to stretch your limbs and flex your bones till the rupture point.

This will be the seventh run, and what is your lucky number?

Again we hear the escort pause a few moments (slow revolutions of his screws tell us this) and then he cranks up his engines to a high whirring noise as he comes in again with the intention of killing us this time. This time all four charges were to port and I was wondering—man! How many charges does this lousey rat carry? These last charges were very effective and we began to worry about

our foward batteries. Someone had passed the word that chlorine was building up, that perhaps salt water was getting into that compartment.

Waiting for the escorts eighth run we noticed that he was waiting longer than usual to start his run. Our Captain brought the sub up to periscope depth and fired one torpedo at him. It was on the mark. We still wondered why had the escort stopped?

THEN, ALL OF A SUDDEN THERE WAS AN EXPLOSION, JUST LIKE A DEPTH CHARGE BUT FURTHER AWAY! But hell, he was starting up again. No! We hear noises, like a ship breaking-up noises. We were totally disoriented. We don't know what the explosion was, or what the heck was going on.

So far we had taken twenty-eight deoth charges with how many more to come? I really got serious about trying to guess how many charges this escort might be carrying. To this day I still do know.

We listen—nothing. No screws, no accelerating whine, what was happening? After one hour the Captain took a sweep with the periscope. Seeing debris and men in the water he then brought the sub to the surface. The escort was gone and no other ships were in sight.

OUR PRAYERS HAD TRULY BEEN ANSWERED! THANK YOU GOD!

What had happened? Why did the jap escort sink? It seems that the "Cutie torpedo" that we had fired a long time ago had finally caught up to the escort and hit him in the screws forcing him to stop dead in the water. The eleven foot long Cutie carried a smaller charge than a regular torpedo and usually ended up hitting its target in the screws.

That long delay before the escorts eighth run was caused because the Cutie had finally caught up to it, hit it in the screws and disabled it. That is when our Captain had brought the USS COD to periscope depth and fired that one torpedo at it. That torpedo apparently finished the job the Cutie had started! The next explosion we heard was determined to be a depth charge that had not been put on safety and it had exploded when it reached the depth it was set for. It exploded just under the escorts crew who were in the water after abandoning ship.

What was interesting was the fact that the "Cutie", which was a sound directed torpedo, persistently went after the escort but was diverted in a different direction each time a depth charge had exploded. It must have traversed some crazy path both up and down, while shifting from side to side. For all this to happen, it was obvious that the timing had to be just right.

The escort had made seven runs on us, his mistake was waiting too long after making his seventh run allowing the "Cutie" to catch up with him and thus ending his harassment of the USS COD.

How did the "Cutie" arm itself when it wasn't deep enough for it to do so in the beginning? A plauseable explanation would be that the depth charges wrre set for 150 feet and the "Cutie" chased the noise to that depth and thus armed itself. No matter how it had armed itself, we were darn lucky it did not home in on some noise coming from our sub. We were truly lucky again when you stop to think that the running time for a torpedo is about thirty minutes and it must have taken this torpedo forty-five minutes to catch the escort, and it still worked.

You can call it luck, fate, or what ever you wish, but I feel that all crew members of the USS COD had a lot to thank God for on that fateful day!

Jack Banks and Friends

USS ENTERPRISE